The Ultimate Guide
TO THE ADVISERS ACT
A PRACTITIONER'S HANDBOOK

BETTINA ECKERLE

ISBN-13: 978 0 9862 7170 0
ISBN-10: 0986 271 705
LCCN: 2014922292

Table of Contents

Introduction

Here I was, in 2007. I had just assumed the position as general counsel of one of the largest conglomerates of independent registered investment advisers in the United States with dozens of advisory firms under our umbrella. It didn't take me long to realize that what I needed was a comprehensive guide for my team to stay on top of the Advisers Act. Something in plain English, concise, and pragmatic, easy to read but with enough detail to answer day-to-day questions and spot issues that we would then be able to tackle with specialists, if necessary. Everything I found was useful in its own right but not right for my audience – executives, chief compliance officers, compliance staff (i.e., the ones in charge of or involved in the day-to-day compliance work at companies that handled other people's money). Most of the writings I came across were too detailed and scholarly, or if not that, then not concise enough, and everything was fragmented. It would take a lot of time and effort to piece it all together, not to mention the lawyer's fees. Then Dodd-Frank came along and reshuffled the rules, complicating things further. So I began writing this book, first and foremost to help myself.

Just as the Investment Advisers Act of 1940 was largely drafted as a response to the stock market crash of 1929 and the depression that followed, Dodd-Frank was the reaction to the 2008 financial meltdown. It required many new advisers to register with the SEC for the first time (namely managers of hedge funds and other private funds), established new exemptions from SEC registration, changed reporting requirements, and reallocated regulatory responsibility for advisers between the SEC and states.

I finally wrote the book I was looking for after starting my own practice, mostly to help clients out. Whether you are wondering if you meet the definition of an investment adviser under the Advisers Act post-Dodd-Frank and need to register or are already involved in compliance at a registered advisory firm or fund, this book is for you. I hope you will find it as helpful as I intended it to be.

Chapter 01

Dodd-Frank and The Advisers Act – an Overview

Dodd-Frank, more precisely Title IV of it, introduced wide-sweeping changes to the regulatory framework that governs the world of investment advisers. With one broad stroke, namely the repeal of the *private adviser exemption*, the Advisers Act suddenly applied to an entire new universe of entities that had not been regulated before or to a much more limited extent. Before Dodd-Frank, many advisers to private funds had relied on the private adviser exemption to avoid SEC registration. This exemption applied to advisers with fewer than fifteen clients, where each fund counted as a client as opposed to each investor in the fund. By eliminating this exemption, Congress generally extended the registration requirements under the Advisers Act to advisers to many private funds, such as hedge funds and private equity funds.

Fig 1.1 *Number of SEC-Registered Investment Advisers by RAUM Category*

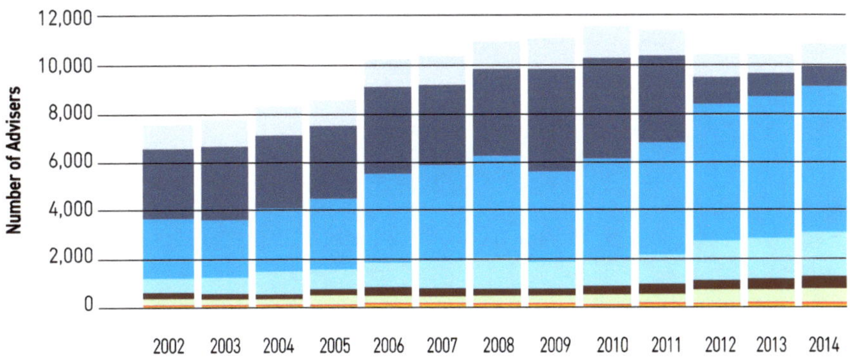

All Advisers	7,581	7,852	8,302	8,614	10,290	10,446	11,030	11,257	11,643	11,539	10,511	10,533	10,895
<$25m	989	1,124	1,137	1,035	1,139	1,077	1,071	1,350	1,305	1,116	852	815	838
$25m to <$100m	2,875	3,020	3,036	3,068	3,492	3,489	3,720	4,259	4,228	3,651	1,245	974	863
$100m to<$1b	2,480	2,474	2,747	2,993	3,812	3,904	4,096	3,780	4,108	4,600	5,680	5,867	6,085
$1b to < $5b	708	727	828	915	1,149	1,173	1,235	1,096	1,176	1,276	1,656	1,747	1,868
$5b to $10b	203	199	206	211	237	284	327	301	318	331	414	429	452
$10b to < $50b	237	221	250	285	334	367	409	346	363	404	485	498	574
$50b to < $100b	37	39	46	51	65	77	90	65	81	83	89	104	103
≤$100b	52	48	52	56	62	75	82	61	64	78	90	99	112

Source: Investment Adviser Association, 2014 Evolution Report

In lieu of the private adviser exemption, Dodd-Frank created new narrow exemptions for advisers to certain types of private funds, such as venture capital funds and midsized private funds with less than $150 million in assets under management, as well as foreign advisers that did not have a place of business in the United States.

At the same time, Dodd-Frank and the new SEC rules raised the minimum threshold of assets under management from $25 million to $100 million for advisers to be eligible to register with the SEC versus registering with the state(s) they do business in.

Additionally, the SEC amended the disclosure requirements for advisers – and particularly for those who advised private funds – on Form ADV, and the SEC and CFTC jointly adopted rules holding advisers to more stringent reporting and registration standards by requiring advisers to hedge funds and other private funds to report detailed information on a new Form PF. Furthermore, Dodd-Frank amended the rules relating to *custody* of client assets and *pay to play*.

Lastly, Dodd-Frank mandated the SEC to conduct studies on whether or not to create a uniform fiduciary standard for investment advisers and broker-dealers and shift the supervision of private funds from the SEC to a self-regulatory organization.

This chapter summarizes the main changes brought about by Dodd-Frank with a closer look at changes that are most relevant to advisers to private funds, such as hedge funds, private equity funds, and venture capital funds, as well as family offices.

Overview

Title IV of Dodd-Frank made numerous changes to the registration and reporting and record-keeping requirements of the Advisers Act. Among these is the requirement that advisers to most private funds (hedge funds and private equity funds) register with the SEC. In adopting the new SEC rules as mandated by Dodd-Frank, SEC Chairman Mary Schapiro stated that they "will fill a key gap in the regulatory landscape. In particular, our proposal will give the [SEC], and the public, insight into hedge fund and other private fund managers who previously conducted their work under the radar and outside the vision of regulators."

Specifically, Dodd-Frank and the SEC's new rules under it did the following:

1) They defined three new exemptions from the Advisers Act registration requirements for:
    - advisers solely to *private funds* with less than $150 million in assets under management in the United States;
    - advisers solely to *venture capital* funds; and
    - foreign advisers without a place of business in the United States.
2) They raised the assets-under-management threshold for advisers to be eligible for SEC registration from $25 million to $100 million.
3) They created a new category of advisers, the so-called *exempt reporting advisers*, who are advisers to private funds that are exempt from registration but nevertheless required to submit periodic reports to the SEC.

4) They created new reporting requirements for advisers on Form ADV, including:
    - ***For private fund advisers***, who need to report basic organizational and operational information about each fund they manage, such as the type of private fund (hedge fund, private equity fund, or liquidity fund), information about the size and ownership of the fund, general fund data, the nature of the adviser's services to the fund, and identification of five categories of "gatekeepers" (auditors, prime brokers, custodians, administrators, and marketers).
    - ***For all advisers***, who need to report information regarding their advisory business, including the types of clients they advise, their employees, and their advisory activities, any business practices that may present significant conflicts of interest (such as the use of affiliated brokers, soft dollar arrangements, and compensation for client referrals), their non-advisory activities, and their financial industry affiliations.
5) They created a novel uniform defined term of *regulatory assets under management* that is used for many different purposes and that looks at gross assets, includes uncalled capital commitments, and values the assets at fair or market value.
6) They amended the pay-to-play rule so that it applies to exempt reporting advisers and foreign private advisers.
7) They defined the term *family offices*, which do not need to register with the SEC or comply with other Advisers Act requirements.
8) They created a new Form PF that requires private funds, such as liquidity funds, hedge funds and private equity funds to disclose extensive information with the SEC.
9) They created/reiterated rules regarding custody of client assets.
10) They mandated studies regarding a self-regulatory organization to oversee Adviser Act compliance and the introduction of one fiduciary standard for investment advisers and broker-dealers.

Even before Dodd-Frank, becoming registered as an investment adviser entailed significant obligations. Post-Dodd-Frank the requirements became even more pronounced and required particular attention by advisers that had not been subject to SEC purview before.

Needless to say, SEC-registered advisers should ensure that they are fully compliant with the Advisers Act by implementing, among other things, an effective compliance program with written policies and procedures designed to prevent and detect violations and to be able to demonstrate their program's effectiveness at the time of an SEC examination. To make this easy, I wrote this book.

Arguably, asset managers (i.e., managers of hedge and other private funds) are the ones most heavily impacted by the new regimes. This chapter will walk you through the aspects of the complicated new regulatory world that I found most noteworthy for them. The main elements of the new rules are then discussed at greater length in chapters 3 through 12 of the book.

Detailed Discussion

Invariably, all these changes to the Advisers Act raise many questions for asset managers and financial advisers alike. The ones that I am asked most frequently are answered in this chapter.

■ What Exemptions Are Available under the New Advisers Act?

The following table provides an overview of registration requirements and exemptions.

Fig. 1.2 *Adviser Registration Requirements and Exemptions*

Type of Adviser	SEC Registration	Registration with State(s)
You manage **solely** private funds and have less than $150 million in regulatory assets under management (AUM).	**Not required**, but subject to filing/ reporting obligations of an exempt reporting adviser.	**Required** based on law of individual states, unless registered with the SEC or state law exemption available. **Exempt** reporting advisers are not considered SEC registered for this purpose.
You manage **solely venture capital** funds.	**Not required**, but subject to limited filing/reporting obligations of an exempt reporting adviser.	**Required** based on law of individual states, unless registered with the SEC or state law exemption available. **Exempt** reporting advisers are not considered SEC registered for this purpose.
You are a **foreign private adviser**.	**Not required.**	**Required** based on law of individual states, unless registered with the SEC or state law exemption available.
You are an **intrastate adviser** and do not advise private funds.	**Not required.**	**Required** in accordance with law of individual states, unless registered with the SEC or exempt under state law.
You are an adviser to **family offices**.	**Not required.**	**Required** based on law of individual states, unless registered with the SEC or state law exemption available.
You are an **SBIC adviser** meeting the conditions under Section 203(b)(7) of the Advisers Act.	**Not required.**	**Required** based on law of individual states, unless registered with the SEC or state law exemption available.

Dodd-Frank replaced the private adviser exemption with a general requirement that an investment adviser to any private equity fund or other private pool of capital must register with the SEC, unless they qualify for one of the few, more limited, exemptions that Dodd-Frank created. They are as follows:

❖ *Venture Capital Fund Exemption*

Dodd-Frank amended the Advisers Act to exempt from registration advisers that only manage venture capital funds and directed the SEC to define the term.

Under the SEC's definition, a venture capital fund is a private fund that:

1) invests primarily in *qualifying investments*, generally, in private operating companies, but may invest in a basket of non-qualifying investments of up to 20 percent of its committed capital;
2) is not leveraged except for a minimal amount on a short-term basis;
3) does not offer redemption rights to its investors; and
4) represents itself to investors as pursuing a venture capital strategy.

Under a grandfathering provision, funds that began raising capital by the end of 2010 and represented themselves as pursuing a venture capital strategy qualify.

❖ *Private Fund Adviser Exemption*

Dodd-Frank amended the Advisers Act to exempt from registration any adviser that:

1) solely advises private funds;
2) advises private funds, with private funds defined as any fund that would satisfy the definition of an investment company under the Investment Company Act but does not have to register under that act because it has fewer than 100 investors or only has super-high net worth "qualified purchaser" investors (i.e., persons who meet the criteria of sections 3(c(1) or 3(c)(7) of the Investment Company Act); and
3) does not exceed $150 million in total assets under management in the United States.

❖ *Foreign Private Adviser Exemption*

Dodd-Frank also amended the Advisers Act to provide for an exemption from registration for foreign advisers that do not have a place of business in the United States and have:

1) less than $25 million in aggregate assets under management from US clients and private fund investors; and
2) fewer than fifteen US clients and US private fund investors.

■ A Quick Guide to Calculating Regulatory Assets under Management

The SEC rules implemented a uniform method for advisers to calculate their assets under management. It is used for multiple purposes in the Advisers Act, including to assess whether an adviser is eligible to register with the SEC or meets one of the exemptions from registration discussed above. The SEC calls this new uniform calculation *regulatory assets under management*.

As a general rule, advisers must include in their regulatory assets under management securities portfolios for which they provide continuous and regular supervisory or management services, regardless of whether these assets are family owned or proprietary, managed without receiving compensation, or of foreign clients.

The SEC clarified that an adviser must calculate its regulatory assets under management on a gross basis – that is, without deduction of any outstanding indebtedness or other accrued but unpaid liabilities.

There are also two different methods of calculation, depending on whether an adviser advises private funds or not.

❖ *Private Funds*

For each private fund, an adviser must include in its calculation the market value (or if the market value is not available, the fair value), on a gross basis, of all assets of the fund, regardless of the nature of the assets, plus uncalled capital commitments.

Advisers may calculate the fair value of their private funds in accordance with generally accepted accounting principles in the United States or another international fair-valuation standard as long as they are acting consistently and in good faith.

❖ *Other Funds and Accounts*

For each fund or account that is not a private fund, an adviser must determine whether 50 percent or more of the total market value of the account or fund consists of securities. Only accounts that consist of 50 percent or more of securities are included in the calculation. For more details on the calculation, please read chapter 8, which is entirely dedicated to the topic.

As a general matter, an adviser must calculate regulatory assets under management based on the current market value of assets, which must be determined within 90 days prior to filing Form ADV.

■ I Qualify for an Exemption – What Are My Reporting Requirements?

Even if exempt from registration, many advisers will nonetheless need to submit regular reports to the SEC as so-called *exempt reporting advisers*. Only advisers that rely on the venture capital funds exemption or the private fund adviser exemption are considered exempt reporting advisers with the corresponding legal consequences. To find out if you qualify, please read chapters 2 and 4. Advisers relying on the foreign private adviser exemption, which is available to advisers without a place of business in the United States, will not need to submit regular reports to the SEC, nor do firms who fall within the new definition of family offices.

Exempt reporting advisers are required to submit regular reports containing a subset of the information that all registered advisers must report on Form ADV.

In addition to regular reporting, the SEC exempt reporting advisers are also subject to record-keeping requirements. While the SEC stated that it does not plan to conduct regular compliance examinations of exempt reporting advisers, it will conduct cause examinations where there are indications of wrongdoing (e.g., prompted by tips, complaints, and referrals).

Exempt reporting advisers are required to complete seven items on Form ADV: Item 1: Identifying Information, Item 2.B: Reporting by Exempt Reporting Advisers, Item 3: Form of Organization, Item 6: Other Business Activities, Item 7: Financial Industry Affiliations and Private Fund Reporting, Item 7A Financial Industry Affiliations and Activities, including Foreign Affiliates, Item 7.B: Information Regarding Private Funds Managed by an Adviser, Item 10: Control Persons, and Item 11: Disclosure Information (disciplinary history and the disciplinary history of all its advisory affiliates).

In addition, exempt reporting advisers must complete corresponding sections of Schedules A, B, C, and D.

Like registered advisers, exempt reporting advisers are required to file updating amendments to reports filed on Form ADV on an annual basis within ninety days of the end of their fiscal year. They must promptly update Item 1 (Identifying Information), Item 3 (Form of Organization), and Item 11 (Disclosure Information) if they become inaccurate in any way, and update Item 10 (Control Persons) if it becomes materially inaccurate.

Exempt reporting advisers should take their reporting obligations seriously whether or not they anticipate to morph into registered advisers or not. One other aspect to consider is that the information on Form ADV is largely publicly available on the SEC website and thus accessible to investors and anyone else who is interested in an adviser's business. I dedicated an entire chapter (chapter 10) to exempt reporting advisers and their obligations for those who fall within this newly created adviser category.

What Do I Need to Know about Revised Form ADV?

All advisers have to submit significant amounts of new information on Form ADV. The SEC views the data collected from Form ADV as critically important to its regulatory program and its ability to protect investors. The information reported by advisers on Form ADV is used for a number of purposes, such as identifying common business activities, creating risk profiles of investment advisers, permitting examiners to better prepare for and conduct examinations, and getting a better understanding of the industry.

Form ADV now requires all advisers to provide additional information about three areas of their operations:

- information about the private funds they advise;
- data relating to their business (including data about the types of clients they have, their employees, and their advisory activities), as well as its business practices that may present significant conflicts of interest (such as the use of affiliated brokers, soft dollar arrangements, and compensation for client referrals); and
- additional information about their non-advisory activities and their financial industry affiliations.

❖ *Private Fund Reporting*

The new ADV requires a host of data on private funds that an adviser manages. Item 7.B and Section 7.B of Schedule D require a private fund adviser to provide information regarding the size and organizational, operational, and investment characteristics of each private fund that it advises. As part of its response, the adviser must indicate whether the fund is part of a master-feeder arrangement or a fund of funds and must provide information about the fund's regulatory status (i.e., the exclusion from the Investment Company Act on which the fund relies). The adviser must also identify the types of strategies employed by the fund, gather information regarding the fund's investors, and report the gross asset value of the fund. In addition, the adviser must identify gatekeepers for the fund, including auditors, prime brokers, custodians, administrators, and marketers.

❖ *All Advisers*

The new Form ADV requires disclosure for all advisers, whether they manage private funds or not, in a number of areas. They are:

- **Item 1.O: Reporting $1 Billion in Total Assets**. An adviser must indicate whether it had $1 billion or more in total assets shown on its balance sheet as of the last day of the most recent fiscal year. This information is used to identify those advisers that could be subject torules regarding certain excessive incentive based compensation arrangements required by Dodd-Frank.

- **Item 5: Advisory Business Information**. An adviser is required to provide basic information concerning its business, including the scope of its business, types of services it provides, types of clients to whom it provides those services, and number of employees.

- **Items 6 and 7: Other Business Activities and Financial Industry Affiliations**. Items 6.A and 7.A require advisers to report those financial services the adviser or a related person is actively engaged in providing.

- **Item 8: Participation in Client Transactions**. An adviser is required to report if it has discretionary authority to select the brokers or dealers for client transactions or if it recommends brokers or dealers to clients, as well as the compensation received for client referrals. Advisers are also required to report if they receive soft dollar benefits and if they qualify for the safe harbor under Section 28(e) of the 34 Act.

- **Item 9: Custody**. An adviser is required to indicate the total number of persons that act as qualified custodians for the adviser's clients, as well as the amount of client assets for which it has custody.

It is crucial to dedicate sufficient time and resources to assembling the information for and completing Form ADV. In addition to the legal consequences of filing an incorrect or incomplete report with the SEC, such as fines and enforcement actions, Form ADV is publicly available and investors rely on the completeness and truthfulness of the information contained in it. Chapter 7 provides more details on Form ADV, and I would urge each applicant or SEC-registered adviser to read it carefully.

Do I Have to Register with the SEC or the State I Do Business In?

Section 410 of Dodd-Frank created a new category of midsized advisers (i.e., advisers with assets under management between $25 million and $100 million) and shifted primary responsibility for their regulatory oversight to the states.

The intent was to allow the SEC to focus its oversight resources on larger advisory firms, and the many private funds that are required to register with the SEC as first time registrants based on the new rules.

As such, the new rules prohibit a midsized adviser from registering with the SEC if it is regulated or is required to be regulated by the state in which it has its principal office and place of business, with the following exceptions:

- the adviser does not meet the criteria for state registration;
- the state does not subject investment advisers to examinations; or
- the adviser advises registered investment companies or business development companies under the Investment Company Act.

For efficiency and convenience, advisers that would have to register with more than fifteen states may register with the SEC. For more details on state vs. federal registration requirements, refer to chapter 6.

What Are the Changes to the Pay-to-Play Rule?

Dodd-Frank and the resulting SEC rules amended the *pay-to-play* rule (Section 206(4)-5). The pay-to-play rule was originally adopted to address the pay-to-play issues relating to relationships between investment advisory firms and political officials who have control over the investment decision making for public pension plans. The rule limits the political contributions (federal, state, and local) that investment advisers and certain current and prospective employees can make.

Specifically, the new rules:

- amend the scope of the existing pay-to-play rule so that it applies to exempt reporting advisers and foreign private advisers;
- add registered municipal advisers to the categories of registered entities excepted from the rule's prohibition on advisers paying third parties to solicit government entities; and
- permit advisers to compensate persons that are registered entities for soliciting government officials, if they are subject to restrictions at least as stringent as the pay-to-play rule.

Am I a Family Office, And if Yes, What Compliance Obligations Do I Have?

Historically, family offices did not have to register with the SEC because they fell within the private adviser exemption or got individual exemptive relief from the SEC. With Dodd-Frank, the SEC defined family office within the spirit of the previously granted exemptive relief. The SEC's new definition is carefully crafted to mimic the organizational, employment, and management structure of a true family office. Do keep this in mind. It will make ploughing through the maze of the technicalities of the definition much easier.

As newly defined, family offices are excluded from the definition of an investment adviser under the revised Advisers Act and, accordingly, are not subject to its registration, record keeping, and other compliance requirements. They are also not exempt reporting advisers and thus not subject to the reporting and compliance obligations applicable to that adviser category.

To fall within the definition, an investment adviser must meet the following criteria:

1) it must provide investment advice only to *family clients*, as defined in the rule;
2) it must be wholly owned by family clients and is exclusively controlled by *family members* and/or *family entities*; and
3) it must not hold itself out to the public as an investment adviser.

The rule also incorporates a grandfathering provision that includes in the definition of "family office" those advisers who would otherwise meet the rule's requirements, but provided investment advice to certain clients before January l, 2010. I provide more details on the family offices in chapter 3.

I Advise a Private Fund. Do I Have to File Form PF?

The adoption of Rule 204(b)-1 under the Advisers Act and the introduction of Form PF was a watershed event for private fund advisers. Rule 204(b)-1 requires SEC-registered investment advisers who manage private funds to report a large amount of data largely dealing with systemic risk exposure to the SEC and other agencies on a consistent basis on Form PF.

What Types of Funds Are Covered?

Many private funds are within the scope of Form PF and subject to various levels of reporting. However, advisers to private funds with less than $150 million in assets under management and advisers to venture capital funds are not required to report on Form PF.

Form PF requires extensive information from three types of funds: hedge funds, liquidity funds, and private equity funds. Hedge funds are generally defined as private funds that are able to earn performance fees based on unrealized gains, permitted to borrow in excess of one-half of net asset value and to have gross notional exposure in excess of twice the net asset value, or permitted to short securities and other assets.

On the other hand, liquidity funds are funds that seek to generate income by investing in short-term securities while maintaining a stable net asset value for investors. Lastly, private equity funds are funds that are not hedge funds, liquidity funds, real estate funds, securitized asset funds, or venture capital funds, and they do not normally provide investors with redemption rights.

When classifying its funds, a manager needs to pay close attention to the instructions and definitions on Form PF and the fund's offering documents, which may give funds more trading latitude than they currently utilize to provide flexibility. This latitude may cause the fund to meet the definition of a hedge fund and, therefore, subject the fund to expanded reporting.

❖ *What Are My Reporting Requirements?*

The extent and frequency of the reporting requirements are determined by the type of fund and the amount of assets under management. Form PF utilizes the SEC's newly adopted definition of regulatory assets under management. Regulatory assets under management are a fund's gross assets under management without subtracting borrowings or other forms of leverage. For a private equity fund, regulatory assets under management includes investors' unfunded capital commitments.

It is important to note that the new metric is different from the more commonly used "net assets under management," which is calculated by subtracting outstanding liabilities from fund assets. Form PF requires the use of regulatory assets under management to determine the requirement to complete certain Form PF sections. If you manage private funds, please read chapter 9, which is entirely dedicated to Form PF.

■ Do I Have Custody? And if Yes, What Does it Mean?

Section 411 of Dodd-Frank amended the Advisers Act by specifically requiring registered investment advisers to "take such steps to safeguard client assets over which such adviser has custody, including, without limitation, verification of such assets by an independent public accountant, as the [SEC] may, by rule, prescribe."

The SEC's existing custody rule, Rule 206(4)-2, imposes various requirements on registered investment advisers that have custody of client funds or securities, including:

1) to maintain client assets with a qualified custodian, and

2) to undergo an annual surprise examination by an independent public accountant to verify client assets, unless an exemption applies.

By virtue of Dodd-Frank and the new SEC rules, many previously unregistered managers of private funds, including venture capital and private equity funds, became subject to the custody rule and its requirements. These requirements are discussed in more detail in chapter 11.

For now, Dodd-Frank appears to do little more than reiterate the obligations of advisers regarding custody of client assets and the SEC's authority to promulgate rules regarding the same.

■ Once Registered, What Are My Ongoing Compliance Obligations?

❖ *SEC-Registered Investment Advisers*

If you conclude that you need to register with the SEC, you generally become subject to the full scope of the Advisers Act. The obligations include:

- filing current disclosures on Form ADV;
- satisfying specified record-keeping requirements;
- establishing, maintaining, and implementing a compliance program;
- establishing, maintaining, and implementing a code of ethics;
- meeting the custody requirements;
- complying with advertising rules; and
- satisfying limitations on marketing.

For the details on what is means to be an SEC-registered investment adviser and a summary of the specific obligations, please read chapter 12 and also chapter 9, which deals with new reporting obligations for managers of private funds on Form PF.

❖ *Special Considerations for Advisers to Private Funds*

While all advisers must comply with the Advisers Act, there are unique issues that advisers to private funds should be aware of when implementing a compliance program and controls in preparation for registration and when conducting business as a registered adviser. Some of these are outlined below.

❖ *Fiduciaries*

Regardless of whether a private fund adviser must register or not, advisers are held to a fiduciary standard of honesty and transparency with investors. All advisers are subject to the antifraud provisions of the Advisers Act, which make it unlawful to "engage in any transaction, practice, or course of business which operates as a fraud or deceit upon any client or prospective client."

Advisers have a duty of loyalty and good faith toward their clients and the obligation to disclose material facts to clients where failure to do so would defraud or operate as a fraud or deceit.

❖ *Conflicts of Interest*

Private equity fund advisers that register with the SEC need to pay careful attention to the conflicts presented by the type and structure of investments those funds typically make and ensure that conflicts are identified, mitigated, and disclosed.

❖ *Allocation of Investments*

When a private equity firm has several funds operating in a similar space, disclosure should also be made to investors as to how allocation decisions are determined. Similarly, when an adviser has two funds that both own a piece of a portfolio company, there should be adequate disclosures around the method of valuation of that portfolio company by both funds. A policy for valuation in such an instance would also be helpful. Cross trades between two funds must also be executed according to established policies and procedures that have been disclosed previously to investors.

❖ *Allocation of Expenses*

Disclosures, policies, and procedures should also address the allocation of expenses between the adviser and the funds. Expenses borne by the funds should be plainly disclosed, and the adviser should ensure that no additional expenses are charged to the funds. Allocation of expenses in cases where there are co-investors with the fund, especially in the case of broken deals, should also be allocated fairly across all funds, including the co-investment vehicles. The adviser and co-investors should have a policy about how such expenses are paid by the various investors and how those expenses will be allocated among the co-investors.

❖ *Successive Funds*

One area of which private equity advisers should be cognizant is the use of successive funds to support older investments. Using newer funds to maintain operations of an older fund's investment until an appropriate exit opportunity arises carries the potential for conflicts of interest between the funds. Policies and procedures must be developed to provide a guide to think through, document, approve, and, importantly, disclose such conflicts.

■ Handling of Material Nonpublic Information

❖ *Insider Trading*

All advisers are required to have policies and procedures to prevent insider trading. A private equity adviser should work to identify all possible sources of material nonpublic information flowing into or out of the firm, and then establish policies to help mitigate any related risk. Due to the complexity of the private equity business, there may be a large number of possible sources. These sources could include discussions in one or more portfolio companies regarding a major supplier, vendor, or customer; employees who sit on outside boards; senior advisers; strategic investors who, in addition to being investors in the fund, are also officers or directors of outside companies or are invested in other funds; and outside consulting/research firms. A compliance program should include regular training on identification and mitigation of risk surrounding material nonpublic information and a legal or compliance-based resource that is available to consult on these issues.

❖ *Public and Private Sides*

Many private equity funds have a public and private side (whether the public side is an equity fund or, more often, a debt fund). A challenge for private equity advisers in particular is the need to carefully enforce and monitor the policies and procedures used to mitigate risk of distribution of material nonpublic information within the investment adviser, such as information walls and restricted and watch lists. It is incumbent upon private equity personnel to be able to identify instances carrying a higher risk of transmission and either avoid them or obtain a reasonable level of comfort that both parties do not intend to share any material nonpublic information.

Advisers should create detailed written policies and procedures surrounding the public and private businesses, including information barriers between the two sides, identifying who sits on top of the wall and what the wall-crossing procedures will be. In addition, compliance might want to chaperone such wall-crossing meetings, or at least maintain a record of such meetings and receive notes as to what was discussed between the public and private sides.

❖ *Custody of Client Assets*

Registered advisers, including private fund advisers, must comply with the custody rule, which applies to client assets, over which the investment adviser has custody. "Custody" is a broad term that covers the holding of cash or securities, as well as the ability to control assets through a related party such as a general partner of a fund. The custody rule creates many requirements, including having qualified custodians sending statements, annual examinations performed by an independent auditor, and internal reports over qualified custodians. Advisers may be exempt from some of these requirements if the client assets are in a pooled investment vehicle meeting an audit exemption. Custody is an important aspect of an adviser's obligations with respect to its clients' assets, and you should read chapter 11, which describes it in greater detail.

For private fund advisers, special care should also be paid to waterfall calculations and other fee provisions that impact client assets. After the legal offering documents establish the fee methodology, a policy should be implemented to monitor the related calculations and provide notice to investors if any changes occur. As discussed above, a fund should disclose expense allocations to investors, but expenses – both routine and those incurred during investment due diligence – should also be monitored. Monitoring provides a record of compliance with policies and legal documents and helps ensure that investor assets are not used for expenses that are the responsibility of the adviser, co-investors, or other client accounts.

❖ *Marketing*

Registering as an investment adviser also results in documentation and retention of record requirements related to marketing. Advisers must maintain documentation to confirm the accuracy of any past performance information given to current and prospective investors. Such documentation to support performance data must be maintained for five years after its last use. Private fund advisers typically use an internal rate for stating fund-performance results. Different than an annual total return metric, internal rate of return is a metric that goes back to the initial close date of the fund. Because an internal rate of return from a previous fund is often used to market a newer fund, private equity advisers will need to ensure they have the appropriate performance backup for a longer period than is traditional with funds (e.g., investment records for performance in 1990 that were used in 2011 must be kept until 2016).

❖ *FCPA*

While this topic is outside the scope of this book, I need to cover it; if only in passing. When an adviser is meeting with clients or potential clients, it is important to also be aware of the Foreign Corrupt Practices Act (FCPA). Private equity firms have likely focused on FCPA issues related to target acquisition due diligence, but they should also actively keep the FCPA in mind after acquisitions and during their own marketing activities. The FCPA prohibits improper payments and other practices (such as bribery), as well as the offer to make payments to a foreign official in order to secure any improper advantage in obtaining or retaining business for or with, or directing business to, any person. The adviser should have policies and procedures for monitoring and reviewing activities at its portfolio companies that could create FCPA risk. The Department of Justice has focused on alternative asset managers as it continues to broaden the number of industries that are investigated under the scope of the FCPA.

❖ *Risk Management*

Private fund advisers should evaluate their risk management structures and processes. Effective risk management starts at the product and asset class levels in accordance with the tolerances and appetites set by the board and senior management.

Risk management functions should be effectively integrated into the structure of the organization while still keeping the necessary independence, standing, and authority to effectively identify, manage, and mitigate risk. Internal audit processes should independently verify the effectiveness of the firm's compliance, control, and risk management functions.

Lastly, senior managers should effectively exercise oversight of enterprise risk management. The tone needs to come from the top.

Chapter 1 **Key Take-Aways**

**It is critical for advisers to accurately assess whether they are required to register with the SEC or if they are exempt from registration.
I urge you to ready the details in the corresponding chapters.**

Advisers who are already registered need to have effective compliance programs and be prepared for the SEC's examination oversight.

All registered advisers are required to provide extensive information on a revised Form ADV.

The reporting requirements for private funds are even more extensive, both on Form ADV and a new Form PF.

Even if exempt from registration, many advisers may be subject to reporting obligations as exempt reporting advisers.

Careful consideration should be given to all the disclosures made. The antifraud rules apply to all communications. In addition, most of them are publicly available.

Chapter 02

Private Fund Advisers – Hedge Funds and Private Equity Funds

If you have read chapter 1, you know by now that Dodd-Frank eliminated the principal Advisers Act exemption on which many hedge fund and private equity fund managers relied to avoid state and federal registration. Pre-Dodd-Frank, an adviser with fewer than fifteen clients (where each fund counted as a client, not each investor in the fund) was generally exempt from registration. Dodd-Frank replaced this general exemption with a number of narrower ones. It also increased the required dollar threshold for advisers to register with the SEC and significantly increased the reporting and disclosure requirements under the Advisers Act for those who were now within the auspices of the SEC.

The overhaul of the Advisers Act affected most advisers, among them many advisers to private equity and hedge funds. Not only did most of them find themselves in a position of having to register with the SEC for the first time, but they were also confronted with a complex new legal framework to contend with enhanced compliance requirements. This chapter is meant to serve as a step-by-step guide to the SEC registration requirements and relevant compliance obligations, as well as the available exemptions for advisers to hedge and private equity funds.

Overview

The answer to the question as to whether or not you need to register with the SEC or state regulators mostly depends on the amount of assets you have under management. If you are an adviser of private funds, you need to register with the SEC if the funds you manage have in the aggregate more than $150 million in assets. If you are below that threshold, you qualify for the newly created private fund adviser exemption with which you still have to file reports with the SEC and satisfy specific record-keeping requirements but are not subject to all the obligations under the Advisers Act. If the private fund adviser exemption is not available to you, you may still qualify for others, such as the foreign private adviser exemption, the venture capital exemption, or the family office exemption. All of them are outlined in separate chapters. If you advise private funds among other clients, you would need to determine whether to register with the SEC or the state regulators.

If you decide that you do need to register, then it is imperative that you have implemented a full compliance program before you make the appropriate filings and that you have created the infrastructure to comply with all the new disclosure requirements.

Detailed Discussion

The following chart may help you with the determination as to whether to register or not:

Fig. 2.1 *Private Fund Adviser Exemption*

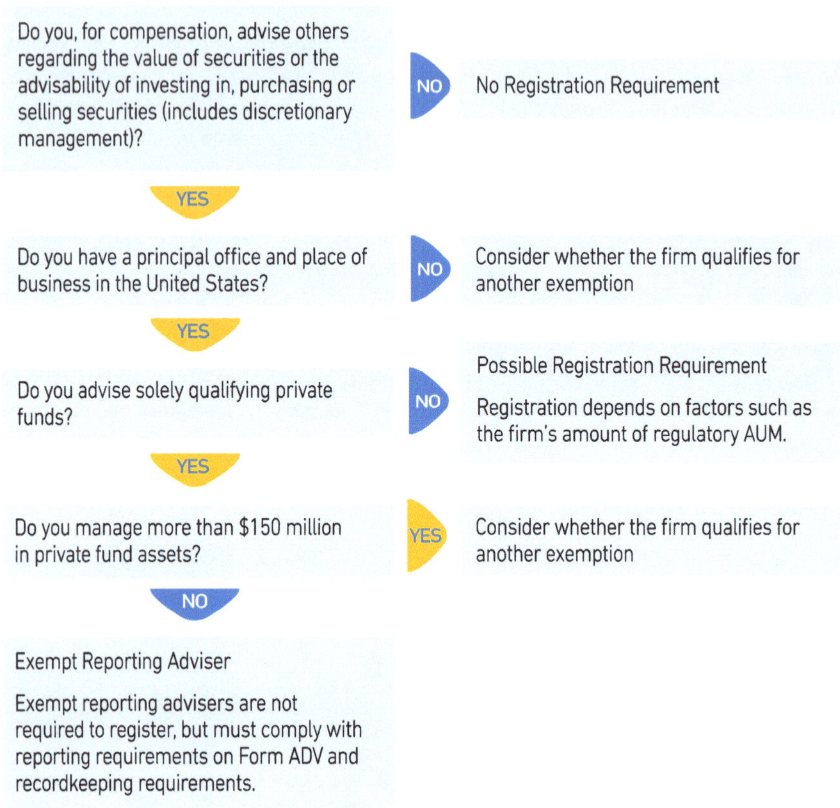

■ Am I an Investment Adviser?

This is the first question you would ask yourself before worrying about registration and exemptions. The registration and compliance obligations under the Advisers Act apply to investment advisers, which are defined as any person who, for compensation, engages in the business of advising others as to the value of securities or as to the advisability of investing in securities, or who, for compensation, issues or promulgates analyses or reports concerning securities. Excluded from the definition are:

1) banks or bank holding companies;
2) lawyers, accountants, engineers, or teachers whose performance of advisory services is incidental to their profession;

3) broker-dealers;
4) newspaper or magazine publishers;
5) advisers whose advice or analysis relates to certain US government related securities;
6) recognized statistical rating organizations; and
7) family offices.

Most hedge fund and private equity fund managers provide advice with respect to securities and would qualify as investment advisers. However, if an adviser exclusively advises about matters other than securities – for example, real estate or gold or foreign currencies – it would not be an investment adviser within the meaning of the Advisers Act and would not be subject to its registration requirements.

■ Do I Have to Register with the SEC/State Regulators?

❖ *Registration Requirements*

You are required to register with the SEC under the Advisers Act if:

1) you have regulatory assets under management of $150 million or more;

2) some of your clients are not hedge funds or private equity funds, and you have regulatory assets under management of $100 million or more;

3) some of your clients are not hedge funds or private equity funds, and you have regulatory assets under management of $25 million or more and a.) your principal office and place of business is in a state where: you are not required to register with the state securities regulator as an investment adviser, or you are required to register with the state securities regulator but are not subject to examination as an investment adviser by the latter (currently, the only states where you are not subject to examination are New York and Wyoming); b.) you act as an adviser to a registered investment company or a business development company, or c.) you hold yourself out to the public in the United States as an investment adviser.

Alternatively, you are not required to register if:

1) you have regulatory assets under management of less than $25 million subject to certain exceptions (note that you may still be required to register in the states in which you do business);

2) you advise solely private funds and have regulatory assets under management of less than $150 million and qualify for the private fund adviser exemption;

3) you advise only venture capital funds and qualify for the venture capital exemption;

4) you are a foreign private adviser and qualify for the foreign private adviser exemption;

5) you are a family office and fit within the definition of family office; or,

6) you are registered with the CFTC as a commodity trading adviser, and your business is not predominantly providing securities-related advice.

❖ *Calculating Assets under Management*

The first step in determining if you must register with the SEC/state regulators is to calculate your assets under management. The SEC has adopted a uniform method for calculating assets under management (which are now called regulatory assets under management), providing that advisers must incorporate securities portfolios, including funds for which they provide continuous and regular supervisory or management services. The definition includes family or proprietary assets, assets managed without receiving compensation, and assets of foreign clients. Under the new rules, advisers must calculate their assets under management on a gross basis; that is, without deduction of any outstanding indebtedness or other accrued but unpaid liabilities.

An important note for managers of private equity funds: the new instructions for Form ADV provide specific guidance to managers of private funds for calculating their assets under management. The instructions provide that:

- Advisers to private funds are required to include the value of any private fund over which they exercise continuous and regular supervisory or management services, regardless of the nature of the assets held by the fund.
- Value is based on the current market value, or, in the case of a private fund, the fair value where current market value is unavailable for the private fund's assets, and the contractual amount of any uncalled commitments.
- Advisers that calculate fair value in accordance with GAAP, or another international accounting standard for financial reporting purposes, are expected to use that same basis for purposes of determining the fair value of their assets under management; but, advisers may use any fair-valuation standard.

■ Can I Still Register with the SEC If I Am a Small or Midsized Adviser?

While advisers with less than $100 million in assets under management are generally prohibited from registering with the SEC, the SEC provided exceptions to this rule. These exceptions apply to:

1) pension consultants,
2) advisers affiliated with an SEC-registered investment adviser,
3) advisers expecting to be eligible for SEC registration within 120 days of filing its Form ADV,
4) multistate investment advisers, and
5) Internet advisers.

The following table illustrates the registration obligations:

The new rules also provide a buffer for advisers close to $100 million in assets under management to help these advisers determine if and when they will be required to switch between state and SEC registration. The buffer provides that advisers with between $100 million and $110 million in assets under management will be permitted, but not required, to register with the SEC

Fig. 2.2 *State vs Federal Registration*

Type of Adviser	SEC Registration	Registration with State(s)
Pension Consultants: Advisers that are "pension consultants" with respect to assets for plans having an aggregate value of at least $200 million meeting certain conditions under Rule 203A-2(a)	**Optional**	**Required** in accordance with state law, unless registered with the SEC or exempt under state law
Multi-State Advisers: Advisers required to register with 15 or more states meeting certain conditions under Rule 203A-2(d)	**Optional**	**Required** in accordance with state law, unless registered with the SEC or exempt under state law
Internet Advisers: Internet investment advisers meeting certain conditions under Rule 203A-2(e)	**Optional**	**Required** in accordance with state law, unless registered with the SEC or exempt under state law
Affiliates of Registered Advisers: Advisers that control, are controlled by, or are under common control with, an investment adviser that is registered with the SEC, and whose principal office and place of business is the same as the registered adviser	**Optional**	**Required** in accordance with state law, unless registered with the SEC or exempt under state law
Advisers Eligible for Registration within 120 days: An adviser that expects to be eligible for SEC registration within 120 days after the date it registers with the SEC and meeting certain conditions under Rule 203A-2(c)	**Optional**	**Required** in accordance with state law, unless registered with the SEC or exempt under state law

and that once an adviser is registered with the SEC, it is not required to withdraw its registration until it has less than $90 million in assets under management.

Whether you are eligible for SEC registration or not is determined annually as part of your annual updating amendment to Form ADV. Since federal registration preempts state law registration, it may be preferable, if possible, for a small or midsized adviser to register with the SEC instead of the state authorities if, for example, it would otherwise be subject to more onerous state rules or would be required to file and pay registration fees in more than one state. Please refer to the separate chapter (number six) for details on when to register with the SEC or with the state securities regulators and the consequences of doing so.

What Are the Requirements for the Exemptions from SEC Registration?

Some hedge and private equity fund advisers may be able to rely on new exemptions from SEC registration that Dodd-Frank created/amended. The main ones are as follows:

Advisers Only to Private Funds with Less than $150 Million in Assets under Management

If you are a manager of hedge or private equity funds, this would be the first exemption to look into. It exempts from registration any adviser that:

- acts *solely* as an investment adviser to one or more qualifying private funds (defined below) and
- has assets under management attributable to private funds of less than $150 million.

For this exemption to apply, all of your clients need to be private funds (i.e., investment companies that would have to register as such under the Investment Company Act, if it weren't for the exclusions in Section 3(c)(1) or Section 3(c)(7) of the Act). What that means is that the funds need to be companies (corporations, business trusts, partnerships, or limited liability companies) that issue securities and are primarily engaged in the business of investing in securities, but are not required to be registered under the Investment Company Act because they have 100 or fewer investors, or whose investors are only qualified purchaser (i.e., ultra-high-net-worth individuals).

The question of whether or not a company is a private fund plays a role in a number of the exemptions, including the venture capital exemption described below. For purposes of the private fund adviser exemption, private funds may also include funds that rely on any of the exemptions under Section 3 of the Investment Company Act, including Section 3(c)(5)(C), which applies to real estate funds. As a result, advisers are permitted to advise a broader category and a greater number of funds and still satisfy this exemption. However, advisers must treat each private fund as such for other purposes of the Advisers Act, including for purposes of calculating the $150 million threshold described below.

Advisers relying on this exemption must annually calculate the amount of the private fund's assets under management and report the amount in the adviser's annual amendment to its Form ADV. Therefore, while advisers may be required to register under the Advisers Act as a result of changes to their assets under management as reported in their annual updating amendments, they will not lose the benefit of this exemption due to fluctuations in the adviser's assets under management during the course of the year.

Foreign advisers take note: the private fund adviser exemption also applies to an adviser with its principal office and place of business outside of the United States if the adviser:

- has no client that is a US person except for one or more qualifying private funds; and
- all assets managed by the adviser at a place of business in the United States are *solely* attributable to private fund assets, the value of which is less than $150 million.

When determining if all of the non-US adviser's clients are private funds, a non-US adviser whose principal office and place of business is *outside* the United States may enter the US market and rely on the exemption without regard to its advisory services, clients, or assets under management outside of the United States. The new rules also clarify that, for advisers whose principal office and place of business is outside the United States, a client will not be considered a US person for purposes of this exemption if the client was *not* a US person at the time it became a client of the adviser.

Managers relying on the private fund adviser exemption will be exempt reporting advisers, which are subject to limited public reporting requirements, including parts of Form ADV, and reporting obligations.

❖ *Advisers Only to Venture Capital Funds*

If you manage private funds and all of them are venture capital funds, you may qualify for the venture capital fund exemption. The Dodd-Frank Act exempts from registration US and non-US fund managers that advise solely venture capital funds, regardless of the number or the size of the funds. Managers relying on the venture capital exemption will not be required to register with the SEC but will be considered exempt reporting advisers. This exemption is described in more detail in chapter 4, which you should read if you call yourself a venture capital fund.

❖ *Foreign Private Advisers*

Some private fund advisers may be able to rely on the newly created foreign private adviser exemption which is available only to advisers that have no place of business in the United States and do not hold themselves out as an investment adviser in the United States. Please read chapter 5 for more details.

❖ *Advisers to Family Offices*

Some private fund managers may fit the new definition of family offices, which are exempt from the registration and compliance requirements under the Advisers Act; although, you should keep in mind that the scope of the definition is quite narrow and tailored to match the true scope of single-family office. Please read chapter 3 for more details.

■ How Do I Register with the SEC?

If you do not qualify for an exemption and meet the asset threshold, you must register with the SEC. Form ADV is the central document for registering as an adviser with the SEC and states. To register, you must electronically file Form ADV with the SEC through the Investment Adviser Registration Depository (IARD), the registration system managed by the Financial Industry Regulatory Authority (FINRA). I provide all the details on how to register in chapter 7.

Chapter 2 **Key Take-Aways**

Dodd-Frank and the amended Advisers Act dramatically changed the regulatory landscape. Not only did it significantly expand the circle of advisers required to be registered but also the disclosure and compliance obligations of registrants once they were registered.

Many hedge and private equity fund managers are now required to register because they do not qualify for an exemption, such as the private fund adviser exemption or the venture capital exemption. You should carefully look at the newly minted calculation of regulatory assets under management to determine if and where you have to register (i.e., with the SEC or your state regulator).

Investment advisers must satisfy filing and reporting requirements on Form ADV and Form PF. Especially Form PF requires lead time and logistics. Keep that in mind.

Registered investment advisers, including those to hedge and private equity funds, are subject to the full set of compliance obligations imposed by the Advisers Act and the rules under it. That requires compliance processes and procedures (i.e., an infrastructure, including a manual, a chief compliance officer, a code of ethics, and an annual compliance review). The substantive rules cover marketing and advertising, custody of client assets, conflicts of interest, personal trading and clear, accurate, and complete disclosures to clients.

Chapter 03

FEDERAL RESERVE NOTE
THE UNITED STATES OF AMERICA
C 81230251 D
WASHINGTON, D.C.
ONE DOLLAR

Family Offices

Family offices are private wealth management firms established by ultra-high-net worth individuals or families to manage their own wealth and to provide other services such as budgeting, insurance, charitable giving, wealth transfer, and tax and estate planning. Under the Advisers Act, pre-Dodd-Frank, most family offices were not required to register with the SEC, because they either fell within the scope of the private adviser exemption in the Advisers Act available to advisers with fewer than fifteen clients, or they obtained individual exemptive orders from the SEC. The Dodd-Frank Act repealed the private adviser exemption effective July 21, 2011 and replaced it with a new exclusion in Section 202(a)(11)(G) of the Advisers Act, under which family offices were not to be treated as investment advisers and not subject to registration. The SEC was tasked with defining what family office means by following its previous exemptive practice and recognizing "the range of organizational, management, and employment structures and arrangements employed by family offices."

A family office that meets the SEC's new definition is not subject to SEC registration since Congress and the SEC view family offices not as arrangements that the Advisers Act was designed to regulate, but rather as private business matters to be handled within the family and, in the event of disputes, in state family law courts.

This chapter explains how the new definition of family office works, what it means to be registered as an investment adviser if the exemption is not available, and how advisers may structure the office to fall within its scope.

Overview

To qualify as a family office for the purposes of the new exemption from SEC registration, a firm must meet the following criteria:

1) It must provide investment advice only to "family clients" (i.e., family members, key employees, family nonprofits, and family trusts and estates).
2) It must be wholly owned by family clients and be controlled, either directly or indirectly, exclusively by "family members" and/or "family entities, such as family trusts and estates."
3) It must not hold itself out to the public as an investment adviser.
4) If an adviser had previously obtained an exemptive order from the SEC, it may continue to rely on it and does not need to meet the above requirements.
5) Advisers may be able to avail themselves to the grandfathering provision. Please read below for the details.

   If a family office fails to meet these conditions, it may still provide advisory services to its clients, but it will need to register with the SEC under the Advisers Act or seek an exemptive order from the SEC.

If you decide that you do need to register, then it is imperative that you have implemented a full compliance program before you make the appropriate filings and that you have created the infrastructure to comply with all the new disclosure requirements.

Detailed Discussion

Fig. 3.1 *Family Offices*

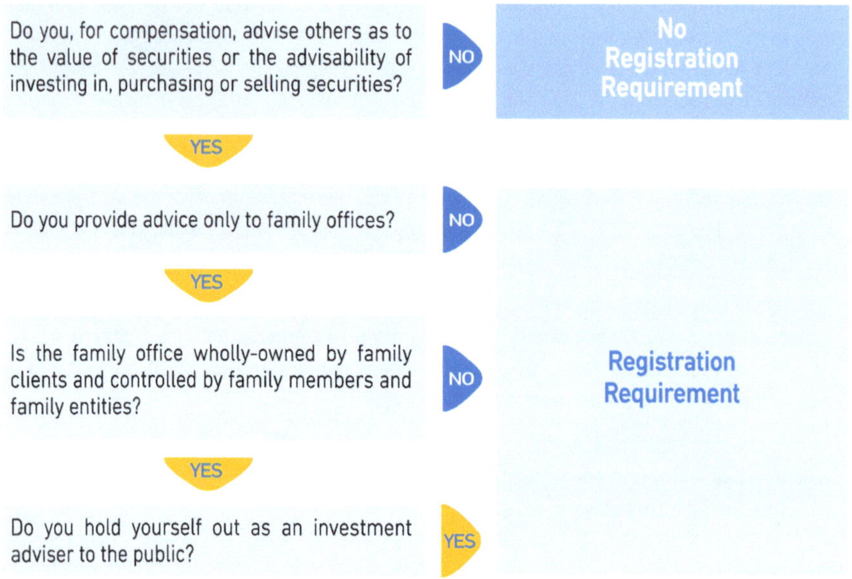

While the family office exemption criteria may seem straightforward, the defined terms, as explained below, can prove quite complex.

■ Family Clients

Family clients fall under the following categories:

❖ *Family Members*

The exemption covers lineal descendants as well as their spouses or spousal equivalents, stepchildren, adopted children, foster children, and persons who were minors when another family member became their legal guardian. The definition of "family member" includes all lineal descendants of a designated common ancestor, as well as their spouses or spousal equivalents within ten generations from that common ancestor.

Under the new rules, the family chooses the ancestor – whether living or deceased – and defines the family members by reference to the lineal kinship to that designated relative. The ancestor is not required to be the individual who originally created the family's wealth, and over time the family may even choose to change the designation and adjust the scope of family members served by the family office.

The most common problem with this definition is with friends and in-laws. The definition of a family member does not include parents, siblings, lineal descendants of an adopted child, stepchild, or foster child, or anyone else in the family of a spouse who is not a lineal descendant of the designated common ancestor.

The following diagram, based on a chart provided by the SEC, illustrates the effect of a family office redesignating its common ancestor. In the top chart, the light blue circles indicate persons in various generations that are "family members" of the family office. The dark blue circles indicate persons in various generations that are outside the 10-generation limit and thus may not be advised by the family office under the exclusion. The lower diagram shows the impact of redesignating the common ancestor from an individual in generation 1 to an individual in generation 5. The gray circles indicate the new group of family clients that the family office may advise and maintain its exclusion. The light blue circles indicate individuals that previously the family office could advise, but that are no longer "family members" due to the re-designation. The dark blue circles indicate individuals that were too remote from the common ancestor in both cases to be considered "family members."

Fig. 3.2 *Family Office Redesignating Common Ancestor*

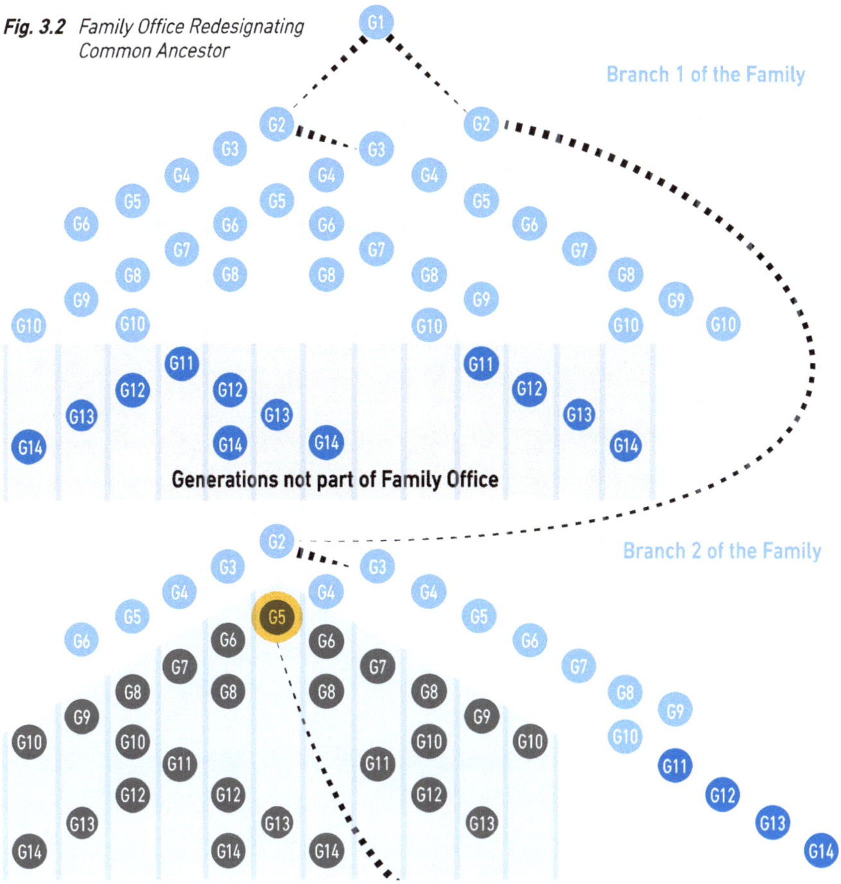

Derived from original SEC chart

❖ *Former Family Member*

A "former family member" is defined as a spouse, spousal equivalent, or stepchild who once was a family member, but is no longer. The exemption treats former family members (i.e., former spouses, spousal equivalents, and stepchildren) as family members.

❖ *Key Employee*

The new rules treat key employees of the family office, as well as their estates and entities through which they invest, as family clients, and they may obtain investment advice from and participate in investment opportunities provided by the family office.

A key employee would be an executive officer, director, trustee, or general partner of the family office, or any other employee who participates in the investment activities of the family office as part of his or her regular job functions, provided he or she has been performing those duties for at least twelve months at the family office or another entity affiliated with the family office.

The definition of a key employee extends to individuals working in a similar capacity for an affiliated family office, as well as their spouses or spousal equivalents, who own joint community property or have other similar ownership interests with the key employee.

Individuals performing only clerical, secretarial, and administrative functions are not considered key employees, nor are employees who do not participate in the family office's investment activities and who are not executive officers. For example, an in-house counsel who is not an executive officer is not considered a "key employee."

❖ *Former Key Employee*

A former key employee can remain a family client after relinquishing his or her duties, but only with respect to those assets managed by the family office prior to the termination of key employee status.

A former key employee is not considered to be a family client with respect to any investment made after the termination of key employee status unless the key employee was contractually obligated to make the new investment prior to the termination of status.

To determine the amount of assets of a former key employee that can still be managed by the family office, the firm need only consider the amount of assets the former key employee invested through the family office as of August 29, 2011 (the effective date of the family office rule) and any other investments the former key employee was contractually obligated to make.

❖ *Charitable Organizations and Trusts*

The new rule treats as family clients any nonprofit organizations and charitable foundations that are funded exclusively by one or more family clients.

To determine which charitable organizations qualify as family clients, the source of investment funds held by each of those organizations must be examined. If all of the funding has come from one or more family clients and no other source, then the charitable organization will qualify as a family client.

❖ *Family Estates*

Under the new rule, any estate of a family member, former family member, key employee, or former key employee may be treated as a family client for the entire period of the estate's administration. The identity of the estate's beneficiaries is not relevant and need not be taken into consideration.

❖ *Family Trusts*

Family trusts established for testamentary and charitable purposes are considered family clients. To qualify for exemption, the trust must fall into one of the following categories:

- An irrevocable trust – a trust that can be modified or terminated only with the consent of the beneficiary/ies – in which one or more family clients are the only current beneficiaries.

- An irrevocable trust funded exclusively by one or more family clients in which the only current beneficiaries are other family clients or nonprofit organizations, charitable foundations, charitable trusts, or other charitable organizations.

- A revocable trust – a trust that can be altered or terminated by the grantor – funded solely by family clients. The designated beneficiaries are not relevant unless the trust becomes irrevocable, at which point it must qualify as a permissible irrevocable trust as described above.

- A trust in which each trustee or authorized decision maker, as well as any person who funded the trust, is a key employee, or the key employee's current or former spouse or spousal equivalent, holding a joint community property or similar shared ownership interest in the contributed assets at the time of contribution.

For purposes of determining if a trust is a family client, contingent beneficiaries are disregarded unless and until they become actual current beneficiaries.

❖ *Family Entities*

The new rule allows the family office to conduct its activities through typical investment structures. Accordingly, the family client definition includes any entity, including a pooled investment vehicle, which is wholly owned, directly or indirectly, by family clients and which operates for their sole benefit. Entities that participate in the control of a family office would include a family client trust, a family client estate, a family client charitable organization or trust, or a family company as described above.

Key employees and their trusts are excluded from the definition of family entity

❖ *Involuntary Transfers*

Under the new rules, an involuntary transfer of assets to a person who is not a family member (for example, a bequest of assets in a family office fund to a friend) does not automatically cause the family office to lose its exemption. Rather, the new rules provide for a one-year grace period to facilitate an orderly transition of the assets out of the family office to another investment adviser.

❖ *Multifamily Offices*

The family office exemption limits the definition of "family office" to offices that exclusively advise a single family. The exclusion does not accommodate a de facto multifamily office, where more than one family attempts to circumvent the family office rule by establishing separate family offices staffed with the same, or substantially the same, employees.

■ Ownership and Control

For the SEC's core policy rationale for the exemption to be fulfilled – that a family office is essentially a family managing its own wealth – the family office must be wholly owned by family clients and be exclusively controlled, whether directly or indirectly, by one or more family members or family entities. While family clients other than family members, such as key employees, may own a portion of the family office, control of the family office must remain, directly or indirectly, exclusively with family members and their related entities (i.e., family owned companies or family trusts).

Assuming there are no special shareholder agreements or other arrangements that would give nonfamily members and/or nonfamily entities control over the management and policies of the family office, nonfamily members are permitted to serve on the board of directors of a family office. However, the board cannot consist exclusively of nonfamily members or entities, unless the governing documents of the family office indicate that only shareholders who are family members may decide on matters relating to the management and policies of the family office.

Since the rule requires that a family office be wholly owned by family clients, a nonfamily client owning nonvoting shares would still disqualify the office from the exemption.

■ Holding Out as an Investment Adviser

To qualify for exemption, a family office cannot present itself to the public as an investment adviser. However, the SEC indicated that a family office already registered as an investment adviser can choose to deregister in order to qualify for the new rule without getting penalized for having previously held itself out to the public as an investment adviser.

It is important to note that a family office cannot market nonpublic offerings to persons or entities that are not family clients.

Previously Issued Exemptive Orders

In the past, the SEC issued orders exempting a number of family offices from registration. The SEC has indicated that a family office currently relying on such orders may continue to do so, even if the order permits activities that are not covered by the new family office exemption.

A family office may also apply for an exemption for any services and activities not covered by the family office exemption rule. However, if a family office is not registered as an investment adviser, it should not provide services that are not exempt from registration until and unless such an exemption is granted.

Grandfathering Provision

Three types of clients are grandfathered as family clients so long as the family office was engaged to provide advice to the client before January 1, 2010. First, a family office may treat as a family client an officer, director, or employee of the family office who is an accredited investor. Second, any company exclusively owned and controlled by one or more family members may be a family client, even if it is operated for the sole benefit of one or more family clients. Third, any investment adviser to the family office that is registered under the Advisers Act who identifies investment opportunities to the family office and co-invests in those opportunities with the family office on substantially the same terms may be a family client, so long as the adviser's co-invested assets, in the aggregate, do not represent more than 5percent of the value of the assets to which the family office provides advice. However, in this last case, the family office will be considered an investment adviser for purposes of the antifraud provisions of the Advisers Act.

Investment managers who believe that they fit within the definition of "family office" should check the definitions and the grandfathering provisions in the final rule carefully to see if they meet every requirement of the rule.

SEC Registration for Family Offices

A family office that does not qualify for the family office exemption under the SEC's definition but does provide investment advice needs to do the following:

- **File Form ADV and Annual Updates.** Form ADV is publicly available and searchable in electronic format and includes information on ownership, structure, and asset values.
- **Prepare a Disclosure Document.** The document must be provided to clients on an annual basis.
- **Designate or hire a chief compliance officer.** This individual is responsible for administering the policies and procedures developed by the adviser.
- **Maintain records.** All nonexempt investmentadvisers must keep true, accurate, and current books and records relating to their investment advisory business.

- **Abide by Enhanced Custody Rules.** The firm's compliance manual must state that the manager maintains custody over the fund's assets.
- **Adopt Operational Procedures.** This would include a code of ethics, conflict of interest and privacy policies, and a business continuity plan with written policies regarding annual reviews of its compliance policies and procedures, the effectiveness of their implementation, as well as a documented process that identifies potential compliance risks and conflicts of interest.
- **Be Prepared for SEC Audit.** All investment advisers are subject to examination and information requests by the SEC.

Alternatives for Family Offices that Do Not Fall within the New Definition of Family Office

There are a number of alternatives for firms who do not fall within the new definition of "family office" that fall short of registering the entire office with the SEC. It may make sense for you to create a separate investment adviser and register that entity with the SEC. Alternatively, you may also choose to outsource the investment advisory function to a third party investment adviser. A number of firms have also restructured as a private trust company. Please keep in mind, however, that to be exempt as a private trust company, your investment advice must be ancillary to your primary function of acting as a trustee. Then there is always the option of to seek an exemptive order if you believe that there are good policy reasons for an order.

Chapter 3 **Key Take-Aways**

Determining if a particular family office qualifies for the new family office exclusion requires a careful legal review of the ownership, control, operations, and clients of the family office. Registration as an investment adviser entails a loss of privacy for the family office, as well as the added burden of ensuring legal and administrative compliance and maintenance of records, policies, and procedures imposed by the Advisers Act on registered investment advisers.

There are several alternatives available to family offices that do not qualify for the family office exemption but wish to avoid the pitfalls of having to register the family office as a whole. The family office should explore the following possibilities with its counsel:

- Set up a single-purpose registered investment adviser such a wholly owned registered investment adviser
- Restructure as an exempt entity
- Outsource to a third-part investment adviser
- Apply for an exemptive order

Family offices that do not meet the family office exemption criteria may need to transition some clients to other advisers if the family office does not wish to register. This rule only applies to investment advice with regard to securities. Family offices may continue to provide other types of administrative services and support to those clients.

Advisers who have fifteen or more clients and cannot transition clients and/or restructure to bring themselves in compliance with the rule may need to register with either the SEC or state authorities, unless another exemption is available.

Chapter 04

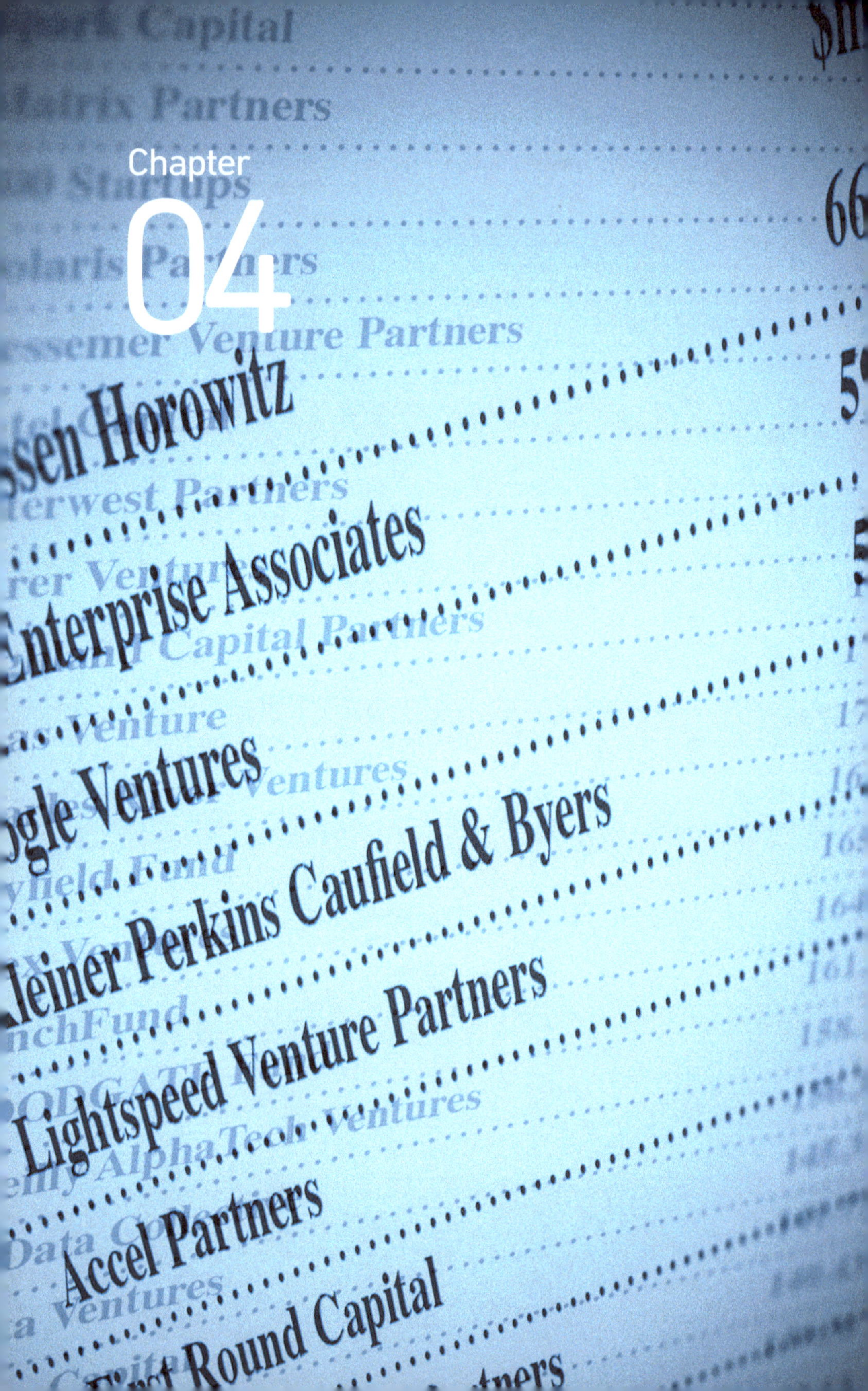
Horowitz
Enterprise Associates
Ventures
Perkins Caufield & Byers
Lightspeed Venture Partners
Accel Partners
Round Capital

Venture Capital Funds

Under the old Advisers Act, most managers of venture capital funds did not have to register as investment advisers because they relied on the private adviser exemption, which exempted from registration advisers who had fewer than fifteen clients.

Title IV of Dodd-Frank eliminated this exemption in one radical move and replaced it with a few new, much more limited, ones. One of them is the exemption for managers of venture capital funds in the new Rule 203(1)-1 of the Advisers Act. To put it all into context, Congress created this exemption mainly for funds that contribute substantial capital to early stage companies and that are generally not leveraged or connected to the public markets (i.e., funds that are not increasing the systemic risk that Title IV of Dodd-Frank was created to address). The SEC was then tasked to craft a definition of venture capital fund with those funds in mind, which it did. It is also worth pointing out that the new definition of a venture capital fund, which we will discuss in detail below, was meant to, and it largely does, successfully encompass most venture capital investing activity found in the market today, while also allowing for some flexibility by introducing a basket for investments that fall outside typical venture capital activities. The rules are technical, though, so I would encourage you to run through the elements of the defined term to ensure that your fund's activities don't put you outside the scope of the exemption accidently.

"Grandfathered" venture capital funds – venture capital funds that sold securities to investors before December 31, 2010 – satisfy the exemption. Readers interested in that category may disregard the detailed analysis that follows and skip to the end of the chapter where I talk more about the grandfathering rules.

I should point out that advisers relying on the venture capital exemption who are not required to register with the SEC, are still considered exempt reporting advisers and as such are subject to limited public reporting and compliance requirements, such as filing parts of Form ADV and record keeping (see chapter 10, "Exempt Reporting Advisers," for more details). It is also important to note that the venture capital exemption applies only to investment advisers who solely advise one or more venture capital funds.

Overview

For the purposes of the venture capital fund exemption, the SEC's new definition of venture capital generally encompasses only funds that engage in traditional venture capital activities and investment strategies. However, it does provide for a 20 percent basket for nontypical venture capital investment activities.

Determining if a fund qualifies as a venture capital fund is complex and requires careful analysis. Specifically, under the new rule, a fund must meet each of the following five criteria.

A venture capital fund is one that:

1. **1.** Venture Capital Strategy
2. **2.** 80 Percent Qualifying Investments
3. **3.** No Leverage
4. **4.** No Redemption
5. **5.** No Investment Company or Business Development Company

1) is a private fund that pursues a **venture capital strategy and is presented to investors as such;**

2) holds **80 percent** of the fund's capital contributions and uncalled capital commitments in "qualifying investments;"

3) **does not borrow** or otherwise incur leverage in excess of 15 percent of the fund's aggregate capital contributions or uncalled capital commitments, and then only on a short-term basis;

4) offers its investors **no redemption** or other similar liquidity rights except in extraordinary circumstances; and

5) is **not registered under the Investment Company Act** or elected to be treated as a **business development company**.

Examples for funds that fall outside the definition of venture capital funds are funds that:

- engage in a broader form of investing, such as growth equity investments or control transactions;
- use leverage in their investments on a regular basis;
- purchase shares from existing shareholders on a regular basis; and/or
- invest in public companies on a regular basis.

This chapter will guide you through what a "qualifying investment" is, how to calculate the 20 percent non-qualifying basket, whether your fund is grandfathered or not, and some factors you might consider when forming a fund.

Detailed Discussion

The SEC distinguishes venture capital funds from hedge funds and private equity funds on the basis of the lack of leverage of venture capital funds, and the nonpublic, start-up nature of the companies in which they invest. The venture capital fund exemption does not impose a limit on the number of funds a venture capital fund adviser may advise. However, an adviser is disqualified if he advises any non-venture capital fund client.

Fig. 4.1 *Venture Capital Fund Exemption*

Do you advise only venture capital funds?

NO → **Consider whether the firm qualifies for another exemption**

YES ↓

Does every fund you advise meet the criteria to be a qualified fund?

1. Represents to investors and prospective investors that it pursues a venture capital strategy
2. Holds no more than 20% of the fund's capital commitment in non-qualifying assets
3. Does not borrow or otherwise incur leverage of more than 15% of committed capital
4. Does not provide investors redemption rights except in extraordinary circumstances
5. Is not registered under the Investment Company Act and is not a business development company

YES → **Exempt Reporting Adviser**

NO ↓

Does any non-qualifying fund satisfy the grandfathering provision?

1. Has the fund represented to investors and potential investors at the time of offering that the fund pursued a venture capital strategy;
2. Has it sold securities to one or more investors prior to Dec 31, 2010; and
3. Has it not sold any securities to, or accepted capital commitment from, any person after July 21, 2011?

YES → **Exempt Reporting Adviser**

Exempt Reporting Adviser

Exempt reporting advisers are not required to register, but must comply with:

- Reporting requirements on Form ADV
- Recordkeeping obligations

NO ↓

Registration Requirement

■ Venture Capital Strategy

To meet the definition of venture capital fund, the fund must represent itself to current and prospective investors as a fund pursuing a venture capital strategy. The SEC will analyze this requirement under a "facts and circumstances" test based on all of the statements (or lack thereof) made in communications by the fund to its investors, including all fund offering and marketing materials. For example, "managerial assistance" to portfolio companies is not considered essential under the definition but would help demonstrate that a fund is indeed a venture capital fund. On the flip side, a fund that includes itself in a hedge fund database or index would have a hard time arguing that it qualifies for the exemption.

It is not necessary that a fund presents itself as pursuing a venture capital strategy to the exclusion of all other strategies, but I would recommend that the fund does not identify itself as a multistrategy fund (i.e., venture capital being one of several investment strategies, along with, for example, a hedge fund strategy) in communications. The SEC also noted that a fund manager representing to its investors that it is pursuing a venture capital strategy, but actually does not, may have made an untrue statement of a material fact in violation of the antifraud provisions under the Advisers Act that does not require scienter/intent.

Further, the fund does not have to include the term venture capital in its name. It is even possible for a venture capital fund to represent itself as pursuing a venture capital strategy without ever using the term "venture capital," but this seems to create unnecessary complications, and I would advise funds seeking to qualify as venture capital funds to use the term "venture capital strategy" in their marketing materials and governing agreements.

■ At Least 80 Percent Qualifying Investments

An exempt venture capital fund must hold at least 80 percent of the firm's capital commitments in qualifying investments. A qualifying investment generally consists of any:

1) *equity security* of a *qualifying portfolio company (QPC)*, or
2) short-term holdings.

More specifically, the equity security must be acquired directly from the portfolio company or as part of a recapitalization of the QPC or acquisition of another entity by the QPC, and then the recap or acquisition equity security must be in exchange for equities directly issued by the QPC.

❖ *Qualifying Portfolio Company*

Venture capital funds as defined in Section 203(l) under the Advisers Act can only invest in qualifying portfolio companies (QPCs). A QPC is defined as a company that:

1. Not a Reporting or Foreign Traded Company
2. No Leverage
3. Operating Company

- *Is not a reporting or foreign traded company* and does not have a control relationship with a reporting or foreign traded company.

Publicly traded companies are not QPCs, so direct investments in those companies must be done within the 20 percent non-qualifying basket (unless the shares are received in exchange for QPC securities in an acquisition as described above). Because the publicly traded status of a QPC is determined only at the time of the fund's investment, a portfolio company will not cease to be a QPC when it goes public, although any new investment in the company post-IPO would need to be included in the basket. Securities issued post-IPO in a conversion of convertible debt, options, or warrants that were acquired by the fund pre-IPO would probably not be counted as new investments for this purpose.

- *Does not incur leverage* in connection with the investment by the venture capital fund and does not distribute the proceeds of any such borrowing to the fund in exchange for the investment. This restriction is intended to distinguish a venture capital fund from a leveraged buyout fund, which has a different risk profile than what Congress had in mind. However, a QPC may borrow for general business purposes and may even borrow to redeem securities held by third parties. Moreover, subsequent distributions by the portfolio company to the fund solely based on the fund's status as an investor would not be subject to the limitation.
- *Is an operating company and not itself a fund*. Generally, a fund or pooled investment vehicle is not a qualifying investment. However, the SEC made clear that the fund may hold the QPC through an intermediate holding company formed solely for tax, legal, or regulatory reasons (such as "blocker corporations"), so long as the holding company is wholly owned by the fund. In this context, the SEC has also clarified that the intermediate holding company may be owned collectively by more than one venture capital fund advised by the same investment adviser.

❖ *Equity Securities or Short-Term Holdings*

Equity Securities The investment must be in equity securities of the QPC or consist of short-term holdings. The new Advisers Act defines *equity security* very broadly (using the definition under the 34 Act) as "any stock or similar security, certificate of interest or participation in any profit sharing agreement, preorganization certificate or subscription, transferable share, voting trust certificate or certificate of deposit for an equity security, limited partnership interest, interest in a joint venture, or certificate of interest in a business trust; any security future on any such security; or any security convertible, with or without consideration into such a security, or carrying any warrant or right to subscribe to or purchase such a security; or any such warrant or right; or any put, call, straddle, or other option or privilege of buying such a security from or selling such a security to another without being bound to do so."

The definition includes many typical forms of hedges, such as puts, calls, and straddles, relating to common or preferred stock but excludes others, such as currency and interest rate swaps. Keep in mind, though, that, as with other types of nonqualifying investments, a qualifying fund may enter into nonqualifying hedges within its 20 percent basket. The fact that preorganization certificates and subscriptions qualify as equity security are particularly helpful to seed-stage funds that acquire interests in companies that have not yet completed their formation process. Debt instruments of a QPC, such as nonconvertible bridge loans, count toward the fund's 20 percent basket.

Short-Term Holdings A fund may also invest in cash and cash equivalents and US Treasuries with a remaining maturity of sixty days or less and shares of registered money market funds. Short-term holdings are treated as qualifying (i.e., count toward the 80 percent) for purposes of determining the 80/20 percent split. Fund managers may want to pay close attention to their idle fund investment practices to meet the qualification. Managers who desire to invest those funds in longer-term or higher-yield instruments need to do the math and make sure they still fall within the 20 percent basket.

❖ *Directly Acquired or Exchanged*

To qualify for the exemption, qualifying investments must be an equity security that was:

- directly acquired from the QPC;
- issued by a QPC in exchange for directly acquired equity issued by the same QPC; or
- issued by a company of which a QPC is a majority-owned subsidiary or a predecessor that is acquired by the fund in exchange for directly acquired equity.

Qualifying investments generally must be acquired directly from the issuer, which means that equity securities acquired on a secondary basis would not qualify. The SEC made two exceptions to the "directly acquired" rule: In the case of a recapitalization, recap securities are qualifying investments when the fund, along with other existing security holders, accepts newly issued equity securities of the QPC in exchange for previously issued equity securities by the same QPC, allowing reclassifications and recapitalizations of the QPC to take place. The other exception was meant to facilitate the acquisition of a QPC using acquirer stock as part of the purchase price, enabling funds to treat them as qualifying even if they were public securities or would otherwise be non-qualifying. This exception allows the fund to acquire securities in connection with the acquisition or merger of a QPC by another company, as long as the QPC becomes a majority-owned subsidiary of the other company or is a predecessor company.

The SEC also recently clarified that the acquisition of "warehoused investments" by the fund still satisfies the QPC requirement, despite the fact that the investment was not strictly "directly" acquired from the QPC. A warehoused investment is an investment in a QPC that was initially made by the adviser because the fund was not yet able to make investments, and that was subsequently transferred to the fund once the fund was established. One caveat: the investment must have been made solely on behalf of a prospective venture capital fund that is actually fundraising and the terms of the investment must be fully disclosed to each investor in the fund prior to the investor's commitment.

Often advisers establish main funds and side funds. Sometimes the adviser closes the main fund, possibly after the main fund has acquired some investments, and transfers them to the side funds. The SEC clarified that it will treat the acquisition of investments by the side fund as if they were directly acquired by the QPC, as long as they occurred within twelve months of the closing of the main fund and the transfer was fully disclosed in the offering documents of the main fund and the side funds.

Lastly, the SEC provided guidance regarding the use of alternative investment vehicles (AIVs) by advisers to venture capital funds to accommodate varying tax, legal, or regulatory concerns of investors, such as US tax exempt and non-US investors. United States tax exempt and non-US investors may invest directly in AIVs, which must be controlled and managed by the adviser, and their sole purpose must be to invest in the venture capital fund. One caveat: the AIV must not be formed to get around the 20 percent basket, but solely for the purpose of addressing the investor's tax, legal, or regulatory concerns.

A final important note: Secondary market shares do not meet the "directly acquired" requirements. They count toward the 20 percent basket for non-qualifying investments.

■ The 20 Percent Non-Qualifying Investment Basket Calculation

The 20 percent non-qualifying basket that the new rules provide for nontraditional venture capital activities and investment strategies provides some flexibility. Within this basket, qualifying funds may make investments more typically associated with hedge funds, private equity funds, or other types of funds, as well as other investments that do not meet the strict qualifying investment tests. At the same time, the 20 percent limit is meant to prevent hedge funds and private equity funds from relying on the venture capital fund exemption by just adding some venture capital investments to their portfolios.

The 20 percent non-qualifying basket includes activities such as acquiring companies on public markets, making investments in debt instruments, creating founder liquidity by acquiring stock from the founder directly, etc. The basket also provides some buffer against accidental violations of the rules.

❖ *Valuation of Non-Qualifying Assets*

Non-qualifying assets may be valued at historical cost or fair value. However, once chosen, the fund must consistently apply the same method to all non-qualifying assets in a consistent manner during the fund's term. Alternating between valuation methodologies is not permitted. Using the assets' historical value would avoid having to account for market fluctuations or other changes in the portfolio value while the investment is held by the fund. Given market volatility and the related uncertainty of whether or not a fund would meet the 80/20 percent test at a given time, I anticipate that most funds will choose to value non-qualifying assets at cost.

❖ *Testing Date and Methodology*

The 20 percent test is applied immediately after the fund's acquisition of a non-qualifying investment. It is important to point out that the test does not have to be performed on a regular basis afterward. Thus, a subsequent change in the value of non-qualifying assets or the amount of the fund's capital will not result in failure to satisfy the 20 percent test.

It is quite possible that a fund may, at multiple times during its term, hold a portfolio that consists substantially of non-qualifying assets without violating the 20 percent test. Having non-qualifying securities in excess of the basket in the portfolio does not violate the exemption but precludes the fund from making another non-qualifying investment until the amount of non-qualifying investments in the portfolio (including the new investment) is reduced to below 20 percent.

❖ *Changes in Qualifying or Non-Qualifying Character*

A qualifying investment will not become non-qualifying just because the underlying portfolio company is no longer qualified. For example, a qualifying investment does not disqualify because the company later files for an IPO.

❖ *Contributed or Committed Capital*

The 20 percent test is applied against the amount of fund capital, which includes called capital and unfunded capital commitments expected to be called.

■ Limitation on Leverage of Fund

In general, a venture capital fund cannot borrow, issue debt obligations, provide guarantees or otherwise incur leverage in excess of 15 percent of the fund's capital – defined as capital contributions and uncalled capital commitments. Also, any such obligations must have a nonrenewable term of no longer than 120 days. The rule was designed to permit short-term borrowing pending capital calls.

Although not clarified by the SEC in its release of the new rules, it appears that the 15 percent limit should be determined by reference to the amount of leverage in effect at any given time, rather than on a cumulative basis over the fund's term. It is also unclear if accrued interest must be taken into account. I would err on the side of caution so not to jeopardize the entire qualification or seek guidance from the SEC.

Many venture capital funds establish lines of credit to bridge capital calls and provide for other short-term capital needs. Such lines of credit may still be used, but a number of previously common terms generally should be changed. For example, such lines of credit should no longer provide for terms longer than 120 days or for automatic renewals.

Furthermore, venture capital funds often engage in activities that under the new rules may be considered "leverage." For example, a fund's general partner may defer receipt of management fees in order to allow the fund to make additional investments. Unless properly structured, such a deferral may be deemed a borrowing or other use of leverage that counts toward the 15 percent limit. It is also advisable to carefully review loan agreements for cross-guarantee provisions. Many loan agreements require cross-guarantees by parallel or affiliated funds. Such cross-guarantees generally would count toward the 15 percent limit.

Lastly, the SEC has added one important exception to the guarantee restriction: venture capital funds may guarantee the obligations of QPCs without charging it against the 15 percent cap, provided that the guarantee does not exceed the fund's investment in the company.

No Redemption Rights for Limited Partners/Investors

A venture capital fund cannot grant investors withdrawal, redemption, or repurchase rights except under extraordinary circumstances. However, the new rules allow pro rata distributions to investors. This rule is based upon a principal distinction Congress made between venture capital funds and hedge funds, which typically grant broad redemption rights. While the SEC does not define what those extraordinary circumstances may be, it appears that the rule is based on an intention to allow redemption rights of the type historically common in the venture capital industry. Extraordinary circumstances could include future amendments to the law that would affect investors' tax treatment or ability to invest in particular countries and industries or unexpected corporate occurrences such as mergers. The determination is based on all the facts and circumstances. Redemption rights not triggered by law changes would need to be reviewed with greater scrutiny to make sure they are truly extraordinary.

Also, a fund cannot qualify as a venture capital fund if it offers quarterly or periodic withdrawal rights, even if the fund has a temporary initial lockup period or other restrictions relating to the right to redeem.

No Registration/Election under the Investment Company Act

The fund must not be registered as an investment company under the 1940 act (i.e., the fund must not be a mutual fund and must not have elected to be a business development company as previously indicated in the discussion of the definition of private fund).

The Grandfathering Provision

The rules "grandfather" any preexisting private fund as a venture capital fund if:

- At the time the fund offered its securities it presented itself to existing or prospective investors as pursuing a venture capital strategy.
- It sold securities to one or more investors prior to December 31, 2010.
- It does not issue securities to any person, including by means of accepting capital commitments, after July 21, 2011. The SEC confirmed that calling capital after July 21, 2011 for commitments existing on July 21, 2011 will not violate this requirement.

Foreign Fund Advisers

Foreign fund advisers may use the venture capital exemption if they qualify. The SEC clarified that a venture capital fund does not need to be managed by a US-based adviser, and, accordingly, non-US-based advisers can also qualify for the exemption (in addition to other available exemptions, such as the foreign adviser exemption discussed in chapter 5). Furthermore, a non-US adviser may treat as a venture capital fund any non-US fund that is not offered through the use of US jurisdictional means but that would be a private fund if the fund conducted a private offering in the United States and met the rule's other criteria.

■ Managerial Assistance

Interestingly enough, the SEC did not adopt a managerial assistance requirement as originally proposed in its rule proposal. Based on commenters' concerns, the SEC eliminated this requirement, following the argument that the business arrangement between the parties should dictate such decisions and that it would be unduly burdensome with no significant benefit for investors.

■ Reporting Requirements

Advisers relying on the venture capital fund exemption remain subject to SEC reporting requirements, including a requirement to file a limited subset of the items in part 1A of Form ADV. For more details see chapter 10, "Exempt Reporting Advisers."

Chapter 4 **Key Take-Aways**

The venture capital exemption for advisers to venture capital funds is significantly narrower than the former private adviser exemption. Careful analysis and structuring is required to make sure all elements are met.

Even if a fund meets the requirements of a venture capital fund, the adviser may still have to file reports as an exempt reporting adviser for purposes of the new Advisers Act and SEC rules and maintain records.

Venture capital funds exempt from the requirements of the Advisers Act may still have to register in accordance with state laws. This again requires careful analysis.

Advisers who do not meet the venture capital exemption may still fall within the scope of another exemption, such as the private fund adviser and the foreign private adviser exemptions.

Chapter 05

Foreign Private Advisers

The passing of Dodd-Frank was one of the most significant overhauls of the financial services industry in the United States; and due to the extraterritorial reach of some of its provisions, it has a significant impact on foreign financial institutions. As of March 31, 2012, many non-US investment advisers are required for the first time to be registered with the SEC under the United States Investment Advisers Act of 1940. Previously, many non-US advisers relied on the private adviser exemption under the Advisers Act, which provided an exemption from registration for investment advisers (whether US or non-US) that had fewer than fifteen US clients and did not hold themselves out to the public in the United States as investment advisers. The private adviser exemption was repealed by Dodd-Frank, which created a number of narrower exemptions that advisers may now rely on, such as the family office exemption, the private fund adviser exemption, the venture capital exemption and the foreign private adviser exemption – which is the focus of this chapter. The other three are discussed in chapters 2, 3, and 4. Not qualifying for the exemption means that you would register with the SEC and comply with the various requirements of the Advisers Act, such as being a fiduciary of client assets with all of its implications, the implantation of a compliance program, maintenance of books and records and publicly available reporting with the SEC.

While non-US advisers may qualify for other exemptions, in this chapter I will guide you through the elements of the foreign private adviser exemption and explain what it would mean for you to be registered with the SEC in the event an exemption is not available to you.

Overview

The Advisers Act defines a foreign private adviser as an investment adviser that meets all of the following criteria. A foreign private adviser:

1) must not have a **place of business** in the United States,

2) must have **fewer than fifteen US clients and US investors** in private funds advised by the adviser,

3) must have **less than $25 million** in assets under management from those US clients and US Investors,

4) cannot **hold itself out** generally to the public in the United States as an investment adviser, and

5) must not be an adviser to a **registered investment company** or **registered business development company**.

> **1.** No US place of business;
> **2.** Fewer than fifteen US clients/ investors;
> **3.** Less than $25M AUM; and
> **4.** No holding itself out as an investment adviser in the United States

The web of defined terms in the new exemption is intricate and stems from different sets of rules, such as the Investment Company Act and Regulation S under the Securities Act. The following flow chart hopefully simplifies the analysis:

Fig 5.1 *Foreign Private Adviser Exemption*

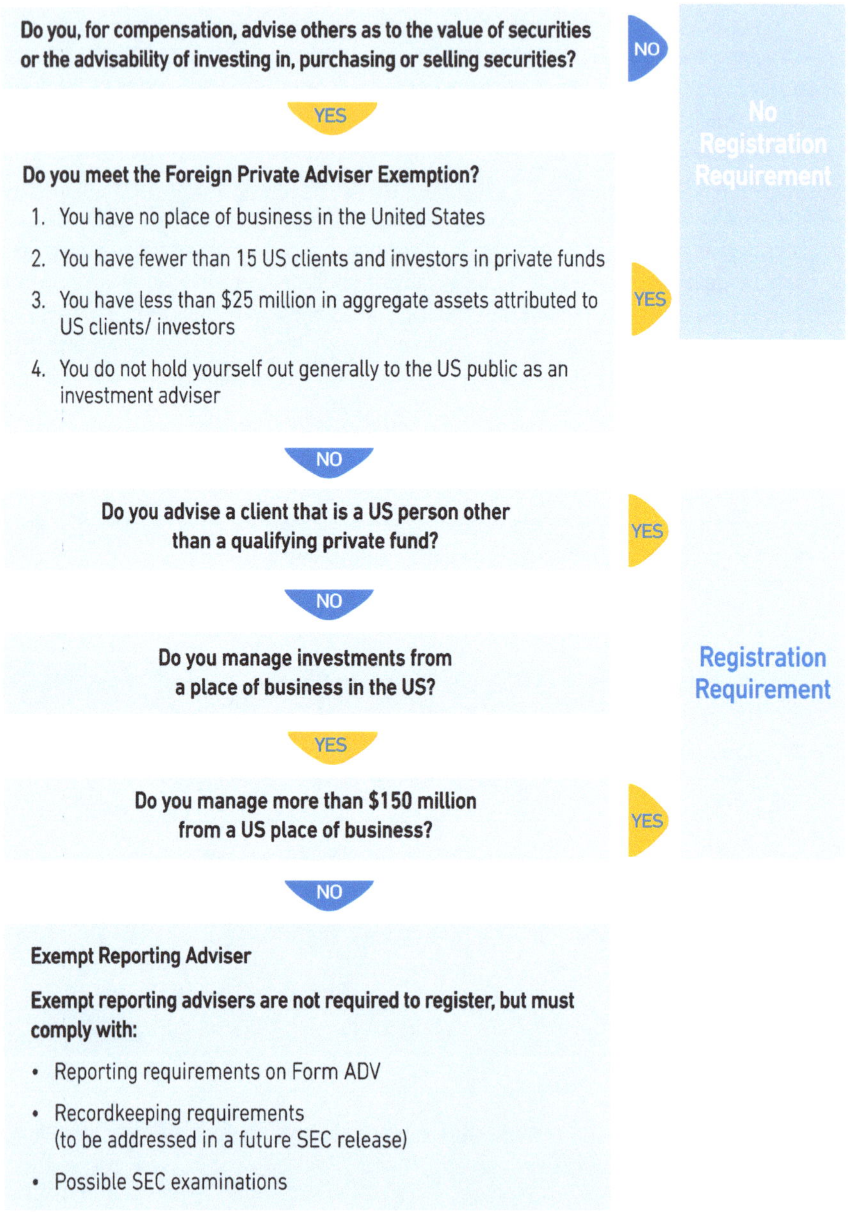

Detailed Discussion

Before you start analyzing your specific situation, let's take a look at the key definitions. They are:

- place of business,
- clients (fewer than fifteen in the United States),
- private fund investors, and
- what "in the United States" means.

A summary of the defined terms and how they relate to each other is set forth below. Let's look at them in detail.

■ Place of Business

To qualify as a foreign private adviser, the investment adviser or fund manager cannot have a place of business in the United States. Under the new Advisers Act rule, "place of business" of an investment adviser means any office in which the adviser regularly provides investment advisory services, solicits, meets with, or otherwise communicates with clients, as well as any other location that is held out to the general public as a location at which the adviser conducts any such activities.

Note that a non-US adviser or manager will not be presumed to have a place of business just because it has a US affiliate. However, if the non-US adviser's personnel regularly conducts advisory activities at the affiliate's place of business, the non-US adviser will be deemed to have a place of business in the United States.

Every adviser must determine if it has a place of business in the United States based on its own facts and circumstances. The SEC provided some specific examples:

- A place of business includes any office from which an adviser regularly communicates with clients, whether they are US or non-US clients.
- A place of business includes any office or other location where an adviser regularly conducts research, including research used to produce nonpublic information relevant to investment decisions and recommendations. While the issue was not addressed in the proposed rule, the final release specifically states that the SEC considers research intrinsic to the provision of investment advisory services.
- A place of business does not include an office where an adviser solely performs administrative and back-office activities that are intrinsic to the provision of investment advisory services. However, these activities cannot involve communication with clients.

A word of caution: the SEC interprets the term very broadly. For example, if you were to use a hotel room or the office of an affiliate or business partner, it could already be viewed as a place of business and would disqualify you from the exemption.

■ Clients (Fewer than Fifteen): How Do You Count Clients/Private Fund Investors?

To qualify as a foreign private adviser, an investment adviser or fund manager must have fewer than fifteen US clients or US private fund investors. Rule 202(a)(30)-1 of the Advisers Act provides the method for counting those clients or investors.

❖ *Clients*

A foreign private adviser may treat as single client any natural person and his/her minor children (regardless of whether or not they share the same principal residence) and any relative, spouse, spousal equivalent, or relative of the spouse or spousal equivalent of that person who has the same principal residence as the person. Also, any accounts and trusts in which that person and his children, etc., are the only primary beneficiaries.

You may treat as a single client a partnership, limited liability company, corporation, trust, or other legal organization (or more than one organization with identical ownership) to which the adviser provides advice based on the organization's investment objectives, rather than the individual objectives of the organization's owners. Two or more legal organizations that have identical shareholders, partners, limited partners, members, or beneficiaries will also be treated as a single client. However, if the legal organization is an investment company as defined under the Investment Company Act, but for the exceptions in sections 3(c)(1) and 3(c)(7) of the Investment Company Act (less than 100 investors or exclusively qualified purchasers), the number of investors in such private funds would be counted as private fund investors as discussed below in more detail.

It is worth pointing out that a person still counts as a client even if the adviser provides services for such person without compensation. Also, a general partner or managing member or similar person acting as an adviser to a partnership or limited liability company is required to count the partnership or limited liability company as a client.

To avoid double counting (i.e., ensure that a client who is also an investor in a private fund advised by the adviser is only counted once), new Rule 202(a)(30)-1 provides that:

- an adviser is not required to count a private fund as a client if he counts any investor in the fund for purposes of determining availability of the exemption; and
- an adviser is not required to count a person as an investor in a private fund, if it counts such person as a client of the adviser.

❖ *Private Fund Investors*

As noted above, special rules apply to legal organizations that constitute private funds. The final Rule 202(a)(30)-1of the Advisers Act, defines an investor in a private fund as any person who would be included in determining the number of beneficial owners under Sections 3(c)(1) or 3(c)(7) of the Investment Company Act. Accordingly, in calculating the number of investors, advisers are required to "look through" nominee and similar arrangements and count the underlying holders of private fund interests. The Investment Company look-through rules seem deceivingly simple at first glance; at second glance they are the opposite. Counting the number of private fund investors will require individual determinations based on the facts and circumstances of each case. However, the SEC does provide specific examples:

- An adviser to a master fund in a master-feeder arrangement must treat as investors the holders of the securities of any feeder fund formed or operated for the purpose of investing in the master fund rather than just the feeder fund itself, the argument being that the feeder only acts as a conduit.
- An adviser must look through any nominee entity or similar arrangement.
- An adviser must look through any entity created for the purpose of making an investment and count each of its beneficial owners as investors.
- An adviser must count as an investor any holder of an instrument – such as a total return swap – that effectively transfers the risk of investing in the private fund from the record owner of the private fund's securities.
- An adviser must count as investors holders of both equity and debt securities.
- In a departure from the Investment Company rules, for purposes of the foreign private adviser exemption, a beneficial owner of short-term paper issued by the private fund would also count as an investor. They need not be counted for purposes of Section 3(c)(1) of the Investment Company Act.
- The final rule also does not count knowledgeable employees of the fund in the investor definition.

Since the number of private fund investors is determined by facts and circumstances specific to each case, an adviser may treat as a non-US investor any person he *reasonably believes* is an actual investor and who he reasonably believes is not in the United States.

❖ *Rules To Avoid Double Counting*

The final Rule 202(a)(30)-1 also contains several provisions that prevent investors from being double-counted. An adviser need not:

- count a private fund as a separate client if the adviser counted any of the investors in that private fund as a client;
- count an individual as a client due to that individual's investment in a private fund if the individual has already been counted separately as a client of the adviser; or
- double-count an individual who is an investor in two or more private funds advised by the adviser.

The requirement to count each investor in a private fund against the fifteen-client limitation is a significant departure from previous practice and will take some time to get used to.

■ What Does "In the United States" Mean?

In general, in the United States in this context is defined as in Regulation S of the Securities Act. Regulation S defines a US person as:

- any natural person residing in the United States;
- any partnership or corporation organized under the laws of the United States;
- any estate of which any executor or administrator is a US person;
- any trust of which any trustee is a US person;
- any agency or branch of a foreign entity located in the United States;
- any nondiscretionary account or similar account (other than an estate or a trust) held by a dealer or other fiduciary for the benefit or account of a US person;
- any discretionary account or similar account (other than an estate or trust) held by a dealer or other fiduciary organized, incorporated, or (if an individual) resident in the United States; and
- any partnership or corporation organized under the laws of any foreign jurisdiction, but only if formed by a US person for the purpose of investing in securities, unless the entity is organized and owned by accredited investors who are not natural persons, estates or trusts.

There are deviations to Regulation S, however. For purposes of the foreign private adviser exemption, a number of persons count as *US persons* that would not under Regulation S. For example, any discretionary account owned by a US person and managed by a non-US affiliate of the adviser would be treated as *in the United States*. This is meant to discourage non-US advisers from creating discretionary accounts to circumvent the limitations imposed by the exemption.

Lastly, I would like to point out one important general principle. Under the new rule, an adviser must determine the number of investors based on all the facts and circumstances and not do indirectly what would be unlawful to do directly. On that note, an adviser must have reasonable belief that an investor is the actual investor and not just a nominee, and that he/she is not located in the United States. Unfortunately, the SEC did not provide examples for what would constitute a basis for the "reasonableness" of the belief, so advisers must use their best judgment.

❖ *Time of Determination*

If a person was not physically in the United States at the time he became a client, or at the time he became an investor in a private fund, that person may be treated as a non-US person.

It is also important to note that in order to avoid requiring an investment adviser to monitor the ongoing location of clients, which would be somewhat impractical, the final rule allows the determination to be made once: at the time the individual or entity becomes a client.

However, the rule dictates that the fund manager make the determination each time an investor acquires an additional interest in the private fund.

How Are Assets under Management Calculated?

The final requirement in the Dodd-Frank Act for an investment/fund manager to qualify for the foreign private adviser exemption is that the adviser/manager has less than $25 million in assets under management attributable to US clients and US private fund investors.

Rule 202(a)(30)-1 of the Advisers Act makes clear that assets under management must be calculated in accordance with the uniform method specified for calculations of regulatory assets under management prescribed in Item 5 of Form ADV. I dedicated an entire chapter (chapter 8) to the new method of calculating regulatory assets under management, which I urge you to read. You will need to familiarize yourself with it to determine if you qualify for the foreign private adviser exemption.

The main principles of the new method are that it: 1) includes clients/investors' gross assets without any deduction for debt or leverage, 2) includes uncalled capital commitments, and 3) requires that all assets must be valued at their market value or fair value.

What Are the US Compliance Obligations If an Exemption Is Not Available?

The Fiduciary Standard

While the Advisers Act contains numerous specific requirements (some of which I summarize below and many of which are discussed in more detail in chapter 12), the core of the regulatory framework applicable to US investment advisers is the obligation to act as a fiduciary to advisory clients. While the term is not defined in the Advisers Act itself, the SEC describes an adviser's fiduciary obligation as follows (the entire statement is available at: **http:/www.sec.gov/divisions/investment/advoverview.htm**).

"As an investment adviser, you are a "fiduciary" to your advisory clients. This means that you have a fundamental obligation to act in the best interests of your clients and to provide investment advice in your clients' best interests. You owe your clients a duty of undivided loyalty and utmost good faith. You should not engage in any activity in conflict with the interest of any client, and you should take steps reasonably necessary to fulfill your obligations. You must employ reasonable care to avoid misleading clients and you must provide full and fair disclosure of all material facts to your clients and prospective clients. Generally, facts are "material" if a reasonable investor would consider them to be important. You must eliminate, or at least disclose, all conflicts of interest that might incline you – consciously or unconsciously – to render advice that is not disinterested. If you do not avoid a conflict of interest that could impact the impartiality of your advice, you must make full and frank disclosure of the conflict. You cannot use your clients' assets for your own benefit or the benefit of other clients, at least without client consent. Departure from this fiduciary standard may constitute "fraud" upon your clients (under Section 206 of the Advisers Act)."

The following guides you through a summary of the main requirements of being registered as a US investment adviser (please read chapter 12 for more detail):

❖ *Filing Form ADV*

Advisers must file Form ADV in an accurate and timely manner. Form ADV Part 1 includes information related to the adviser's business, ownership, and disciplinary history. Form ADV Part 2 is a narrative statement requiring plain English descriptions of conflicts of interest and other matters to be provided to clients and prospective clients and to be publicly available at least in part on the SEC's website.

❖ *Implementing a Compliance Program*

Advisers must adopt and implement a compliance program reasonably designed to prevent violations of the Adviser's Act. They must also designate a chief compliance officer (CCO), implement comprehensive written compliance policies and procedures, and undergo an annual compliance review.

❖ *Code of Ethics and Personal Trading*

Advisers must adopt a written code of ethics that sets forth the standards of business conduct expected from firm employees, and addresses conflicts that may arise from personnel and proprietary trading and gifts and entertainment, among others. The code of ethics must also require that certain firm employees report their personal securities transactions to the CCO or another person, and it should establish how insider trading is to be prevented.

❖ *Books and Records*

Advisers must maintain their books and records, and keep them accurate and current for at least five years. These include advisory business and financial records, client records regarding advice and trades for clients, advisory agreements, records supporting and evidencing advertising and performance, among others.

❖ *Advertising and Third-Party Solicitors*

The Advisers Act specifically prohibits certain forms of advertising, including testimonials and the use of past specific recommendations. The use of business referral arrangements (persons who refer are called solicitors) is regulated as well and requires that the solicitor provide written disclosures to solicited clients.

❖ *Custody Rule*

The Dodd-Frank imposed overhaul of the Advisers Act also impacted the rules governing custody of client assets.

The notion of "custody" is a perennial concern for the SEC. It means that an adviser has possession of client funds or securities, as well as the control to withdraw or transfer such funds, securities, etc. Registered advisers who have custody of client assets must keep them with a qualified custodian that sends account statements directly to the clients. This custodian may also be required to undergo a surprise examination and obtain an internal control report prepared by an independent accounting firm. I included an entire chapter (chapter 11) on the topic, which I urge you to read if you have any doubt as to whether or not you have custody, and if you do, what your obligations are under the Advisers Act.

❖ *Best Execution*

Advisers must seek to obtain the best price and best execution on client trades from the firms executing the trades. Any conflicts must be fully disclosed or eliminated, including advisers' trading for their own principal account with a client account.

❖ *SEC Exams*

Registration with the SEC is a significant undertaking but not rocket science. Upon registration, advisers must be operating in accordance with fiduciary standards and must be in compliance with the full range of requirements under the Advisers Act. Once registered, advisers become subject to examination oversight by the SEC. It is critical for advisers to establish and maintain a strong compliance program to be prepared for an SEC examination.

■ Are There Other Exemptions Available to Me If I Fail the Foreign Private Adviser Test?

The new Advisers Act contains a number of other exemptions that may be available to you even if you don't meet the criteria of the foreign private adviser exemption. Those are: 1) the private fund adviser exemption for advisers to private funds with less than $150 million of assets under management and 2) the venture capital exemption for advisers to venture capital funds. You may also consider whether or not your activities encompass a family office and fall within the exemption created for them. All of these exemptions are discussed elsewhere in this book (chapters 2, 3, and 4).

Chapter 5 **Key Take-Aways**

Most asset managers that target the United States as a desirable market and have a meaningful presence here will probably not be able to benefit from the foreign private adviser exemption due to the exemption's limited scope as to number of allowed clients and total assets in the United States.

If the foreign private adviser exemption is not available, you may be able to satisfy the requirements of another exemption, such as the private fund exemption or the venture capital exemption, or fall within the new definition of "family office", depending on your circumstances.

If you do fall within the exemption, you would not be an "exempt reporting adviser" under the Advisers Act and would thus not have to comply with the SEC reporting and compliance obligations of an "exempt reporting adviser" (advisers relying on the private fund and venture capital fund adviser exemptions would).

If no exemption is available, you would need to satisfy all the reporting and compliance requirements of the Advisers Act, which are extensive.

Chapter 06

State vs. Federal Regulation

Dodd-Frank reallocated the primary responsibility for supervision over investment advisers by delegating responsibility for midsized advisers – those with $25–100 million of assets under management – to state securities regulators.

Under the new rules, larger investment advisers – generally those with over $100 million of assets under management – must be registered with the SEC and are subject to the Advisers Act and SEC oversight. Many midsize investment advisers with between $25 million and $100 million of regulatory assets under management and small advisers with assets under management of $25 million or less are subject to state law and the oversight of one or more state securities authorities. They generally must register with the state(s) in which they transact business or have a place of business.

Overview

New Section 203A of the Advisers Act prohibits an investment adviser that is regulated by the state in which it transacts advisory business from registering with the SEC unless it has at least $25 million assets under management; it also preempts state laws applicable to advisers that are registered with the SEC. This provision makes the states the primary regulators of small and midsize advisers and the SEC the regulator for larger ones.

Dodd-Frank created a new category of **midsized advisers** and shifted primary responsibility for their regulatory oversight to the states by prohibiting SEC registration advisers that have assets under management between $25 million and $100 million if they transact business in states that regulate investment advisers and conduct examinations of them.

A few advisers are exempted from this prohibition to register with the SEC, including those who expect to be eligible for SEC registration within 120 days of filing Form ADV, multistate advisers, and advisers providing their services over the Internet.

Detailed Discussion

This chapter will assist you in determining where to register and why, and what it means to register and be subject to the oversight of a state.

How to Determine Whether to Register with the SEC or the State(s)

The new thresholds and requirements for determining whether to register with the SEC or the state(s) in which you maintain your primary office and transact business are as follows:

1) **Small advisers** with less than $25 million of assets under management are prohibited from registering with the SEC if their principal office and place of business is in a state that regulates advisers (currently all states except Wyoming).

2) **Midsized advisers** with assets under management between $25 million and $100 million of assets under management are required to register with their state securities regulators. They only need to register with the SEC if their principal office and place of business is in New York or Wyoming, unless they qualify for an exemption from registration – such as for advisers to private funds, venture capital funds, and foreign private advisers. Midsized advisers in any other state are prohibited from registering with the SEC and must register with their state securities regulator.

3) **Large advisers** with assets under management above $100 million are generally required to register with the SEC.

An adviser approaching $100 million of assets under management may rely on a "buffer" that ranges from $90 million to $110 million. What that means is that the adviser may register with the SEC when it reaches $100 million of assets under management, must register with the SEC once it reaches $110 million of assets under management, and, finally, it must withdraw from SEC registration and register with the states when it has less than $90 million of assets under management.

The following chart illustrates the filing obligations:

Fig. 6.1 *State vs. Federal Filing Obligations*

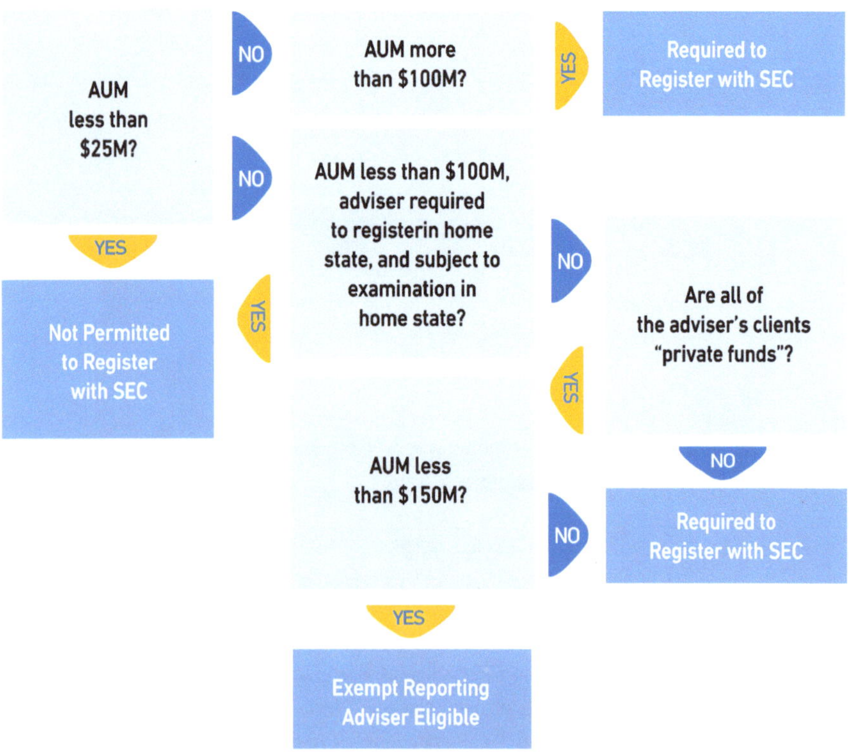

■ I Am Not Required to Register with the SEC. May I Register Anyway?

Generally speaking, investment advisers must register with the SEC or with one or more states and may not choose with whom they can register, subject to the exceptions below. If you are exempt from SEC registration because you advise solely hedge funds and/or private equity funds and have regulatory assets under management of less than $150 million, or you advise solely venture capital funds, or you are a foreign private adviser, you may elect to register with the SEC unless you are prohibited from registering as described in the next few paragraphs.

If you are a small adviser (i.e., have less than $25 million in regulatory assets under management), you are prohibited from registering with the SEC unless you fall within the five categories spelled out below. If you are a midsize adviser (i.e., have between $25 million and $100 million in regulatory assets under management), you are generally prohibited from registering with the SEC, unless:

1) you are not required to be registered as an investment adviser in the state in which you maintain your principal office and place of business;
2) if, once registered, you would not be subject to examination as an investment adviser by the applicable state securities commissioner; or
3) you fall within the five categories listed below. Currently, the only states that do not meet these requirements are New York and Wyoming. Accordingly, if you have $25 million or more of regulatory assets under management and maintain your principal office and place of business in New York or Wyoming, you must register with the SEC (of course, unless an exemption is available, which I discuss in detail elsewhere in this book).

However, there are five categories of small and midsized advisers that may still register with the SEC even if they would otherwise be prohibited from doing it. Those are:

1) affiliates of SEC-registered investment advisers,
2) pension consultants,
3) investment advisers expecting to be eligible for SEC registration within 120 days of filing Form ADV,
4) multistate advisers (i.e., advisers that would have to register with fifteen states or more), and
5) Internet advisers.

When Am I Not Required to Register with the SEC?

You are not required to register with the SEC if:

1) you are an adviser to Small Business Investment Compaies licensed by the Small Business Administration;
2) you advise only venture capital funds and qualify for the venture capital exemption;
3) you advise only private funds and have total regulatory assets under management of less than $150 million and qualify for the private fund adviser exemption;
4) you are a foreign private adviser and qualify for the foreign private adviser exemption;
5) you are a family office and therefore outside the definition of investment adviser under the Advisers Act; or
6) you are registered with the CFTC as a commodity trading adviser and your business is not predominantly the provision of securities-related advice.

However, in the scenarios listed above, you may still be subject to registration and supervision in the state(s) of your principal place of business and office and other states in which you conduct advisory business. Each state has different laws, and I would urge you to retain local counsel to assist with the analysis. You should check with each state in which you intend to transact business, not just the state in which your principal place of business is located, for information regarding investment adviser regulation. The names and addresses of the appropriate regulating official for each state can be obtained by contacting the North American Securities Administrators Association, Inc. (NASAA) at One Massachusetts Avenue, N.W., Washington, D.C. 20001.

What Are Regulatory Assets under Management and How Do I Calculate Them?

For purposes of assessing whether or not you have to register, and if yes, with whom to register, the SEC requires that you determine your regulatory assets under management by calculating the value of the securities portfolios for which you provide continuous and regular supervisory or management services.

Regulatory assets under management are calculated based on a new uniform method the SEC created that includes: 1) proprietary assets, 2) assets managed without receiving compensation, 3) assets of foreign clients, and 4) uncalled capital commitments. You are not permitted to subtract outstanding indebtedness and accrued but unpaid liabilities, and you must value assets at their market value or fair value where market value is unavailable.

Regulatory assets under management must be calculated annually to confirm if you meet the threshold for registration. After reaching the threshold, you will then generally have up to ninety days to register with the SEC.

■ What Is the Difference between an Investment Adviser and an Investment Adviser Representative?

The term *investment adviser* refers to the firm (legal entities or sole proprietorships) that provides investment advice, whereas the term *investment adviser representative* refers to the individual who actually gives advice to clients. Investment advisers and investment adviser representatives are subject to different licensing/registration rules, which vary from state to state. Most states follow a uniform definition of investment adviser representative. An investment adviser representative is generally a person who, for compensation:

1) makes recommendations or otherwise renders advice regarding securities;
2 manages accounts or portfolios of clients;
3) determines which recommendation or advice regarding securities should be given;
4) solicits, offers, or negotiates for the sale of, or sells investment advisory services; or
5) supervises employees who perform any of the foregoing.

Investment adviser representatives can only register with states, not the SEC. You should take note, however, that investment advisory firms that are registered with the SEC may have to register their investment adviser representatives with the state or states they do business in, depending on state requirements.

In many states, investment adviser representatives must pass the Series 65 exam (or equivalent), file an application, pay a fee, and comply with the other requirements, such as a background check, to get licensed. Many states also require that adviser firms file a Form U4 for investment adviser representatives employed by the firm once the firm itself is registered.

Individual investment adviser representatives generally must be registered in states where they have a place of business. Some jurisdictions base registration on the number of clients. This applies to individuals affiliated with both state and SEC-registered advisers.

■ What Do State Securities Regulators Require? How Do I Register As an Investment Adviser with a State?

All states (except Wyoming), the District of Columbia, and Puerto Rico each have a registration or licensing requirement for investment advisers. The requirements vary by state, but they may include:

1) State advisers to register or become licensed by filing Form ADV.
2) SEC-registered advisers to make a notice filing of their Form ADV in states in which they conduct business.
3) A passing score on a competency examination for each individual acting as an investment adviser or investment adviser representative.
4) Payment of a fee for processing the applications.
5) Certain disclosures to the securities agency and/or the public.
6) Registration of branch offices of the adviser.
7) A bond or minimum net capital.

❖ *The Registration/Licensing Process*

The application/licensing process and requirements vary from state to state, but they typically include filing a complete Form ADV with the state in which the adviser wants to offer services, providing any state-specific forms required, filing a Form U4 application for each investment adviser representative who will provide services on behalf of the adviser, and paying all required fees for the adviser and their representatives.

❖ *Filing Form ADV*

All states require that an investment adviser applicant file a Form ADV with the state securities authorities. The form has two parts. The first part requests information about an adviser's business, as well as about the persons who own or control the adviser, and inquires about whether the adviser or certain of its personnel have been sanctioned for violating the securities or other laws. The second part comprises Part 2A (brochure) and Part 2B (brochure supplement). Part 2A provides clients, in narrative format, with information about the adviser's business practices, fees, and conflicts of interest the adviser may have with its clients.

Advisers must deliver Part 2A to each client before or at the time they enter into an advisory agreement with that client pursuant to applicable state rules.

As a first step, the adviser should download and fill out an entitlement package, then mail it to FINRA – the vendor that operates the IARD for NASAA and the SEC. A CRD number and password are assigned to enable access to the secure "WebIARD" site where online forms are completed. Before submitting the forms electronically, applicable IARD system fees and state registration fees must be paid to FINRA.

Once the firm is licensed, it can register individuals as investment adviser representatives utilizing Form U4 if its respective state registers investment adviser representatives. Before starting, firms and individuals should consult with investment adviser licensing departments of securities regulators in the states where they have a place of business or expect to have clients.

❖ *State Notice Filings*

SEC-registered advisers must make a notice filing with the state if they have a place of business in the state or six or more clients in that state in a twelve-month period, regardless of the place of business. A state notice filing for an SEC-registered adviser is made by:

- Filing with the state(s) the adviser conducts business in a complete copy of Form ADV as filed with the SEC.
- Filing a Form U4 application for each investment adviser representative who will provide services on behalf of the adviser.
- Payment of any required notice-filing fees.

■ I Am Registered with the SEC. Do I Also Have to Register with State Securities Authorities?

Once you are registered with the SEC, you are not required to register with a state. Individual states, however, may require notice filings. A state may also institute licensing, qualification, or registration requirements for advisory personnel (investment adviser representatives) who have a place of business in that state. State rules vary considerably, and you should consult with your counsel as to your particular circumstances.

■ I Am Exempt from Registration under the SEC Rules. Do I Still Have to Register with a State or States?

If you are exempt from SEC registration because you qualify for an exemption (such as the private fund adviser exemption and the foreign private adviser exemption), you may still have to register with state securities authorities in the state or states in which you conduct business. You should consult with your state securities authorities to make the determination.

■ How Do I Convert My Firm from Being State Registered to Being SEC Registered or Vice Versa? When Do I Submit My Partial ADV-W?

To convert from being a state-registered adviser to being a SEC-registered adviser, submit the filing type, "Apply for registration as an investment adviser with the SEC." After the SEC approves your registration, you should file a "Partial ADV-W" to withdraw your state registration(s).

Do not file your Partial ADV-W until your application for SEC registration is approved, or you may be unable to conduct your business during this period of time. To convert from being a SEC-registered adviser to being a state-registered adviser, submit the filing type, "Apply for registration as an investment adviser with one or more states." After your state registration has been approved, then you should file a Partial ADV-W to withdraw your SEC registration.

Do not file your Partial ADV-W until your state registration application(s) is approved, or you may be unable to conduct your business during this period of time. The Gateway Call Center at (240) 386-4848 or iard@finra.org can provide additional assistance.

■ When Must Form ADV be Amended?

Whether you are registered with the SEC or with a state, a firm must file the annual updating amendment within ninety days of the close of its fiscal year (e.g., by March 31 for firms on a calendar-year basis). The firm should update all information that has changed, including a recalculation of its regulatory assets under management. During the year, if there are material changes to the information on the Form ADV, the firm should file an "other-than-annual" amendment promptly. State registrants pay no IARD fees for filing the annual update or other amendments to Form ADV other than a once-a-year system fee covering computerization costs.

■ What Is Form U4 and How Do I File It?

Form U4 is the form investment advisers must use to register investment adviser representatives with state securities authorities as required by the state. It must be filed through the IARD system.

■ What Is My Registration/Licensing Period?

Investment advisers and investment adviser representatives must renew their registration/ license annually. For investment advisers, this is accomplished by updating Form ADV; for more details see chapter 7 regarding filing the regular updating amendment to Form ADV and how to keep your registration current.

States send out a notice to renew a registration or license some time in advance of the end of the year. Check with each state for specific details. The renewal process for investment advisers will be handled via IARD.

■ What Are My Ongoing Compliance Obligations?

A state-registered investment adviser is generally subject to the statutes, rules, and regulations of the states in which the investment adviser transacts business. A number of state laws and regulations apply even to an investment adviser that is not registered in that state by virtue of the fact that it has some other nexus to the state such as clients or a place of business in that state. Advisers Act registration generally preempts only registration and related requirements with the states, rather than all regulation.

In addition, a limited number of Advisers Act compliance obligations will apply to investment advisers that are not registered under the Advisers Act, including the following:

❖ *Antifraud Provisions*

The antifraud provisions of the Advisers Act prohibit advisers from employing any device, scheme, or artifice to defraud any client or prospective client, and, among other things, require advisers to disclose all material facts (and not to make any material omissions) and to disclose to their clients actual and potential conflicts of interest. I urge you to spend significant time and thought on your disclosures in your Form ADV and your marketing/offering materials.

❖ *Pay-to-Play Rules*

The SEC's pay-to-play rules 1) prohibit payments to certain third parties to solicit government clients on the adviser's behalf, 2) restrict contributions and payment to certain government officials and political parties, and 3) prohibit an adviser from receiving compensation for advisory services within two years after a political contribution has been made by the adviser (or its covered associates) to an official of certain government entities.

❖ *Supervisory Requirements*

All unregistered exempt investment advisers are subject to the supervisory requirements in Section 203(e)(6) of the Advisers Act, which requires advisers to supervise those who act on their behalf with a view to preventing violations of securities laws.

❖ *Principal Transactions*

Section 206(3) of the Advisers Act provides that it is unlawful for an investment adviser acting as principal for its own account to knowingly sell or purchase any security from a client, or to act as broker for a person other than such client, without disclosing to such client in writing before the completion of such transaction the capacity in which he is acting and obtaining the client's consent for such transaction.

Chapter 6 **Key Take-Aways**

Dodd-Frank and new SEC rules allocated primary responsibility for oversight of small and most midsize investment advisers to the states.

Small advisers (less than $25 million under management) and most midsize advisers ($25-100 million under management) are prohibited from registering with the SEC and must register with the state of their principal place of business or primary office.

All states (other than Wyoming) regulate investment advisers. The rules governing the licensing and registration requirements for investment advisers vary from state to state. You should retain local counsel to assist you with the analysis.

All states (other than Wyoming) require a complete Form ADV in the application/licensing process.

As a general rule, being subject to the jurisdiction of the SEC preempts most state laws regulating advisers, so that advisers either have to follow state or federal laws, but not both.

Even state-registered advisers must comply with some significant Advisers Act requirements. If uncertain, obtain experienced counsel to assist with the analysis.

Chapter 07

How to Register with the SEC/ The New and Improved Form ADV

Form ADV – where ADV stands for "adviser" – is the document used by investment advisers to register with and report to the appropriate securities regulator. Generally speaking, with Form ADV, larger firms register with the SEC, whereas small and midsized advisers register with the state or states in which they conduct business.

The SEC uses data collected from Form ADV for a number of purposes, including the allocation of its own resources, the creation of risk profiles for advisers, and the preparation of examinations. The SEC also reviews the information to process registrations and to manage its regulatory and examination programs.

Form ADV must be kept current, which ensures that new clients of advisory firms have the opportunity to acquire detailed information about their advisers and registered representatives before they enter into an advisory relationship and that existing clients can stay educated about changes occurring in their adviser's business and operations.

In July 2011, the SEC adopted a number of significant amendments to the requirements for Form ADV, many of which were mandated by Dodd-Frank. The amendments require advisers to provide more detailed information regarding their business, business practices, and non-advisory activities, which I describe in more detail below. The SEC also changed Form ADV's format by splitting it into Parts 1 and 2. While Form ADV Part 1 is still in check-the-box format, Part 2 is a new narrative brochure that needs to be written in plain English.

This chapter guides you through the process of becoming registered with the SEC and describes in detail the elements of Part 1 and 2 of Form ADV and its delivery and filing requirements.

Overview

Form ADV Part 1 serves two purposes: 1) It is the vehicle to get an adviser registered with the SEC or the state securities regulators, and 2) it is a report that provides basic information about an adviser's business, ownership, clients, employees, business practices, affiliations, and advisory personnel. It is organized in check-the-box format.

Part 2 of Form ADV is intended primarily for clients and fund investors and therefore contains more detailed information regarding the adviser's business practices and conflicts of interest. Part 2 consists of a narrative brochure (Part 2A) and a brochure supplement (Part 2B), both of which need to be written in plain English.

The brochure (Part 2A) contains a description of an adviser's advisory business and the types of clients it has, a discussion of material changes to the brochure since the last annual update, risk factors involved in its investment strategy and legal and disciplinary matters.

The brochure supplement (Part 2B) discloses information about an adviser's personnel that provide advisory services to clients. An adviser must provide a brochure supplement for each person of the firm who provides advisory services to clients.

Overall, on Form ADV, an adviser must disclose all material facts to clients to ensure that they are making an informed decision before they enter into an advisory relationship. The adviser's disclosure must be thorough, accurate, and timely. Form ADV Part 1 and Part 2A of a registered adviser are available to the public on the SEC's Investment Adviser Public Disclosure (IAPD) website at **www.adviserinfo.sec.gov**.

How Do I Prepare for Getting Registered?

At the time the registration becomes effective (note that the applicant will have no control over when this happens once it files its Form ADV), the firm's business and operations must be fully compliant with the Advisers Act. There is no grace period after the date it is registered. Accordingly, before a firm files its application to register, it should make sure that its business and operations comply with the Advisers Act. This may include a number of operational changes, such as enhancing its operations by purchasing and installing new software to capture all its records and e-mails and hiring additional personnel. What typically requires the most lead time is the development of a compliance manual and compliance infrastructure. The firm will need to adopt and implement policies and procedures that are reasonably designed to prevent violations of the Advisers Act, and it must designate a chief compliance officer to be responsible for developing and enforcing these policies and procedures. The policies and procedures must be tailored to the firm's specific structure, investment strategy and operations, and need to reflect the firm's actual practices. You should not adopt an off-the-rack compliance manual, which may impose unnecessary or inappropriate compliance burdens on your business and attract undue SEC scrutiny. You should also test the effectiveness of the compliance procedures internally prior to their implementation. The diagram on the following page shows an example of a timeline for registration.

How Do I Register?

To register, an applicant must electronically file Form ADV Part 1 and Part 2A through the IARD, an electronic clearinghouse for investment adviser registration maintained by FINRA. The applicant must first request access to the IARD through FINRA's entitlement program by completing and submitting originally executed copies of the forms contained in the IARD entitlement packet, which can be found online at **http://www.iard.com/GetStarted.asp**.

It may take up to two weeks to receive the account number for the firm (which is called the IARD number) and a user ID and password, though, typically, it takes just a few days.

Once the applicant receives the IARD number, it should prefund the account with the initial setup fee, which is based on its assets under management. The setup fee will be deducted from the account once the initial Form ADV filing is made.

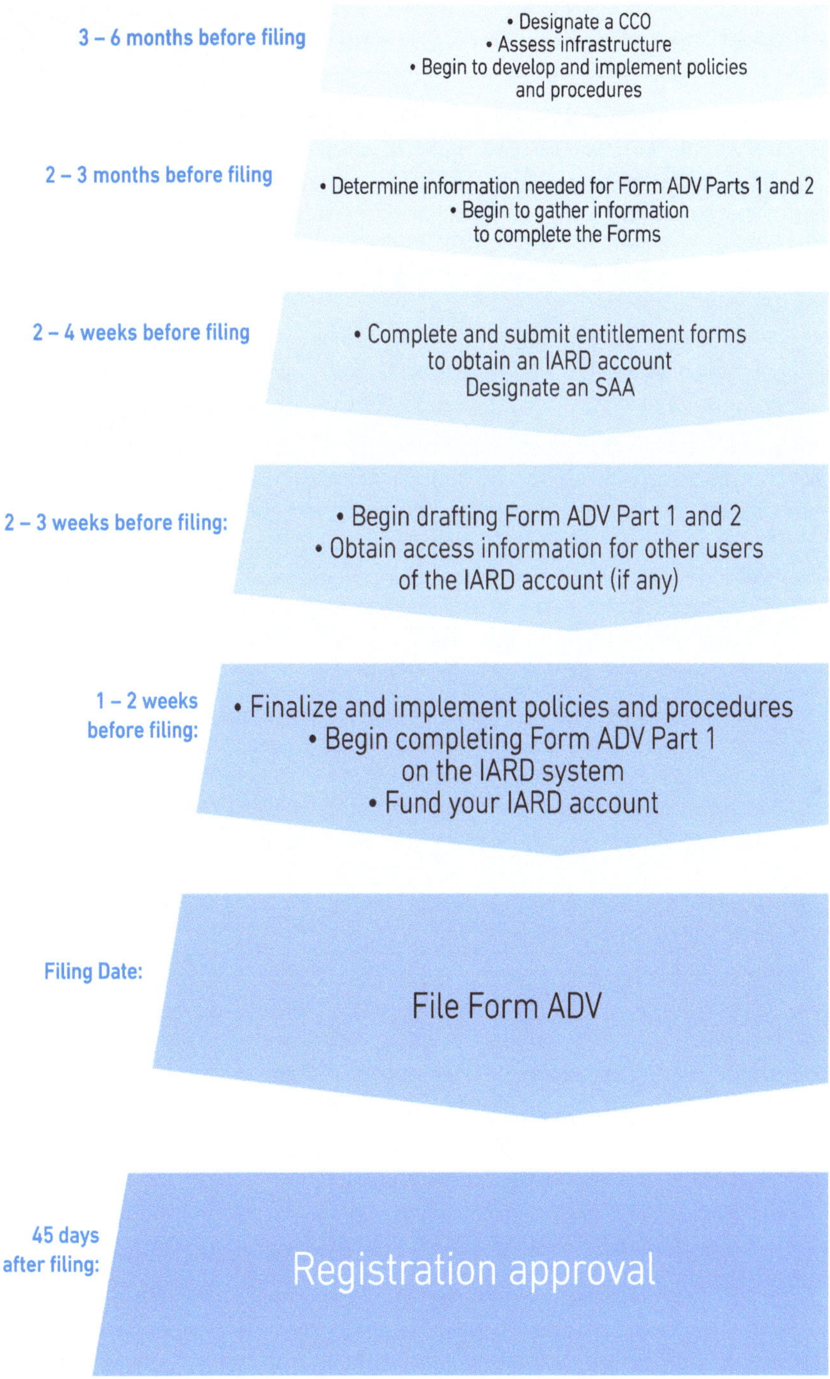

Fig 7.1 *Example of a timeline for registration*

When IARD access is granted, Form ADV Part 1 can be filled out online and submitted electronically. Form ADV should only be filed once the applicant is ready to be fully compliant with the Advisers Act. It is the last step in the registration process.

The SEC then has forty-five days to approve the registration or ask additional questions, in which case the forty-five day approval period is stalled until the SEC obtains satisfactory answers. As part of the approval process, the SEC verifies that all appropriate questions have been answered and conducts a background check on all listed principals and owners. If the SEC does not identify a deficiency in Form ADV, it will mail the applicant an Effective Order, which would make the registration effective. After that, Form ADV Part 1 and Part 2A will be publicly available through the SEC's website.

How Long Does the Entire Registration Process Take and How Much Does it Cost?

Preparation for registration typically takes three to six months and may take significantly longer depending on the size of the business and the complexity of a firm's operations. As I said above, you should make sure to be Advisers Act compliant when you file the application. Once the application is filed, the SEC makes sure that all appropriate questions have been answered and conducts a background check on all listed principals and owners. Going forward, the SEC may begin to undertake a substantive review of Form ADV. Once the Form ADV is filed, the SEC must approve registration or begin proceedings to deny registration within forty-five days. The more complete the application is, the faster the process.

The initial compliance costs vary greatly by adviser. For example, a firm may have already implemented policies and procedures when it started operations and so find that it may not need to make many changes to become Advisers Act compliant. On the other hand, a firm starting from scratch will likely incur ramp-up costs, such as legal and consulting fees and implementation costs, which could include costs associated with meeting e-mail review and retention requirements and implementing a disaster recovery program or hiring a chief compliance officer. Of course, the extent of the ramp-up efforts will also largely depend on the size and complexity of the adviser.

The state or SEC registration process requires an initial setup fee, which currently ranges from $40 to $225, based on assets under management. There may also be an IARD processing fee. A firm may also be subject to notice-filing fees with the states it does business in. These fees vary by state and generally range from $30 to $500.

A firm will be subject to ongoing compliance costs once it is registered. The amount will vary substantially based on a variety of factors, such as the size of the business, the strategies it uses, and its existing infrastructure.

The Elements of Form ADV Part 1A and 1B

Form ADV Part 1A

Form ADV Part 1A identifies the following information about the applicant: (a) basic contact information such as the investment adviser's legal and "doing business as" names, the investment adviser contact person's name, office address and telephone number of the investment adviser, and office hours of the investment adviser; (b) the basis for a new investment adviser's SEC registration; (c) the states whereby an SEC-registered investment adviser will request notice filing (i.e., where it does business); (d) the investment adviser's organizational form; (e) description of the investment advisory business; (f) the types of investment advisory clients; (g) the investment advisory fee and compensation arrangements; (h) the types of investment advisory activities; (i) the investment adviser's other business activities; (j) the location of books and records of the investment adviser; (k) financial industry affiliations of the adviser's related persons; (l) the investment adviser and its related persons' involvement in client transactions such as a proprietary or sales interest or use of discretion; (m) if the investment adviser maintains custody of an investment advisory client's assets; and (n) whether the investment adviser or affiliate has been convicted of a felony or investment-related misdemeanor or is subject to an adverse regulatory finding, censure or fine, or a court judgment related to violation of investment-related statute or regulation.

Form ADV Part 1A also includes several schedules:

- **Schedule A** – Lists all of the executive officers, which includes the chief compliance officer, the chief executive officer, the chief operations officer, the chief financial officer, and any other C-level associates. It also includes all direct owners of the registered investment adviser who have a 5 percent or more ownership interest.
- **Schedule B** – Lists all indirect owners who have a 25 percent or more ownership interest of a direct owner.
- **Schedule D** – Lists other miscellaneous information, such as other business names used, other office locations, Internet address, location of books and records, and affiliated registered investment advisers and broker/dealers.
- **Schedule G** – This is used when a registered investment adviser is required to provide a balance sheet for its most recently completed fiscal year. Schedule G must only be completed if the firm requires prepayment of more than $500 in fees per client, six or more months in advance. Further, state-registered investment adviser firms that maintain custody (as defined by the respective state) may also be required to complete Schedule G.
- **Disciplinary Reporting Page (DRP)** – Provides details about felonies or investment-related misdemeanors, regulatory disciplinary actions, or court judgments related to violation of investment-related statutes and regulations by the investment adviser or its affiliated persons.

Form ADV Part 1A and the schedules above are examined by both the SEC and state securities regulators.

❖ *Form ADV Part 1B*

Form ADV Part 1B must be completed by adviser firms who are registered or are applying for registration with a state securities regulator. Form ADV Part 1B requires the following key information: (a) the states where the investment adviser is applying for registration; (b) the supervisory and compliance principal; (c) information about the surety bond if required by the investment adviser's home state; and (d) information about unsatisfied judgment and liens, and investment-related arbitrations and civil judicial action.

The Elements of Part 2A (Brochure) and Part 2B (Brochure Supplement) of Form ADV

The primary objective of Part 2 of Form ADV is to enable clients to make informed decisions when hiring advisers. The new Part 2 requires an adviser to make plain English disclosures about the adviser's business, conflicts of interest, and the disciplinary history of the adviser's personnel. To achieve this objective, the SEC split Part 2 of Form ADV into Part 2A, which is also called the brochure and contains eighteen disclosure items, and Part 2B, which is called the brochure supplement, and includes information about the adviser personnel that dispenses investment advice.

The Brochure – Form ADV Part 2A

Form ADV Part 2 requires advisers to disclose detailed information that would help clients make an informed decision prior to hiring them. The information must be in narrative format and plain English and address the eighteen items prescribed by the SEC in the instructions for Part 2A of Form ADV (which can be found at

http://www.sec.gov/about/forms/formadv-part2.pdf).

The information covers who the advisers are, their methods and strategies, modes of compensation, the types of clients they serve, and the conflicts of interest that arise as a result of their strategies and dealings. Key disclosures are as follows:

- **Material Changes.** Advisers are now required to update information in Part 2 regularly and describe how the information differs from last year's Part 2.
- **Advisory Business.** Advisers have to check mark the different types of advisory services they provide, such as financial planning, portfolio management, and pension consulting, and they must state their total regulatory assets under management, which is newly defined. I dedicate an entire chapter (chapter 8) to the new definition, and you should familiarize yourself with it. Advisers are permitted to use different methods to compute regulatory assets under management in Part 1 and Part 2 of Form ADV (Part 1 requires disclosure of gross assets, whereas in Part 2 advisers may use net assets), provided they keep documentation describing the different methods in their files.
- **Fees and Compensation.** Advisers need to disclose how they are compensated, including their fee schedules, if fees are negotiable, and whether clients are billed or their fees are deducted directly from their accounts. Also, other costs, such as brokerage fees, custody fees, and fund expenses have to be disclosed.
- **Performance-Based Fees.** Advisers have to disclose if they charge performance-based fees and any related conflicts of interest that may arise when the adviser has accounts that are billed both based on performance and flat fees.

- **Type of Clients.** Form ADV Part 2 must describe the types of clients served by the adviser, such as individuals, trusts, investment companies, or pension plans, as well as the requirements for opening and maintaining an account, such as the minimum account size.
- **Method of Analysis, Investment Strategies, and Risk of Loss.** Advisers must describe their investment strategies and candidly disclose the risks associated with them. Clients must be made aware of how the investment strategies could affect investment performance.
- **Disciplinary Information.** Advisers are expected to list all material facts about any legal or disciplinary events that clients would need in order to evaluate the integrity of an adviser's personnel.
- **Other Financial Industry Activities and Affiliations.** Part 2 requires disclosure of any material relationships or arrangements that advisers have with related financial industry participants and any conflicts of interest that would arise from such relationships. If advisers suggest any other advisers to clients, then the advisers' fee arrangements (i.e., referral or finder's fees) with the other adviser and the associated conflicts have to also be disclosed.
- **Code of Ethics, Participation, or Interest in Client Transactions and Personal Trading.** Part 2 requires a description of the adviser's code of ethics, any existing practice of buying and selling securities in which the adviser or any of its related persons have a material financial interest, and practices of personal trading by the adviser or its related persons in the same securities as the clients.
- **Brokerage and Soft Dollar Practices.** Advisers have to disclose the process of selecting brokers and the reasonableness of broker's compensation, including client referrals, directed brokerage, trade aggregation, and soft dollar arrangements. "Soft dollars" refers to a common industry practice under which an adviser obtains products or services from a broker-dealer other than trade execution (such as research) in exchange for the adviser directing client-brokerage transactions to the broker-dealer.
- **Review of Accounts.** Advisers must state if and how often they review accounts or financial plans of clients, and they must also identify the person conducting the reviews and the circumstances under which an exceptional review was triggered.
- **Client Referrals and Other Compensation.** Advisers must disclose arrangements with third parties and the compensation paid for client referrals.
- **Custody.** If an adviser has custody of clients' assets and clients receive account statements directly from qualified custodians, Part 2 should have a conspicuous legend advising the client to carefully review these statements. If clients also receive statements from the adviser in addition to the account statements customarily provided by the brokerage firm, then the adviser should urge clients to carefully compare the two sets of statements. "Custody" means that the adviser is holding client funds and

securities or has the authority to obtain possession of them. For example, if the adviser has power of attorney to sign checks on a client's behalf, or withdraw funds or securities from the client's account – including fees – or otherwise dispose of a client's assets for any purpose other than authorized trading, then that adviser has custody. For more information on custody refer to chapter 11.

- **Investment Discretion.** If an adviser has discretionary authority to manage client accounts, then Part 2 must say so. It must also explain if clients place limitations on the authority, such as to not execute specified trades, only buy a certain category of securities, etc.
- **Voting Client Securities.** Advisers must describe their proxy voting practices, which need to keep the clients' best interests in mind and address potential conflicts. For example, conflicts may arise if the adviser has a personal relationship with senior management of a company, which could make it difficult to vote against management, or if the adviser or an affiliate does business with the company issuing the proxy (for example, manages its pension plan), which could also make it difficult to vote against management.
- **Financial Information.** If an adviser requires prepayment of more than $1,200 in fees per client, six months or more in advance, it must provide clients with an audited balance sheet showing the adviser's assets and liabilities at the end of the most recent fiscal year and disclose any financial conditions that are reasonably likely to impair the ability of the adviser to meet its contractual commitments to clients. The threshold is $500 for state-registered investment advisers.

❖ *The Brochure Supplement – Form ADV Part 2B*

Advisers must also prepare a brochure supplement. The "brochure supplement" is a disclosure document that contains information regarding each member of the adviser's personnel that provides investment advice to a client, has direct client contact, or has discretionary authority over a client's assets whether or not the person has direct client contact. The brochure supplement must contain the person's educational background, business experience, and disciplinary information regarding the person, including criminal actions, administrative proceedings, or proceedings before a self-regulatory organization (such as FINRA) in which the person was involved. The supplement must also contain a description of other business activities of the person, for example if he or she is also a broker-dealer representative or a commodity pool operator and if the person derives additional compensation from sources other than advisory clients – for instance, from sales awards and prizes. A firm that is state registered would have to disclose additional events, such as a bankruptcy.

■ Special Considerations for Private Funds

The SEC's rules impose significant disclosure requirements on advisers to private funds such as the size, and the organizational, operational, and investment characteristics of each private fund and whether the fund is part of a master-feeder arrangement or a fund of funds. The adviser must also provide information regarding the fund's regulatory status (i.e., the exclusion from the Investment Company Act upon which the fund relies), the types of strategies employed by the fund, and information regarding the fund's investors, as well as The "gatekeepers" to the fund, including prime brokers, auditors, custodians, administrators, and marketers.

More specifically, private fund advisers have to report:

> **Item 1.O: Reporting of $1 Billion in Total Assets.** This information must be given as of the last day of the most recent fiscal year. The additional reporting is meant to enable the SEC to address compensation arrangements for large advisers, as required by Dodd-Frank.
>
> **Item 5: Advisory Business Information.** This requires disclosure of additional information about the business, such as the number of employees registered as investment adviser representatives and insurance agents, the numbers and types of clients, and the number of clients that are US persons.
>
> **Items 6 and 7: Other Business Activities and Financial Industry Affiliations** requires additional reporting of related persons, including those who are major swap participants or swap dealers.
>
> **Item 7.B. and Schedule D** requires reporting on private funds advised by the adviser, including their organizational and operational information, size (including gross or net assets), type of investment strategy, number and types of investors in the fund, and breakdown of assets and liabilities held by the fund, as well as the identities of the fund's gatekeepers (i.e., auditors, prime brokers, custodians, administrators, and marketers).
>
> **Item 8: Participation in Client Transactions** requires additional reporting of compensation received from referrals, any soft dollar benefits, and if they qualify for safe harbor under Section 28(e) of the 34 Act.

■ Filing Requirements – Periodic Amendments to Form ADV

❖ *Annual Updating Amendments*

An adviser, whether it is registered with the SEC or a state, must amend Form ADV each year by filing an annual updating amendment within ninety days after the end of its fiscal year. When the firm submits its annual updating amendment, it must update its responses to all items, including corresponding sections of Schedules A, B, C, and D. It must also submit the summary of material changes required by Item 2 of Part 2A, either in the brochure (cover page or the page immediately thereafter), or as an exhibit to the brochure.

❖ *Other-than-Annual Amendments*

In addition to the annual updating amendment, if the firm is registered with the SEC or a state securities authority, it must amend Form ADV, including corresponding sections of Schedules A, B, C, and D, by filing additional amendments promptly if any changes to Items 1 (Identifying Information), 3 (Form of Organization), or 11 (Disciplinary Information), occur or if there are material changes to the information in Item 10 (Control Persons).

Delivery of Brochures and Brochure Supplements

Initial Delivery of Part 2A and B

Advisers, whether state or SEC registered, must deliver the brochure and the brochure supplement (Form ADV Parts 2A and B) to a prospective client before or at the time the advisory agreement is executed. Advisers should make sure that clients acknowledge receipt of both documents and that their books and records contain evidence of such receipt.

Advisers are required to provide clients with brochure supplements for each supervised person who:

- formulates investment advice for those clients and has direct contact with them; or
- makes discretionary investment decisions for the clients' assets, even if the supervised person has no direct client contact.

If investment advice is provided by a team consisting of more than five supervised persons, an adviser only has to provide brochure supplements for the five supervised persons with the most significant responsibility for day-to-day advice given to the client.

Although SEC-registered investment advisers need not file brochure supplements with the SEC, they need to ensure that they are readily available for inspection during an SEC examination. State-registered investment advisers are required to file their brochure supplements with the appropriate state regulator through the IARD.

Annual and Interim Delivery Requirements Part 2A and B

Advisers have 120 days from the end of the firm's fiscal year to deliver to their clients either:

1) a copy of the latest brochure that includes or is accompanied by a summary of material changes since the last brochure was delivered. or
2) a summary of material changes from the last brochure that includes an offer to provide a copy of the entire current brochure.

Keep in mind that advisers must promptly deliver to clients an updated brochure whenever that is amended and add any disciplinary events or revise material disciplinary information regarding the firm and its personnel. In lieu of the updated brochure, an adviser may deliver a document describing the material facts surrounding the disciplinary event.

Once brochure supplements are delivered to clients, there is no annual offer or delivery requirement. Firms are only required to deliver an updated brochure supplement if there is a new disciplinary event requiring disclosure or a material change to disciplinary information previously disclosed. If the updated brochure supplement is sent electronically, the adviser may provide in its electronic communication a hyperlink to the BrokerCheck or IARD systems. If an adviser hires a new employee to help service a client's account, then a copy of the employee's brochure supplement should be provided to the client before or at the time that the transition occurs.

■ What Exactly Is "Plain English"?

The items in Part 2 of Form ADV are designed to promote effective communication between the adviser and its clients. What that means is that you should write the brochure and supplements in plain English, taking into consideration the clients' level of financial sophistication. It should be easily understandable even for nonfinancial experts and should be concise and direct. I often get asked how to write in plain English. For that, I tend to give the following pointers:

- Use short sentences.
- Use definite, concrete, everyday words.
- Use the active voice.
- Use tables or bullet lists for complex material, whenever possible.
- Avoid legal jargon or highly technical business terms unless the adviser explains them or believes that the clients will understand them.
- Avoid long sentences, superfluous words, and weak verbs.
- Avoid multiple negatives.

You should also consider providing examples to illustrate a description of the firm's practices and policies.

For more information regarding "plain English," please consult the SEC's handbook at https://www.sec.gov/pdf/handbook.pdf.

Chapter 7 Key Take-Aways

Form ADV is the document used to register with the state securities regulators and the SEC and to report to them on a regular basis. It consists of two parts, the check-the-box Part 1 and Part 2, which needs to be written in a narrative format and in plain English. Both provide all the information the client needs regarding the business of an advisory firm and its personnel.

All information in Form ADV needs to be truthful. As a fiduciary, you must make full disclosure to your clients of material facts relating to your relationship with them, including any conflicts of interest.

You should also make certain you are not making statements to clients that are contradicted by your disclosure brochures. As an example, advisers sometimes claim that they are unbiased and have no conflicts of interest. A quick look at the firm's brochure will often contradict those statements.

Before registering with the SEC, every applicant should make sure it has implemented a compliance program that satisfies the requirements of the Advisers Act. Once the SEC deems the registration effective, you must be ready for prime time.

Chapter 08

How to Calculate Regulatory Assets under Management

The SEC, as mandated by the Dodd-Frank Act, introduced significant changes to the disclosure requirements for registered investment advisers in 2011. One of these changes was the adoption of the newly defined term "regulatory assets under management." The amount of an adviser's regulatory assets under management is critical in a number of ways, including determining if the adviser qualifies for the new exemptions from registration and whether the adviser is eligible to register with the SEC or is subject to the purview of state securities authorities. The method used to calculate regulatory assets under management must also be used to calculate and report assets under management on Form ADV and the newly created Form PF that many private fund advisers now have to file with the SEC. The purpose of the reform of this defined term was to create a multipurpose uniform method for calculating assets under management for regulatory purposes.

Overview

The Advisers Act defines "regulatory assets under management" as securities portfolios for which an adviser provides "continuous and regular supervisory or management services," regardless of whether the assets are family or proprietary assets, assets managed without receiving compensation, or assets of foreign clients. Advisers must calculate their regulatory assets under management on a gross basis, which means without deducting outstanding indebtedness or other accrued but unpaid liabilities.

The following two figures indicate how regulatory assets under management need to be calculated for clients other than private funds and private fund clients.

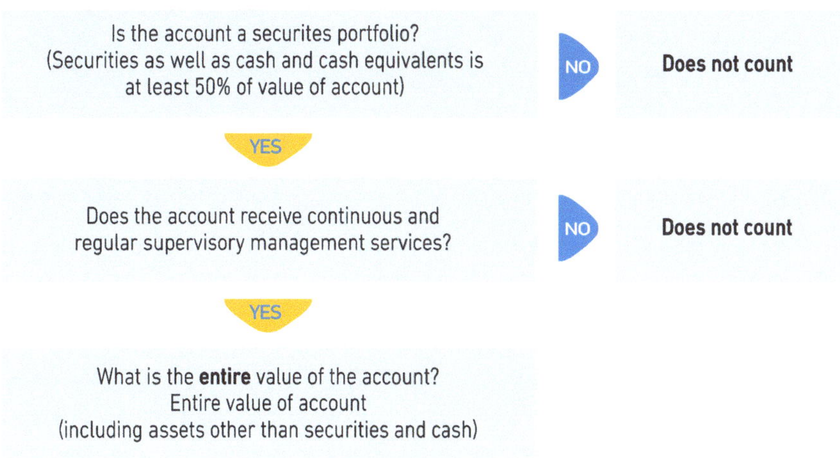

Fig. 8.1 *Calculation of RAUM for Clients other than Private Funds*

Fig. 8.2 *Calculation of RAUM for Private Fund Clients*

Current market value (or fair value)	**PLUS**	Uncalled capital commitments

Detailed Discussion

The term regulatory assets under management is key to the answer to important questions, including whether or not to register and with whom. You will find the new calculation to be quite a deviation from the way "AUM" had been calculated before. For the details, read on.

■ What Are the Instances Where Regulatory Assets under Management Play a Role?

There are a number of important instances where the calculation of regulatory assets under management is relevant. Those are:

❖ *ADV Reporting*

Form ADV requires the disclosure of regulatory assets under management, and it is used for a number of different purposes. As you may have read in chapter 7 where I discussed Form ADV in detail, investment advisers, including many advisers to private funds, must register with the SEC or with state securities authorities by filing Form ADV, and then file periodic reports on it. In addition, private fund managers exempt from registration must submit data on Form ADV as exempt reporting advisers.

❖ *Availability of an Exemption*

The Advisers Act exempts some investment advisers from registration. The exemptions apply to advisers to private funds that have less than $150 million in assets under management (the private fund adviser exemption), to advisers to foreign private funds (the foreign private adviser exemption), and to advisers solely to venture capital funds (the venture capital fund exemption). All three exemptions require a calculation of regulatory assets under management to determine if advisers meet the requirements. See chapters 2, 4, and 5 for details on these exemptions.

❖ *Federal or State Registration*

You will have to look at your regulatory assets under management to determine if you are eligible to register with the SEC or whether you must register with the securities regulators of the state or states you do business in instead. Generally, no adviser with less than $25 million in regulatory assets under management is permitted to register with the SEC. A midsize adviser with assets between $25 million and $100 million that is required to register with the state in which it maintains its principal office and place of business and where it is subject to examination as an adviser, is also not eligible to register with the SEC. Read chapter 6 for details on registering with the SEC or state securities regulators.

❖ *Form PF*

Regulatory assets under management determine if advisers to private funds are required to file the new Form PF with the SEC, as well as how frequently and extensively they are required to do so. Generally, large funds are required to submit more data and more frequently. The threshold for Form PF is $150 million or more. Generally, advisers to funds with assets of more than $1.5 billion must file most frequently and provide the most data. See chapter 9 for details on Form PF filing requirements.

How Do I Calculate Regulatory Assets under Management?

Advisers need to include the value of securities portfolios for which they provide continuous and regular supervisory or management services. You will notice if you read on that the calculation is quite different depending on whether or not you advise private funds.

❖ *Investment Advisers (Other than Advisers to Private Funds)*

The SEC's instructions for filing Form ADV treat an account as a securities portfolio if at least 50 percent of the total value of the account consists of securities. For this purpose, cash and cash equivalents (i.e., bank deposits, certificates of deposit, banker acceptances, and similar bank instruments) may be treated as securities, suggesting that it is also permissible to treat cash and cash equivalents as other than securities. If an account is a securities portfolio, its entire value is included in calculating regulatory assets under management.

All of the following must be included in the calculation:

- Family or proprietary accounts
- Accounts managed without receiving compensation
- Accounts of foreign clients

❖ *Advisers to Private Funds*

The calculation of regulatory assets under management for advisers to private funds is different. You may remember from prior chapters that a private fund is any fund that would be an investment company as per Section 3 of the Investment Company Act but is not because it is owned by 100 investors or less, or it is exclusively owned by ultra-high-net-worth individuals or institutional investors. Private fund advisers must treat all of the assets of a private fund as a securities portfolio, regardless of the nature of the assets of the fund. In addition, advisers must include in the securities portfolio any uncalled capital commitments.

What Are Continuous and Regular Supervisory or Management Services?

Advisers must only include assets for which they provide continuous and regular supervisory services. The general rule is that an adviser satisfies this requirement if it has either discretionary authority over the accounts or has an ongoing responsibility to make recommendations as to specific investments and is responsible for making the trade.

The SEC has provided a number of factors and examples to make the determination. Those include:

❖ *The Terms of the Advisory Contract*

If the adviser and the client agree in their advisory contract that the adviser provides ongoing management services over all the client's assets, the presumption is that the adviser provides these services. Make sure your client contract is unambiguous and you follow its terms in real life.

❖ *Form of Compensation*

If the adviser is compensated based on the average value of the client's assets it manages over a period of time, this suggests that the adviser provides continuous and regular supervisory services for the account. On the flipside, if the adviser is paid based on hours spent with a client during a client visit, or it is paid a retainer based on a percentage of assets covered by a financial plan, this would suggest that the adviser does not provide continuous and regular management or supervisory services.

❖ *SEC Examples*

The SEC provides examples in its Instructions for Part 1A of Form ADV for when the requirement may be satisfied:

- If the adviser has discretionary authority to allocate client assets among various mutual funds
- If the adviser does not have discretionary authority, but makes the same allocations and makes trades
- If the adviser allocates assets among other managers (manager of managers), but only if the adviser has discretionary authority to hire and fire managers and reallocate assets among them
- If the adviser is a broker-dealer and treats the account as a brokerage account, but only if it has discretionary authority over the account

The SEC indicates that the following would not meet the definition:

- If the adviser provides market-timing recommendations (i.e., buy or sell), but has no ongoing management responsibilities
- If the adviser provides only impersonal investment advice (such as newsletters)
- If the adviser makes an initial asset allocation, without continuous or regular monitoring and reallocation
- If the adviser provides advice on an intermittent or periodic basis, such as upon client request, in response to a market event, or on a specific date (for example, quarterly account reviews)

Excluded would also be, for example, the portion of an account that:

- is under management by another person, or
- consists of real estate or businesses whose operations an adviser manages on behalf of its client but not as an investment.

Calculating the Value of the Assets

Market Value and Fair Value

For *nonprivate fund assets*, advisers should value regulatory assets under management based on the market value of the assets used to report to clients or to calculate fees for investment advisory services.

Private fund assets must also be valued at market value or, where that is unavailable, at fair value. The new rules do not specify the methodology for reporting fair value beyond requiring that investment advisers report consistently and in good faith. The SEC noted, however, that the use of appraisers, pricing services, or other third parties is not required. A private fund adviser that calculates fair value for financial reporting purposes is expected to use the same basis for reporting fair value to determine its regulatory assets under management whether that basis is GAAP or something else. There is a limited exception to the fair value requirement for real estate assets where fair valuing of real estate assets is not required for financial reporting purposes under accounting principles. If this exception applies, real estate assets may be valued the same way as the private fund does for financial reporting purposes.

Gross Assets

Pursuant to the new instructions to Form ADV, an adviser must calculate its regulatory assets under management on a gross basis without deducting any outstanding indebtedness or other accrued but unpaid liabilities. This means that an adviser cannot deduct accrued fees or expenses either. Much has been made of this departure from prior practice. However, it serves as a much better indicator of funds at risk in a worst-case scenario, and the reform was necessary for effective systemic risk reporting.

The SEC indicated that an adviser may choose to report net assets in Part 2 of Form ADV, which contains the brochure an adviser provides to clients.

Can You Give A Real Life Example?

Let's assume you have a client with an account consisting of $500,000 in mutual funds, stocks and bonds, $100,000 in cash and $400,000 in real estate. The total value of the account is $1,000,000, so $600,000, or more than 50 percent of it, is securities and cash. Accordingly, the account would be considered a securities portfolio. Keep in mind that for purposes of this 50 percent test, you *may* treat cash and cash equivalents (i.e., bank deposits, certificates of deposit, bankers' acceptances, and similar bank instruments) as securities, but you do not have to. The next step would be to determine whether you provide continuous and regular supervisory or management services for the entire account. If the entire account is discretionary and does receive ongoing supervisory and management services, you would include the entire account ($1,000,000) in the calculation of your total regulatory assets under management, not just the amount of securities and cash in the account. If you only manage a portion of the account, only include that portion.

Chapter 8 **Key Take-Aways**

The method for calculating regulatory assets under management plays an important role in a number of ways and has implications on if an adviser is required to register at all, and if yes, whether the registration needs to be with state regulators or the SEC and if an exemption from registration is available to the adviser.

The calculation is uniform for regulatory purposes and is designed to prevent advisers from opting in and out of federal and state registration by choosing to include or exclude classes of assets.

Assets must be calculated on a gross rather than net basis. This may require many advisers to private funds to register with the SEC rather than rely on the private fund exemption.

Every adviser should pay close attention to the calculation and after reading this chapter review the SEC Instructions for Part 1A of Form ADV available at: http://www.sec.gov/about/forms/formadv-instructions.pdf

Chapter 09

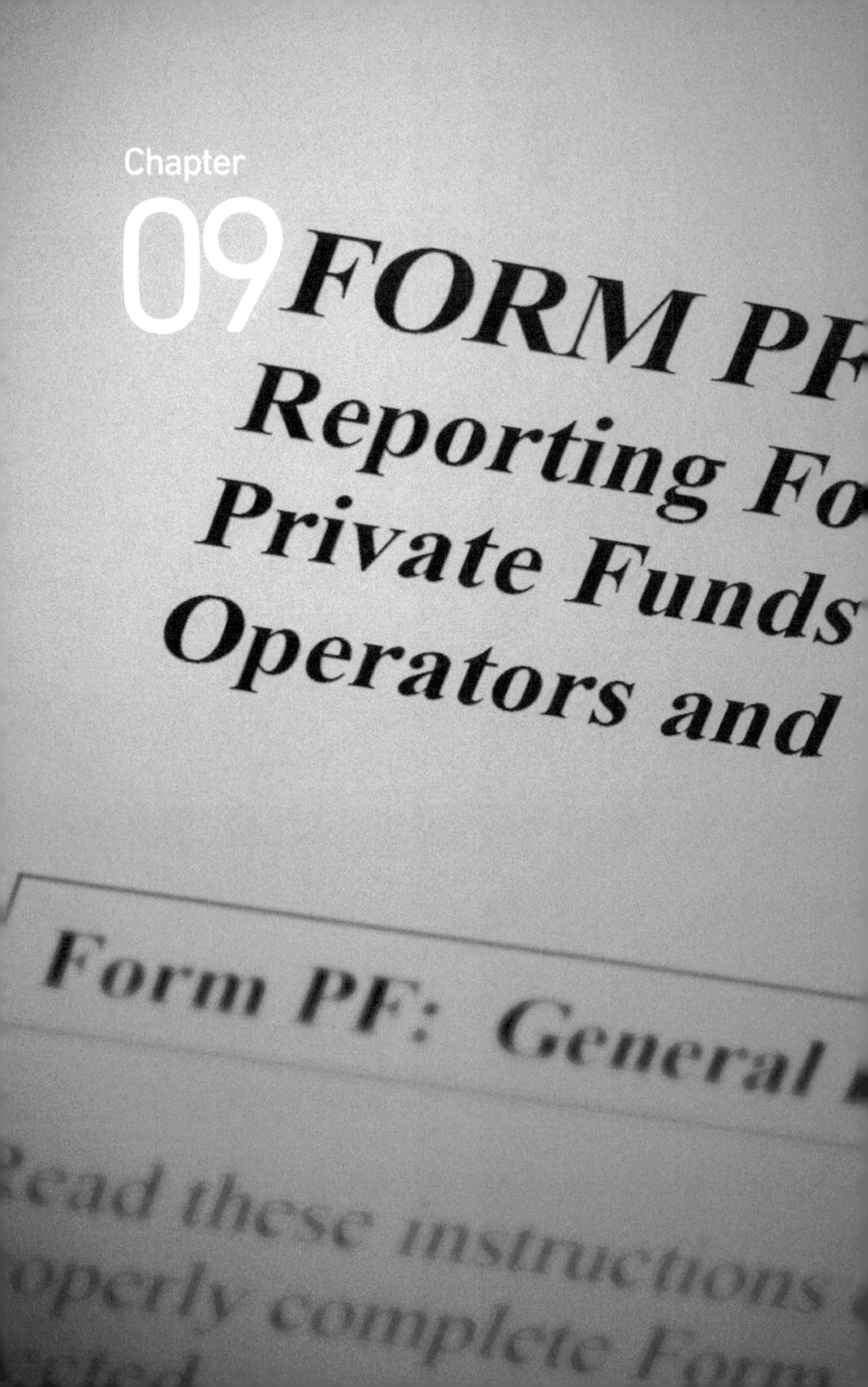
FORM
Reporting
Private Funds
Operators and
Form PF: General
these instructions
complete

The New Form PF

Dodd-Frank amended the Advisers Act requiring that the SEC establish reporting and record-keeping requirements for advisers to private funds. Dodd-Frank also established the Financial Stability Oversight Council (FSOC), a council of banking and securities regulators, to promote financial stability by monitoring systemic risks and collect information.

In October 2011, the SEC and the CFTC jointly adopted the final rules as mandated by Dodd-Frank that require registered investment advisers to report information concerning the private funds they advise on the new Form PF. The information gathered via Form PF was designed to assist the SEC, the CFTC, and the FSOC to better assess the risks to the US financial system in order to prevent future financial meltdowns similar to the one of 2008.

Overview

1) **Minimum reporting threshold.** There is a minimum fund size for reporting. Advisers with $150 million or more in private funds under management are required to file Form PF. Smaller registered advisers to private funds are not required to file.

2) **Large private fund advisers.** The required data depends on size and fund type. The rules require more frequent reporting by large private fund advisers, defined as hedge funds with at least $1.5 billion in assets under management, private equity funds with at least $2 billion in assets under management, and liquidity funds with at least $1 billion assets attributable to liquidity funds and registered money market funds.

3) **Frequency of filing.** The filing frequency varies based on size and type of fund. Large private equity fund advisers must file annually within 120 days of their fiscal year end. Large hedge fund advisers must file quarterly within 60 days of the quarter end. Advisers to large liquidity funds and registered money market funds must file quarterly within 15 days of the quarter end.

4) **Data required**. Depending on the size and type of private fund, advisers need to complete specific sections of the Form; all of them need to submit a completed Section 1. The data includes: a fund's gross and net asset values; aggregate value of derivative positions; percentage of fund ownerships; gross and net performance information; financing information, including secured and unsecured borrowing; information regarding a fund's valuation and methodology; liquidity of holdings; and portfolio company information.

Form PF is complex and requires significant data collection. Be prepared to dedicate sufficient resources to gather the required information and complete the form. The first steps would obviously be to determine if you are required to submit Form PF and, if yes, which fund category you fall in.

This chapter is meant to help you with these determinations and to provide details regarding filing logistics.

Detailed Discussion

■ What Is the Purpose of Form PF?

Unlike Form ADV, which focuses on providing investors with information that may be material to their decision whether or not to choose a particular adviser or stay with the adviser they are currently working with, Form PF is not an investor disclosure form. Form PF is designed to allow the FSOC to monitor systemic trends for the broader private fund industry and to provide tools to identify correlations in behavior of different fund types under various economic conditions to identify systemic risks. More specifically, the form helps measure the systemic exposure to specific financial institutions and credit counterparties, the concentration of fund investments by industry and geography, and the concentration of investor base.

Needless to say, expect the SEC and CFTC to also use the data to improve their oversight of investment advisers and to enhance their investor protection efforts.

■ Who Must File?

The following chart provides the overview of the filing obligations:

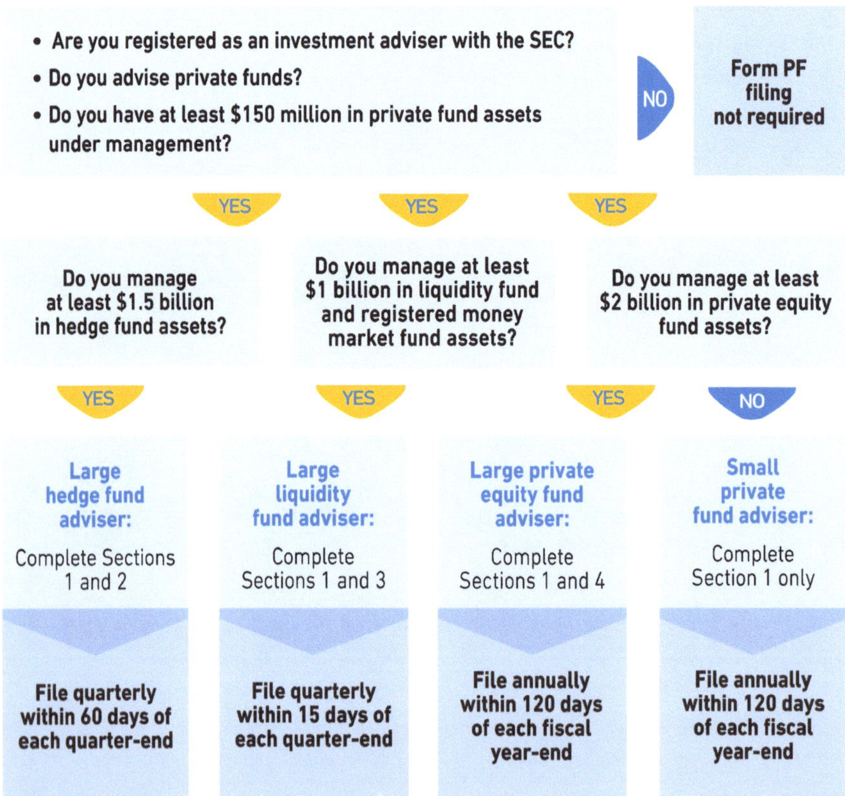

Fig 9.1 *Determining whether and how to file Form PF*

An investment adviser that meets each of the following criteria must file Form PF:

1) It is registered or required to register with the SEC.
2) It manages one or more private funds.
3) It and its related persons (other than any related persons that are separately operated) collectively had at least $150 million in regulatory assets under management attributable to private funds as of the end of its most recently completed fiscal year.

How Is Private Fund Defined?

A private fund for the purposes of Form PF is an issuer that would be an investment company under the Investment Company Act but is not because it has less than one hundred investors or its investor base consists exclusively of super-high-net- worth-qualified purchasers.

A "related person" has the same meaning for Form PF as it does for Form ADV and generally includes 1) officers, partners, and directors of the adviser and individuals performing similar functions, 2) any individuals or entities that directly or indirectly control, are controlled by, or are under common control with the adviser, and 3) all current employees of the adviser other than those that perform only clerical, administrative, support, or similar functions.

Where an adviser and a related person both have an obligation to file Form PF, the adviser and the related person may file Form PF together or separately, but the reporting thresholds are calculated as described below regardless of any separate filings.

How Do I Calculate Regulatory Assets under Management?

Regulatory assets under management are calculated in the same manner as they are for Form ADV and other purposes of the Advisers Act and generally refer to the gross current market value (or fair value) of managed assets (without deduction for outstanding indebtedness or other liabilities) plus the amount of uncalled capital commitments.

If an adviser's principal place of business is outside the United States, the adviser may exclude from this asset calculation any private fund that, during the adviser's last fiscal year, was not a US person, did not offer securities in the United States, and was not beneficially owned by any US person. As per SEC guidance, a non-US fund that has never used US jurisdictional means in the offering of its securities would not be a private fund in any event.

Who Doesn't Have To File?

Exempt reporting advisers (i.e., advisers solely to venture capital funds and solely to private funds that in the aggregate have less than $150 million in assets under management in the United States) are not required to file Form PF. Similarly, advisers solely to real estate funds that rely on the exemption under Section 3(c)(5)(C) of the Investment Company Act are not required to file. These funds are not believed to be interconnected with the global financial system in the same way that other funds are and, therefore, are not viewed as creating the type of systemic risk that Form PF seeks to evaluate.

■ What Types of Funds Must File?

❖ *Hedge Funds*

Form PF defines hedge fund broadly to include any private fund (other than a securitized asset fund) that:

1) is able to earn a performance fee or allocation based on unrealized gains,
2) is permitted to borrow in excess of one-half of its net asset value,
3) is permitted to have gross notional exposure in excess of twice the net asset value, or
4) is permitted to short sell securities or enter into similar transactions (other than for the purpose of hedging currency exposure or managing duration).

A private fund is not considered a hedge fund just because its organizational documents do not prohibit the fund from borrowing or incurring derivative exposure in excess of defined amounts or from engaging in short selling. What matters is that the fund does not actually engage in these practices and that a reasonable investor would understand, based on the fund's offering documents, that the fund would not engage in these practices. What this means is that you have to pay close attention to the instructions and definitions on Form PF and the fund's offering documents when you classify your funds.

Solely for purposes of Form PF, any commodity pool reported on Form PF is treated as a hedge fund. Accordingly, registered commodity pool operators filing Form PF solely for those pools need only complete the sections of Form PF applicable to hedge fund advisers, which are outlined below.

Vehicles established for the purpose of issuing asset backed securities (securitized asset funds) are excluded from the hedge fund definition.

❖ *Liquidity Funds*

A *liquidity fund* is any private fund that seeks to generate income by investing in short-term securities in order to maintain a stable net asset value or minimize principal volatility for investors.

❖ *Private Equity Fund*

A *private equity fund* is any private fund that is not a hedge fund, liquidity fund, real estate fund, securitized asset fund or venture capital fund and does not normally provide investors with redemption rights.

What Is a Large Private Fund Adviser?

Large private fund advisers are required to submit more information on a more frequent basis than other private fund advisers. The information submitted will depend on the types of funds managed and concerns areas of financial activity that have the potential to raise systemic concerns. All reporting advisers, large or small, must complete Section 1.

A large private fund adviser is defined as a large hedge fund adviser, large liquidity fund adviser, or large private equity adviser. The status as a large private fund adviser is determined solely by the assets under management attributable to one particular type of fund, as specified below.

As I explained above, the reporting thresholds were designed to keep the group of filers relatively small in number but to capture a large share of the overall market. To put some numbers behind the concept, the SEC estimates that approximately 230 US-based advisers with at least $1.5 billion in hedge fund assets represent over 80 percent of the US hedge fund industry based on assets under management and that 155 US-based advisers managing over $2 billion in assets each represent approximately 75 percent of the US private equity market.

Large Hedge Fund Adviser – Any adviser that has at least $1.5 billion in regulatory assets under management attributable to hedge funds as of the end of any month in the prior fiscal quarter. These advisers must complete Form PF Section 2.

Large Liquidity Fund Adviser – Any adviser that manages a liquidity fund and has at least $1 billion in combined regulatory assets under management, which are attributable to liquidity funds and registered money market funds as of the end of any month in the prior fiscal quarter. These advisers must complete Form PF Section 3.

Large Private Equity Advisers – Any adviser that has at least $2 billion in regulatory assets under management attributable to private equity funds as of the last day of the adviser's most recently completed fiscal year. These advisers must complete Form PF Section 4.

Accordingly, an adviser that has $1 billion in regulatory assets under management attributable to hedge funds and another $1 billion in regulatory assets under management attributable to private equity funds would not be a large private fund adviser even though it has a total of $2 billion in total regulatory assets under management.

Aggregation of Assets under Management for Determining Threshold Amounts

To determine whether an investment adviser meets the $150 million minimum reporting threshold or if it is a large private fund adviser, an adviser must aggregate:

1) *Parallel managed accounts* (i.e., any managed accounts advised by the adviser or a related person that pursue substantially the same investment objective and strategy and invest in substantially the same positions as private funds advised by the same adviser), unless the value of the parallel managed accounts exceeds the value of the private funds with which they are managed.

2) Private funds that are part of the same master-feeder structure.

3) Private funds that pursue substantially the same investment objective and strategy and invest side by side in substantially the same positions (parallel funds).

These aggregation requirements are designed to prevent an adviser from creatively designing a specific fund structure to avoid Form PF reporting requirements.

One note: Funds that are managed by related persons that are separately operated do not have to be aggregated. Instructions to Section 7.A. of Schedule D to Form ADV provide that a related person is "separately operated" from an adviser if:

1) the adviser has no business dealings with the related person in connection with advisory services provided to its clients;

2) the adviser does not conduct shared operations with the related person;

3) the adviser does not refer clients or business to the related person, and the related person does not refer prospective clients or business to the adviser;

4) the adviser does not share supervised persons or premises with the related person; and

5) the adviser has no reason to believe that its relationship with the related person otherwise creates a conflict of interest with its clients.

In completing Form PF for each private fund, advisers may either aggregate a fund's parallel vehicles and master-feeder structures with that fund and report them together as a single private fund or report them as separate private funds. Whatever methodology you chose, however, you must adopt a single convention and apply it consistently throughout the form.

Also, for purposes of the filing threshold and responding to most questions on Form PF, an adviser may disregard any private fund's investments in other private funds. Moreover, if a private fund invests substantially all of its assets in the equity of other private funds and holds only cash, cash equivalents and instruments to hedge currency risks otherwise, the adviser may complete only Section 1b of Form PF with respect to that fund and otherwise disregard it.

❖ *Affiliated and Subadvised Funds*

As a general principle, each adviser that meets the criteria for reporting on Form PF has an independent obligation to file Form PF with respect to private fund(s) it advises. However, once one adviser files Form PF with respect to any private fund for a given reporting period, any other applicable advisers are relieved of their obligation to file the Form for the same private fund for that reporting period.

Accordingly, where a private fund has an adviser and a subadviser, both firms must count the same private fund assets for purposes of determining if they meet Form PF filing thresholds and pass large private fund adviser tests. However, only the firm reporting for that fund in section 7.B.1 of Schedule D to Form ADV should report for that fund on Form PF unless the firm doing the Form ADV reporting for that fund is not required to file Form PF. The goal is to ensure reporting but to avoid duplicative reporting.

Calculation Methodologies

Form PF permits advisers to submit data that is presented using methodologies consistent with the information the adviser uses for internal and investor reporting purposes as long as the information supplied on Form PF is consistent with Form PF instructions. If audited information is available at the time an adviser files Form PF, the adviser is expected to provide Form PF responses that are consistent with the audited data. Advisers must report gross and net fund-performance information that is consistent with the results reported to investors (or consistent with the one used internally if not reported to investors). Form PF also allows an adviser to provide its methodologies as supplemental information and explain the assumptions on which the calculations were based. Although such explanation is optional, it can be illuminating and help resolve doubt and confusion with the SEC and CFTC.

Non-US Advisers

If an adviser's principal office and place of business is outside the United States, the adviser may exclude any private fund that, during the adviser's last fiscal year, was not a US person, was not offered to investors in the United States and was not beneficially owned by a US person. Advisers that are exempt from registering as investment advisers with the SEC because they solely advise either venture capital funds or private funds that have aggregate assets under management in the United States of less than $150 million are not required to file Form PF.

Investor Information

Question sixteen of Section 1(b) of Form PF requires advisers to specify the percentage of each private fund that is beneficially owned by the enumerated categories of investors. Note that advisers are not required to collect separate data from investors that held their interests prior to March 31, 2012. For these investors, advisers may respond using good faith estimates based on data otherwise available to them without making additional inquiries to establish more precise answers. However, advisers must collect sufficient information from investors that acquired their interests after March 31, 2012 to respond to these questions accurately. For many advisers, this will require gathering information that goes beyond what they usually include in their investor subscription materials. To avoid duplicate inquiries, you may consider adding appropriate inquiries to your subscription materials if you have not already done so.

Examinations and Enforcement

Although Form PF was created to provide the FSOC with critical data necessary to monitor systemic US financial risk and not as an investor disclosure tool, both the SEC and the CFTC are permitted to use Form PF filings in their examinations, investigations, investor protection efforts, and enforcement programs. Pursuant to Section 207 of the Advisers Act, any willful misstatement or omission of a material fact in any Advisers Act report filed with the SEC is unlawful. Also, the CFTC has taken the position that any false or misleading statement of a material fact or material omission in Section 1 or Section 2 of Form PF filed by a commodity pool operator or commodity trading adviser will constitute a violation of Section 6(c)(2) of the

Commodity Exchange Act. Accordingly, advisers should apply the same level of diligence and truthfulness in the completion of Form PF as they devote to the completion of Form ADV and other securities law disclosures.

■ Future Inquiries

Data provided on Form PF is not intended to be the exclusive source of information available for systemic risk analysis for the private fund industry, but to set a baseline for the ongoing financial stability analysis of the industry. The FSOC expects to work with the Office of Financial Research (OFR) to conduct an in-depth review of specific firms identified through the information on Form PF and other data. Both the FSOC and OFR may collect additional, targeted information from specific investment advisers. Accordingly, you may receive future inquiries from FSOC and OFR and should be prepared to respond.

■ Periodic Reporting

Advisers are required to file periodic Form PF updates either quarterly or annually, depending on their fund size/category. Unlike Form ADV, there is no requirement to make interim filings to report changes to information reported on Form PF as long as the information was accurate for the applicable period at the time it was reported. Form PF filing deadlines for the different categories of advisers are as follows:

Category of Adviser	Filing Obligation
Large hedge fund advisers	Quarterly within 60 days after the end of each fiscal quarter as to each hedge fund.
Large liquidity fund advisers	Quarterly within 15 days after the end of each fiscal quarter as to each liquidity fund.
All others (including large private equity advisers and smaller private fund advisers)	Annually within 120 days after the end of each fiscal year of the adviser as to each private fund not picked up by one of the other deadlines.

Fig 9.2 *Filing deadlines for Form PF*

If an adviser advises more than one type of fund – for example, a large hedge fund and a large private equity fund – the adviser is required to only update the information relating to its large hedge fund in its quarterly filings and the information relating to is large private equity fund in its annual filings. An adviser updating a portion of its Form PF for a fund with a quarterly filing requirement is not treated as having affirmed its prior responses for a fund with an annual filing requirement simply because the annual information was not updated in the quarterly filing.

■ Transition and Final Filings

If your Form PF filing obligation terminates or decreases in frequency because of a change in the adviser's status or assets under management, the adviser must make a transition filing to report the change. In particular, if you are transitioning from quarterly to annual filing because you are no longer a *large hedge fund adviser* or *large liquidity fund adviser*, then you must complete and file Item A of Section 1a and check the box in Section 1a indicating that you are making your final quarterly filing. You must file your transition filing no later than the last day on which your next *quarterly update* would be timely.

If you are no longer required to file Form PF, then you must complete and file Item A of Section 1a and check the box in Section 1a indicating that you are making your final filing. You must file your final filing no later than the last day on which your next Form PF update would be timely. This applies to all Form PF filers. This avoids the SEC and CFTC pursuing advisers for what may otherwise be perceived as missed filings.

■ Temporary Hardship Exemption

A limited scope "temporary hardship exemption" is available in cases where an adviser is unable to file Form PF electronically in a timely manner because of unanticipated technical difficulties. A request for the exemption must be filed no later than one business day after the Form PF filing was due. This exemption does not permit you to file on paper; instead, it extends the deadline for an electronic filing for seven business days. To request a temporary hardship exemption, you must complete and file on paper Item A of Section 1a and Section 5 of Form PF, checking the box in Section 1a indicating that you are requesting a temporary hardship exemption.

■ Filing Technicalities

Form PF is filed with the SEC through the IARD filing system maintained by FINRA. Please keep in mind that the IARD system is available only during certain prescribed hours and is generally not available on days the securities markets are closed. Advisers should allow sufficient time to upload Form PF information during the IARD's available hours, typically Monday through Friday from 7:00 a.m. to 11:00 p.m. Eastern Time. Where an investment adviser is also registered with the CFTC as a commodity pool operator or commodity trading adviser, Form PF is not separately filed with the CFTC, but the filing made with the SEC is treated as also having been made with the CFTC.

■ Filing Fees

Pursuant to Rule 204(b)-1, an adviser's complete Form PF will not be accepted by the system and will not be considered filed until the filing fee has been paid. As a technical matter, the IARD filing system requires that advisers fund their firm's IARD Daily Account before submitting Form PF. The funding process may take several days, and I would urge you to make sure that sufficient funds are in your Daily Account before making the filing to avoid causing bouncing/delays.

■ Confidentiality

The SEC suggested that it does not intend to make any Form PF information that is identifiable to any particular adviser or private fund public, although it has made clear that it may use the information in an enforcement action. Dodd-Frank amended the Advisers Act to ensure that the SEC may be compelled to reveal Form PF information only in very limited circumstances. Similarly, Dodd-Frank exempts the CFTC from being compelled under the Freedom of Information Act (FOIA) to disclose to the public any information collected through Form PF and requires that the CFTC maintain the confidentiality of the data consistent with the level of confidentiality that applies to the SEC. While the SEC may share Form PF information with other federal departments or agencies or with self-regulatory organizations, these agencies/organizations are also exempt from responding to FOIA requests and must agree to a confidentiality undertaking.

Chapter 9 Key Take-Aways

Form PF imposes voluminous disclosures that will take a fair amount of time and resources to identify, assemble, aggregate, and verify.

Any adviser managing private funds should start with an assessment of its filing obligations, namely if they pass the filing threshold and, if so, what type of filer they are. This will determine the amount of data that will need to be gathered.

Next, an adviser should define a process with clear tasks allocated to specific staff members and corresponding timelines.

There may be inconsistencies between an adviser's Form ADV and Form PF. The SEC acknowledges that. Be prepared to explain them.

Chapter 10

Exempt Reporting Advisers

The SEC's new Advisers Act rules, as mandated by Dodd-Frank, created a new class of investment advisers, exempt reporting advisers, which are not required to register but must still file reports with the SEC and are subject to a limited set of rules applicable to advisers under the Advisers Act. Exempt reporting advisers are investment advisers that rely on one of two newly created exemptions:

- Venture capital fund advisers
- Private fund advisers with less than $150 million in regulatory assets under management.

Although exempt reporting advisers do not have to register with the SEC or become compliant with the entire Advisers Act, they are subject to obligations such as filing reports, record keeping, pay to play, and other rules. Please note that advisers relying on the exemption for foreign private advisers and advisers to family offices are not considered exempt reporting advisers and, therefore, are not subject to the obligations imposed on them. As a starting point, you should read chapters 2 and 4 to determine whether you qualify for the venture capital exemption or the private fund adviser exemption.

Overview

Exempt reporting advisers are not required to register with the SEC, but are subject to reporting, record keeping, and other obligations under the Advisers Act. In addition to compliance requirements that apply to advisers regardless of their registration status (most importantly, the Advisers Act antifraud provisions), exempt reporting advisers must file a portion of Form ADV, enforce policies and procedures to prevent the misuse of material, nonpublic information, and comply with the Advisers Act pay-to-play rule. Exempt reporting advisers may also become subject to record-keeping requirements and they are subject to the SEC's examination authority. Form PF is complex and requires significant data collection. Be prepared to dedicate sufficient resources to gather the required information and complete the form. The first steps would obviously be to determine if you are required to submit Form PF and, if yes, which fund category you fall in.

This chapter is meant to help you with these determinations and to provide details regarding filing logistics.

Detailed Discussion

■ Who Is an Exempt Reporting Adviser?

Exempt reporting advisers are investment advisers that rely on either the venture capital fund adviser exemption in Section 203(l) of the Advisers Act or the private fund adviser exemption in Section 203(m) of the Advisers Act. Generally, the venture capital fund adviser exemption is available to advisers that solely advise venture capital funds. The private fund adviser exemption is available to advisers that only manage private funds and have less than $150 million of regulatory assets under management.

The rules to determine if you qualify for the exemption are complex. I dedicated two separate chapters to them, chapters 2 and 4, which I urge you to read. Advisers relying on the foreign private fund adviser exemption or the family offices are not exempt reporting advisers and, therefore, are not subject to the obligations associated with that status.

■ What Are My Filing Obligations?

❖ *Initial Filing*

Exempt reporting advisers must submit their initial filing within sixty days of relying on the private fund adviser exemption or the venture capital fund exemption.

❖ *Annual/Other-than-Annual Filings*

After the initial filing, advisers have to keep the information current by filing annual updating amendments within ninety days of their fiscal year end. When you submit your annual updating amendment, you must update your responses to all required items, including corresponding sections of Schedules A, B, C, and D.

In addition to your annual updating amendment, you must amend your Form ADV by filing additional amendments (other-than-annual amendments) promptly if:

- information you provided in response to Items 1 (Identifying Information), 3 (Form of Organization), or 11 (Disclosure Information) becomes inaccurate in any way; or
- information you provided in response to Item 10 (Control Persons) becomes materially inaccurate.

❖ *Transition to SEC-Registered Adviser*

If you are an existing exempt reporting adviser and no longer qualify for the exemption, transition rules apply. Exempt reporting advisers relying on the private fund adviser exemption that have complied with all reporting obligations may continue to advise private funds for up to ninety days after filing their annual updating amendments by stating that their assets under management in the United States are now $150 million or more; after that grace period, you must become a registered adviser. This period will not be available, however, to any adviser that has not met all reporting requirements or who would like to start advising clients that are not private funds. Similarly, it does not apply to an exempt reporting adviser that relies on the venture capital fund adviser exemption and anticipates losing the benefit of that exemption.

Accordingly, an exempt reporting adviser relying on the private fund adviser exemption who would like to advise nonprivate fund clients must become registered with the SEC (i.e., the registration must be accepted by the SEC and be effective) before taking on these clients, while an adviser relying on the venture capital fund adviser exemption must become registered with the SEC before taking on any client that is not a venture capital fund or before making an investment that would cause the adviser to lose its exemptive status. To switch from exempt to fully reporting adviser, an adviser would file a final report as an exempt reporting adviser and apply for SEC registration in the same filing.

Exempt Reporting Advisers that Change Status but Are Not Switching to SEC Registration

If you are no longer an exempt reporting adviser but are not required to register with the SEC – for example in the case where you stop being an investment adviser or become eligible for an exemption that does not require reporting – you must submit a final report as an exempt reporting adviser to update only Item 1 of Part 1A of Form ADV. You may still be required to register or remain registered with a state or the states you do business in.

You should consult with state registration requirements to make that determination.

What Do I Have to Report?

Exempt reporting advisers must report on the same Form ADV as registered advisers, but they are not required to file a full Form ADV. Specifically, they are required to complete Form ADV Items 1 (Identifying Information), 2.B (SEC Reporting by Exempt Reporting Advisers), 3 (Form of Organization), 6 (Other Business Activities), 7 (Financial Industry Affiliations and Private Fund Reporting), 10 (Control Persons) and 11 (Disclosure Information), along with the corresponding sections of Schedules A, B, C, and D.

The answers to these items provide basic information about the adviser, details about the private funds it advises (name, domicile, investment strategy, gross assets, etc.), other business interests of the adviser and its affiliates, and the disciplinary history of the adviser and its employees.

Will the Reports be Publicly Available?

All of the information filed by exempt reporting advisers on Form ADV becomes available to the public through IARD. Advisers should anticipate that bloggers, competitors, journalists, and potential investors will review the filings and make inquiries or write articles about the data.

How Do I File?

Exempt reporting advisers must file reports electronically through the IARD system. Each exempt reporting adviser reporting for the first time must complete the entitlement process, which provides access to IARD.

To file electronically, an adviser must obtain a copy of the IARD entitlement packet (available at www.iard.com) and submit it to FINRA, which assigns the adviser a CRD number (the Central Registration Depository ID number) and a user ID code and password. FINRA also creates a financial account for the firm from which the IARD system will deduct filings fees. Once the adviser has obtained the CRD number, ID code, and password and has funded its account, it is ready to file electronically.

■ What Are My Record-Keeping Requirements?

The SEC has signaled that it will adopt record-keeping requirements for exempt reporting advisers. In the meantime, I would advise you to at least maintain records regarding your relationship and communications with investors and supporting your disclosures on Form ADV until the SEC provides more details.

■ What Are My Obligations Regarding Material Nonpublic Information?

Exempt reporting advisers are subject to Section 204A of the Advisers Act, which requires that advisers establish, maintain, and enforce written policies and procedures reasonably designed to prevent the misuse of material, such as nonpublic information by investment advisers or any person associated with them. Exempt reporting advisers should consider the nature of their businesses and establish appropriate written policies that are designed to prevent the misuse of material nonpublic information.

■ What Other Rules Apply? Will I Have to Comply with the Antifraud Rules?

Exempt reporting advisers (as well as other registered and unregistered advisers, whether registered with the SEC or a state), are subject to the Advisers Act antifraud rule, which prohibits the use of any device or scheme to defraud clients or prospective clients. To that end, advisers should carefully review all marketing and subscription materials provided to investors to prevent misstatements or omissions of material facts.

■ Will I Be Subject to SEC Examinations?

The new rules do not subject exempt reporting advisers to routine SEC compliance examinations. However, the SEC has the authority to examine exempt reporting advisers' records, which leaves the door open for more regular and robust noncause examinations. The SEC has signaled that it expects to conduct cause examinations of exempt reporting advisers when it has cause to suspect them of wrongdoing (such examinations are usually prompted by tips, complaints, and referrals).

■ As an Exempt Reporting Adviser, Am I Also Subject to State Regulation?

Even if you qualify as an exempt reporting adviser the SEC, you may also be required to register with or submit a report to one or more state securities authorities. Every state has different rules for registration and reporting, so please check with the securities authorities in each state you do business in to make sure you are compliant. If you are required to register with one or more states, you must complete all of Form ADV. If you are required to submit a report to one or more state securities authorities, you must check the box(es) in Item 2.C. of Part 1A next to the state(s) that you would like to receive the report. Please refer to chapter 6 ("State vs. Federal Registration") for details on registration/reporting with individual states.

What Are My Obligations under the Pay-to-Play Rule?

All investment advisers, including exempt reporting advisers, are subject to the revised Advisers Act pay-to-play rule. Pay to play refers to various arrangements through which investment advisers seek to influence the award of advisory business by making or soliciting political contributions to the government officials charged with awarding such business. The cornerstone of the pay-to-play rule is a two-year time-out from providing compensated advisory services following certain triggering contributions. Specifically, Rule 206(4)-5 under the Advisers Act prohibits advisers from receiving any compensation for providing investment advice to a government entity within two years after a contribution has been made by the adviser or one of its covered associates.

Chapter 10 Key Take-Aways

Even if exempt from registration, advisers will need to assess if they are subject to the obligations of exempt reporting advisers. If so, they are subject to reporting requirements, as well as the SEC's antifraud rules and requirements regarding material nonpublic information.

The reporting obligations of exempt reporting advisers are significant and require the collection of timely, complete, and accurate information, which requires preparation and foresight. Do also keep in mind that whatever you report will eventually become publicly available.

Although the SEC has stated that it does not anticipate that it will conduct regular compliance exams of exempt reporting advisers, it may conduct cause examinations where there are indications of wrongdoing (i.e., through tips, complaints, and referrals).

Until the SEC publishes specifics regarding record-keeping requirements, advisers should adapt a commonsense approach to record keeping. At a minimum, record keeping should support disclosures on Form ADV and serve as evidence of the exempt reporting adviser's compliance with the rules.

Chapter 11

Custody

The custody rule (Rule 206(4)-2) is one of the more significant rules in the Advisers Act, as it requires SEC-registered investment advisers to implement a set of controls to prevent customer assets from being misappropriated, lost, or misused and to increase chances for earlier detection of fraudulent activity.

Overview

The custody rule broadly states that "it is a fraudulent, deceptive, or manipulative act" for registered advisers to have custody unless the adviser meets the requirements of the custody rule. Subject to a number of exceptions discussed below, the custody rule obligates an adviser with custody to satisfy a number of requirements:

1) The adviser must maintain the client assets with a US bank, broker-dealer, or other qualified custodian and must have a reasonable belief after due inquiry that the custodian sends account statements directly to the clients at least quarterly.
2) The adviser must undergo an annual surprise examination by an independent public accountant to verify client assets.
3) If client assets are maintained by a custodian that is not "operationally independent" from the adviser (i.e., is the adviser itself or a related person), the adviser must obtain an internal control report from an independent public accountant that is registered with the Public Company Accounting Oversight Board (PCAOB) and must have the surprise examination referred to in Item 2 performed by a PCAOB-registered public accountant.

Detailed Discussion

What is Custody?

The Advisers Act defines custody as "holding, directly or indirectly, client assets, or having any authority to obtain possession of them" by an investment adviser or its related persons in connection with advisory services. The SEC defines custody to include:

- actual physical possession of client assets by the adviser or a related person (unless the adviser receives them inadvertently and returns them to the sender promptly but in any case within three business days of receiving them);
- any arrangement, including a general power of attorney, under which an adviser or a related person is authorized or permitted to withdraw client assets; or
- any capacity that gives the adviser legal ownership of or access to client assets.

Note that the custody rule only applies to client funds and securities, not other assets.

Moreover, the above extends to the investment adviser and related persons, with *related person* being defined as any natural person or entity directly or indirectly controlling or controlled by the adviser and any person under common control with the adviser.

Examples of custody include:

- The adviser's personnel or related person serve as trustee or have been granted a power of attorney for client accounts.
- The adviser provides bill-paying services for clients and is authorized to withdraw funds or securities from clients' accounts.
- The adviser manages portfolios by directly accessing online accounts using clients' personal user names and passwords without restrictions and, therefore, has the ability to withdraw funds and securities from client accounts.
- The adviser has signatory and check-writing authority for client accounts.
- The adviser received checks made out to clients and failed to promptly return them to the sender.
- The adviser serves as the general partner of a limited partnership or holds a comparable position for a different type of pooled investment vehicle, such as the manager or managing member of a limited liability company or the trustee of a business trust.
- The adviser has the right to deduct advisory fees or other expenses directly from client accounts.
- The adviser has physical possession of client assets such as share certificates.

It is important to note that the mere fact that the adviser has discretionary authority over accounts does not amount to custody. To avoid acquiring custody inadvertently, an adviser should ensure that the power of attorney or other instrument granting authority to the adviser to execute transactions on a client's behalf only grants trading authority or the ability to transfer client assets between a client's own custodial accounts. To be sure, any power of attorney or other similar arrangement should specifically disclaim other powers.

What Are the Key Requirements of the Custody Rule?

Once you have custody, you must comply with a number of conditions, which are more or less onerous depending on the status of the custodian of the client's assets. They are as follows:

■ Use of a Qualified Custodian

❖ *Who Can Serve As Qualified Custodian?*

The custody rule requires that all client assets managed by the adviser for which the adviser has custody be held by a qualified custodian in a separate account. The account must be held either in the client's name or under the adviser's name as agent or trustee for the client. A qualified custodian is the type of financial institution that clients and advisers customarily turn to for custodial services and include:

1) a US bank that has its deposits insured by the Federal Deposit Insurance Corporation (FDIC),
2) an SEC-registered broker-dealer,

3) a registered futures commission merchant registered with the CFTC, and

4) a foreign financial institution that customarily holds financial assets for its customers provided that it keeps assets in client accounts that are segregated from its proprietary assets.

❖ *Delivery of Account Statements to Clients*

The adviser with custody of client assets must have a reasonable belief after due inquiry that the qualified custodian holding the assets sends quarterly account statements directly to clients. The statements must include all transactions during the quarter and the ending balances. The SEC has stated that the "due inquiry" standard would be satisfied where the qualified custodian provides the adviser with a copy of the account statement that was delivered to the client. If the adviser sends its own statements to its clients, they should contain a legend urging clients to compare the adviser's statement with those provided by the custodian. The legend should also be included in notices sent by the adviser to clients of the opening of the custodial account.

The custodian may deliver the account statements electronically if a) the client consented to electronic delivery, b) the client can effectively access the statements, and c) the custodian receives an e-mail return receipt or other confirmation that the information was accessed. In that case, the adviser may satisfy its due inquiry obligation, for example, by being copied on the e-mail notifications and having access to client statements on the custodian's website.

The SEC recently clarified that for pooled investment vehicles (which include private equity and hedge funds), the statements should include the cash and securities held by the fund and transactions by the fund in the statement period, and they must be sent to all investors in the fund, not just the fund itself.

❖ *Privately Issued Securities*

The SEC made an exception for the qualified custodian requirement for securities that meet the definition of a privately offered security. *Privately offered securities* are defined as securities that are 1) acquired in a nonpublic offering from the issuer; 2) uncertificated, with ownership only recorded on the issuer's register or by the transfer agent; and 3) not freely transferable without the consent of the issuer or the other holders. The SEC deemed these impediments to transferability sufficient to prevent the kind of abuse the custody rule is designed to prevent.

There is one caveat: limited partnerships and other pooled investment vehicles may not rely on the relief offered for privately offered securities unless the partnership is audited annually and the audited financial statements distributed to investors as described in more detail below.

■ Surprise Examination

An adviser with custody of client assets must undergo an annual surprise examination of those assets by an independent public accountant. This requirement does not apply to advisers who have custody solely because they are authorized to deduct their own fees and expenses from client accounts. Moreover, the annual surprise audit is not required of advisers to pooled investment vehicles that deliver audited financial statements to investors. It is also not required if an adviser has custody only because the qualified custodian is a related person of the adviser and the adviser has determined that the related custodian is operationally independent of the adviser (the decision must have been documented and be available for examination by the SEC).

Audits must be conducted on a surprise basis, so they should not be conducted at the same time every year. Accordingly, the accountant should select a time that varies each year without notice to the adviser. Any adviser subject to the surprise audit requirement must enter into a written agreement with the accountant requiring the accountant to:

1) file a report on Form ADV-E describing the nature and scope of the examination;
2) notify the SEC within one business day of any finding of material discrepancies during the course of the examination; and
3) file Form ADV-E within four days of resignation or dismissal from the engagement or upon a voluntary or involuntary removal from reconsideration for reappointment, along with an explanation of the circumstances that contributed to the event.

The accountant must electronically submit its report of the examination on Form ADV-E within 120 days of the surprise examination date. The report is available publicly on the SEC website.

■ Internal Control Report

If the adviser or one of its related parties acts as the qualified custodian, the adviser must obtain an internal control report (such as a Type II SAS 70 report, AT 101 report, etc.) from the custodian prepared by an independent PCAOB-registered public accountant that needs to address effectiveness of controls over custodial services. Note that pooled investment vehicles must still comply with thisrequirement even if they meet the requirements of the audit exception outlined below.

■ Exceptions

❖ *Advisers with Custody Due Solely to Fee Deduction*

An investment adviser that has custody of client assets solely because of its authority to deduct its advisory fees is not required to obtain annual surprise examinations. However, the requirements that the client's cash and securities be maintained by a qualified custodian and that the adviser have a reasonable belief that account statements are being delivered to clients at least quarterly still apply.

❖ *Pooled Investment Vehicles Subject to Audit*

The SEC provides an exception from several of the requirements outlined above for advisers to pooled investment vehicles that a) are subject to an annual audit of their financial statements by an independent public accountant and b) deliver the audited financial statements to the pool's investors. Specifically, advisers that satisfy the audit exception are deemed to have met the annual surprise examination requirement and are not required to have a reasonable belief that a qualified custodian will deliver account statements to investors. To qualify for the exception, the audit must be performed by an independent public accountant registered with and subject to regular inspection by the PCAOB.

Note that an adviser that relies on the exception must nonetheless undergo an annual surprise examination of assets held by nonpooled investment vehicles of which it has custody.

When assessing if it may use the audit exception, an adviser should consider the following factors:

1) The accountant performing the audit must be independent from the adviser under SEC standards. This is a stricter form of independence than the American Institute of Certified Public Accountants' (AICPA) standards that many unregistered advisers and their accountants operated under in the past.
2) The accountant must be registered with and subject to inspection by the PCAOB.
3) The adviser must have a reasonable belief that the audit will be completed and distributed to all investors within 120 days of the fiscal year end of the pooled investment vehicle. If the investment vehicle is a fund of funds (i.e., more than 10 percent of a pooled investment vehicle's net assets are invested in an unrelated pooled investment vehicle), the audit may be completed and delivered within 180 days of the fiscal year end.
4) The financial statements must be prepared under US generally accepted auditing standards (US GAAS). For those pools audited under other auditing standards, a dual opinion referencing US GAAS and the other standard may be issued. The financial statements must also be prepared under US GAAP. Non-US pools may have financial statements prepared in accordance with accounting standards other than US GAAP so long as they contain information substantially similar to statements prepared in accordance with US GAAP, with any material differences reconciled to US GAAP. This reconciliation only needs to be delivered to US investors.
5) The adviser must obtain a final audit of the pooled investment vehicle upon liquidation. Often, private equity funds may significantly wrap up their operations before final liquidation. In these cases, advisers should be mindful of the need to continue conducting annual audits and obtain a final liquidation audit.
6) The audited financials must actually be distributed to all pooled investment vehicle investors, not just made available upon request.
7) Investors cannot waive these requirements.

❖ *Custody through Operationally Independent Related Persons*

An investment adviser that 1) is deemed to have custody solely because a related person holds or has authority to obtain possession of clients' assets and 2) is operationally independent of the custodian is not required to obtain an annual surprise examination.

A related person is presumed to be operationally independent unless:

- client assets in the custody of the related person are subject to claims of the adviser's creditors,
- personnel of the adviser has access to the client assets (or the power to control the disposition of such assets to third parties for the benefit of the adviser or its related persons),
- personnel of the adviser and personnel of the custodian are under common supervision, or
- personnel of the adviser hold positions with the custodian or share premises with it.

What Are My Disclosure Obligations Concerning Custody?

Registered advisers are required to provide information about their custody practices in Form ADV. Part 1, Item 7 of Form ADV asks the adviser to identify all qualified custodians used, including broker-dealers. Item 9 requires the adviser to disclose the accountants used for the audit, surprise examination, and internal control report. Item 9 also requires the adviser to report:

- Whether the adviser or a related person has custody of client assets
- What the total amount of those assets is, as well as the number of clients whose accounts the adviser or its related person has custody of
- If any pooled investment vehicle advised by the adviser is audited, and if the qualified custodians send account statements to investors
- If the adviser serves as a qualified custodian for the adviser's clients

Depending on the responses to these items, the adviser may be required to provide additional information on Schedule D.

Additionally, advisers with discretionary authority or custody of client cash or securities must disclose on Form ADV Part 2 any material financial condition that may impair their ability to meet contractual commitments to clients. If an adviser collects more than $1,200 of fees six months or more in advance, the adviser must include with Form ADV Part 2 an independently audited balance sheet for the most recent fiscal year and disclose any material financial condition that may impair the ability to meet contractual commitments to clients.

What Policies and Procedures Should I Implement Regarding the Custody Rule?

An adviser's policies and procedures must address, among other things, the safeguarding of client assets from conversion or inappropriate use by advisory personnel. Compliance with Rule 206(4)-7 under the Advisers Act requires an adviser with custody to adopt controls that are reasonably designed to prevent misappropriation or misuse of client assets, to develop systems/procedures to assure prompt detection of any misuse, and to take appropriate action if any misuse does occur. To put this into practical terms, advisers with custody should consider the following policies and procedures as part of their compliance programs:

1) Conduct background and credit checks on employees of the investment adviser who have access (or could acquire access) to client assets.
2) Authorize more than one employee for the movement of assets in and transfers from a client's account, as well as for changes to account ownership information.
3) Limit the number of employees who are permitted to interact with custodians and rotate them on a periodic basis.
4) If the adviser also serves as a qualified custodian, segregate the duties of its advisory personnel from those of its custodial personnel to make it difficult for any one person to misuse client assets without being detected.
5) Require that problems be brought to the immediate attention of management and the adviser's chief compliance officer.
6) Prevent custody issues by prohibiting personnel from becoming trustees for client assets or obtaining powers of attorney for clients separate from the advisory firm.
7) Ensure that the adviser's chief compliance officer has access to sufficient information on these matters to enforce the adviser's policies and procedures.

The CCO should also periodically test the effectiveness of the firm'scontrols; for example, reconcile client account balances at the adviser with the custodian's records and comparing, on a sample basis, client addresses obtained from custodians with client addresses in its own files to look for inconsistencies or patterns that suggest possible manipulation.

In addition, the SEC suggests that advisers that have the authority to deduct advisory fees directly from client accounts should have policies and procedures in place that address the risk of advisory personnel deducting fees to which the adviser is not entitled. In that regard, good practices would include:

- Periodic testing on a sample basis of fee calculations for client accounts to determine their accuracy.
- Testing of the overall reasonableness of the amount of fees deducted from all client accounts for a period of time based on the adviser's aggregate assets under management.

- Segregating duties between those personnel responsible for processing client invoices or fees and those personnel responsible for reviewing the invoices for accuracy.

Advisers should also consider the following additional controls as part of an overall robust control environment:

- Periodically assess the adviser's securities in each entity or portfolio company structure for accuracy of the certificates and proper placement with qualified custodians.
- Ensure that current privately offered securities have not changed status under the definition in the custody rule.
- Ensure that policies and procedures address expenses and ensure proper allocation of expenses to each pooled investment vehicle and/or accounts, especially related to diligence on new deals and acquisitions.
- Examine limited partnership agreements and investment advisory contracts when calculating expenses and waterfalls.
- Prohibit commingling of assets.
- Send all certificates directly to the qualified custodian and have policies and procedures on inadvertently receiving client assets.
- Perform periodic oversight of the qualified custodian, including obtaining controls reports, on-site reviews, and reconciliations.
- Ensure that all employees with responsibility for custody controls are adequately trained and understand their obligations.

Chapter 11 **Key Take-Aways**

The custody rule imposes detailed requirements regarding the manner in which SEC-registered advisers must safeguard client cash and securities, which range from the selection of qualified institutions to hold the assets as custodians to undergoing surprise examinations to verify that no improper transactions have occurred.

Custody is defined very broadly and goes far beyond being in possession of assets. Every adviser should familiarize itself with the scope of the rule and carefully consider its ramifications. This means reading up on the rule's wording, SEC releases, and staff interpretations, or the retention of competent counsel.

To avoid inadvertent custody, you should ensure that powers of attorneys or similar arrangements are limited to trades or transfers within clients' custodial accounts. Discretionary authority alone, however, does not give rise to custody.

The SEC has issued a multitude of recommendations for effective compliance processes and procedures concerning custody. You should carefully consider adopting the ones that are appropriate for your firm.

Chapter 12

Consequences of Being an SEC-Registered Investment Adviser

With or without the help of this book, you have determined that you are an investment adviser that is subject to SEC oversight and have successfully registered with the SEC. Now what? You will have to comply with the Advisers Act. The Advisers Act, together with the rules adopted by the SEC under it, are the main body of law applicable to investment advisers. In addition, the SEC provides interpretive guidance in instructions to forms, guidance updates, no-action letters, and interpretative letters and releases, all of which are publicly available.

The Advisers Act consists of a complex set of rules that govern all aspects of an adviser's operations, such as its client contracts, how and with whom it executes trades, broker arrangements, advertising, referral arrangements, having possession of client assets, conflicts of interest, ethics, disclosures, record keeping, etc. In addition, advisers always have to keep in mind their underlying duties of care and loyalty, which are the underpinnings of their role as fiduciaries of their client's assets.

If you have read the chapter on how to become registered (chapter 7), you know that there is no grace period, so applicants must be in full compliance with the Advisers Act at the time their registration becomes effective. Since the SEC's approval typically occurs within forty-five days after filing an initial Form ADV, advisers should begin taking steps to become compliant several months prior to filing the Form ADV. The first and vital step is for an adviser to take stock of its business and operations and plan a timeline on how to become compliant. It should adopt customized policies and procedures that really match the business at hand, as opposed to taking a cookie-cutter approach to the process.

It will take a while to become compliant. Action items may include long-lead items, such as hiring additional or reallocating existing personnel, outsourcing functions or purchasing new software. There will be a lot of drafting required, such as the compliance manual, a code of ethics, client contracts, a privacy policy, and the various forms that go with the policies and procedures that you are adopting. In addition, advisers should review their websites, blogs, marketing materials, social media communications, offering documents, subscription agreements, counterparty agreements, and other existing legal documents to assess if any modifications need to be made, notices need to be given, consents to be obtained, and/or other actions are required.

This chapter is meant to guide you through the main rules and assist you with the task of becoming and staying compliant, whether you just launched a brand-new advisory business or are a seasoned veteran that has just registered for the first time because you finally exceeded the SEC's asset under management threshold or have grown out of an exemption. It obviously only hits the highlights, as there is a lot of ground to cover, but it felt important to include this chapter in the book for completeness' sake.

Overview

What is important to understand about the Advisers Act is that is does not provide a comprehensive regulatory regime for advisers, but rather imposes a broad fiduciary duty on an adviser to act in the best interest of its clients. What I am trying to say is that the regulation of investment advisers is principles-based rather than rules-based, and there are five sources for the regulatory framework:

1. A fundamental fiduciary duty to clients, consisting of the duty of care and loyalty that transcends the specific regulations and rules in the Advisers Act.
2. Specific substantive prohibitions and requirements, such as the advertising rules, use of solicitors, etc.
3. Contractual requirements, most of which are contained in the advisory agreement between the adviser and the client.
4. Record-keeping requirements prescribed by the SEC.
5. Administrative oversight by the SEC, including inspection.

The following highlights the key compliance obligations of advisers and identifies the applicable section/rule of the Advisers Act:

- **Fiduciary Duties:** Each advisory firm, whatever its size, type, or history, owes its advisory clients a fiduciary duty.
- **Compliance Program:** Rule 206(4)-7 requires each adviser to adopt written policies and procedures designed to prevent violations of the securities laws, conduct an annual review, and appoint a chief compliance officer.
- **Code of Ethics:** Rule 204A-1 requires each adviser to adopt and enforce a written code of ethics that sets forth a minimum standard of conduct for its personnel and reflects the adviser's fiduciary duties to its clients.
- **Insider Trading:** Section 204A requires written policies and procedures designed to prevent the use of material, nonpublic information.

■ **Privacy Policy:**	Regulation S-P requires advisers to adopt policies and procedures that address safeguards for the protection of customer records and information.
■ **Disclosure:**	Rules 203-1 and 204(1) require advisers to provide initial and periodic disclosures to clients through the completion, filing and delivery of Form ADV.
■ **Proxy Voting:**	Rule 206(4)-6 governs an adviser's voting of proxies on behalf of clients.
■ **Record Keeping:**	Rule 204-2 requires advisers to maintain records for its activities and its compliance program.
■ **Performance-Based Fees**	Section 205 imposes minimum standards for the terms of the contract between the adviser and its clients, including performance-based fees.
■ **Solicitation Agreements:**	Rule 206(4)-3, imposes a number of requirements on solicitation arrangements
■ **Custody:**	Rule 206(4)-2 governs client funds and securities over which an adviser has custody.
■ **Advertising and Other Client Communications:**	Rule 206(4)-1 restricts among other things, the use of performance data, client testimonials, and past recommendations.
■ **Pay to Play:**	Rule 206(4)-5 sets forth the rules for campaign contributions by advisers.
■ **Advisory Contracts:**	Section 205 prescribes minimum requirements for advisory contracts.
■ **Antifraud:**	Advisers are subject to the broad antifraud provisions of Sections 206 and 207.
■ **Social Media:**	Social media activities are subject to the Advisers Act and the rules under it. See SEC.
■ **Self-Dealing:**	Section 206(3) and Rule 206(3)-2 impose restrictions on principal and agency cross-trade transactions.
■ **Wrap Fee Programs:**	Rule 204-3(d) under the Advisers Act imposes obligations on sponsors of wrap fee programs.
■ **SEC Examinations:**	Section 204 grants the SEC the authority to examine the records of advisers registered with it.

Understanding the Adviser's Fiduciary Duty

Understanding an adviser's fiduciary duty is so critical to the role of being an adviser that I dare to say that if you don't have a good grasp of what it means, you will not be able to be (or will have a hard time being) compliant. It is its essence. While the term "fiduciary" is nowhere to be found in the Advisers Act itself, in 1963 the US Supreme Court held in *SEC v. Capital Gains Research Bureau, Inc.*, that the Advisers Act "reflects congressional recognition of the delicate fiduciary nature of an investment advisory relationship as well a congressional intent to eliminate, or at least to expose, all conflicts of interest which might incline an investment adviser-consciously or unconsciously-to render advice which was not disinterested." Section 206 of the Advisers Act generally prohibits an adviser from engaging in any practice that is fraudulent, deceptive, or manipulative. Aside from Section 206, the fiduciary standard is also embodied in the various disclosure obligations and prohibitions in the Advisers Act described in this chapter. The general purpose of an investment adviser's fiduciary duty is to eliminate/mitigate conflicts of interest and to prevent an adviser from taking unfair advantage of a client's trust. The SEC has continuously made it clear subsequent to capital gains that the Advisers Act imposes on investment advisers an affirmative duty to their clients of utmost good faith, full and fair disclosure of all material facts, and an obligation to employ reasonable care to avoid misleading them. There are several responsibilities that flow from an adviser's fiduciary duties, such as:

1. Placing clients' interests first.
2. Treating clients fairly.
3. Acting with utmost good faith.
4. Providing full and fair disclosure of all material facts, especially conflicts of interest.
5. Rendering suitable advice and having a reasonable, independent basis for recommendations.

What does all of this mean in real life or in concrete terms? It means that an adviser's fiduciary responsibility must permeate its entire business operation and every aspect of its client relationships. It requires more than a mere attempt at compliance and following technical rules; it requires that you undertake reasonable ongoing and continuous efforts to comply with your obligations under the Advisers Act and putting clients' interests first.

■ **Compliance Program** (Rule 206(4)-7)

Rule 206(4)-7 is the most basic rule advisers have to contend with. It is the compliance program rule. Rule 206(4)-7 requires each SEC-registered investment adviser to satisfy a number of minimum requirements. They must:

1. adopt and implement written policies and procedures reasonably designed to prevent violation of the federal securities laws;
2. review those policies and procedures annually for their adequacy and the effectiveness of their implementation; and
3. designate a chief compliance officer to be responsible for administering the policies and procedures.

❖ *Compliance Policies and Procedures*

Each adviser is required to adopt and implement written policies and procedures reasonably designed to prevent violations of the Advisers Act and the rules adopted under it. The scope of this rule is extremely broad, and the SEC has not provided much guidance. However, it has indicated that an effective processes and procedures manual should at least address the following:

- portfolio management processes, including allocation of investment opportunities among clients and consistency with client objectives;
- trading practices, including best execution, soft dollar arrangements (use of advisory fees to obtain research, etc.), and trade allocation among clients;
- proprietary and personal trading activities;
- protection from the misuse of material nonpublic information;
- accuracy of disclosures made to investors, clients, and regulators;
- safeguarding of client assets (i.e., issues related to custody);
- creation and maintenance of required records;
- marketing;
- use of solicitors;
- valuation of client holdings and assessment of fees based on them; and
- business continuity plans, including disaster recovery plans and deaths of owners and/or key personnel.

By now I probably sound like a broken record since you have read me saying this before in my blog and previous Chapters: There really is no "one-size-fits-all" approach to creating, maintaining or enforcing policies and procedures, and every compliance manual should be tailored to your specific structure, investment strategy and the operations of your firm. Adopting generic compliance policies and procedures without undergoing a thorough review of the nature of the business and the operations of the firm typically results in a manual that is overly burdensome, impossible to implement and test, and, worst of all, in violation of the rules. To make things worse, compliance programs that look ill-suited or ineffective may lead the SEC staff to conclude that compliance is not a priority and that the firm is at high risk of violations.

Any new or amended policies or procedures should be carefully reviewed by all affected personnel and should be tested prior to becoming effective. This process should involve senior management and the appropriate business units. In my experience, the "tone from the top" makes or breaks the success (i.e., the effectiveness of a compliance program). Moreover, the SEC staff has indicated on more than one occasion that management's participation in this process helps demonstrate a firm-wide commitment to compliance. Some policies or procedures might also require coordination with outside service providers, such as IT providers (e.g., for e-mail retention and disaster recovery).

Aside from the general mandate in the compliance program rule, several other rules under the Advisers Act require that advisers adopt written policies and procedures. I will discuss these in more detail below.

❖ *Appointment of Chief Compliance Officer*

Each advisory firm must appoint a chief compliance officer (CCO) to be responsible for administering the firm's compliance policies and procedures. A CCO should be competent and knowledgeable regarding the Advisers Act, have full responsibility and authority to develop and enforce appropriate policies and procedures, and have sufficient seniority and authority to compel others to adhere to the firm's compliance program. For smaller firms where the CCO may wear more than one hat, the firm should make sure that dual responsibilities of the CCO do not lead to untenable conflicts of interest and that the person in that role is qualified and dedicated. Some firms even decide to outsource such functions. However, advisers with outsourced CCOs need to make sure that there is one point person within the firm "on the ground," who is in charge of the relationship to make sure that the outside CCO has the access he or she needs to be effective at his or her job.

Since the selection of CCO can be a long-lead item, I recommend that a firm commence the process and designate a CCO as soon as the decision to register is made, so that the CCO can be actively involved in the development of the compliance policies and procedures from the outset. The CCO should not automatically be placed in the legal department, which could lead to conflicts in the implementation and examination of the compliance program. The SEC staff has cautioned that if the CCO reports through the general counsel instances of attorney-client privilege must be clearly articulated and that any dual responsibilities should be segregated. On a related note, the SEC has taken the position that routine compliance monitoring is not subject to attorney-client privilege.

❖ *Annual Review*

Each advisory firm must review the adequacy of its compliance policies and procedures and the effectiveness of their implementation on an annual basis. Firms should maintain written evidence of the review. The annual review should consider matters that arose during the previous year and that might require changes to the policies and procedures, such as internal compliance matters, changes in the firm's business activities, as well as changes in the Advisers Act or other regulations or SEC guidance on matters.

■ **Code of Ethics** (Rule 204A-1)

Each adviser must establish, maintain, and enforce a written code of ethics reflecting the adviser's fiduciary duties to its clients. At minimum, the code of ethics should require:

1. a standard of conduct for firm personnel;
2. supervised persons to comply with federal securities laws;
3. the firm's access persons to report securities holdings and transactions to the CCO;
4. the CCO to preapprove investments by access persons in IPOs or limited offerings;
5. supervised persons to report any violations of the code of ethics to the CCO; and
6. the firm to provide each supervised person with a copy of the code of ethics and obtain a written acknowledgment from the supervised person of receipt of the code.

The code of ethics must require all access persons to periodically report, and for the CCO to review, their personal securities transactions and holdings. Specifically, each access person must provide the CCO with a quarterly report of all of his or her personal securities transactions and an annual report that lists his or her personal security holdings. A firm must also require preclearance of any investments in IPOs or private placements by access persons. For many fund managers, it is often appropriate that these requirements apply to all officers and employees, not just access persons. An adviser should consider including other provisions that are not required but, nevertheless, might be good business practices, such as restrictions on receiving gifts, and the preclearance, as opposed to just a review, of all personal securities transactions.

The adviser must keep copies of the code of ethics, records of violations of the code, actions taken against violators of the code, and the acknowledgments of receipt of the code by firm personnel in the firm's records.

An *access person* is any of an adviser's personnel who: 1) has access to nonpublic information regarding any client's purchase or sale of securities or nonpublic information regarding the portfolio holdings of any reportable fund or 2) is involved in making securities recommendations to clients or who has access to such recommendations that are nonpublic.

Insider Trading (Section 204A)

Each firm must establish, maintain, and enforce written policies and procedures reasonably designed to prevent the misuse of material, nonpublic information by any person associated with the firm. The misuse of this information may include trading based on the information, either personally or on behalf of others, or communicating the information to others (i.e., "tipping."). While the scope of the rules against insider trading are not always clear, as a general rule of thumb a firm cannot use material, nonpublic information obtained from an issuer or another third party for client or personal trading. In addition, an adviser cannot use material, nonpublic information about current or pending client investments (e.g., actual or pending purchases and sales of securities) other than in connection with the investment of client accounts. Advisers should consider adopting insider trading policies and procedures that require as a minimum:

1) Distribution of the insider trading policy to all employees at least annually and to new employees when they are hired. The acknowledgment of receipt should be kept in the files.
2) Maintenance of a list of clients that may have material nonpublic information.
3) Maintenance of a blackout list for both employee and client accounts. Be sure that review of communications, including e-mail, takes place against the companies on the list.
4) Polling of employees to find out whether they have personal or business relationships that may result in access to material, nonpublic information.
5) Review of the trading activity reports submitted by access persons for transactions or trading patterns that suggest violations. For example, trading reports should be reviewed against market news.
6) Ongoing training relating to insider trading at least annually. Employees should learn what procedures to follow if they believe they have received material, nonpublic information.
7) Review of the policy on a periodic basis. Advisers should document any changes; if there are no changes, advisers should document that a review took place and the process.

Insider trading is a large risk for advisory firms, with violations resulting in enforcement proceedings, fines, and other sanctions.

■ **Privacy Policy** (Regulation S-P)

Title V of the Graham-Leach-Bliley Act and Regulation S-P adopted by the SEC in response to it protect the privacy of consumers of financial services, including clients of SEC-registered investment advisers. Each adviser must adopt policies and procedures that address administrative, technical, and physical safeguards for the protection of customer records and information.

❖ *What Are the General Requirements of the Privacy Rule?*

There are three fundamental rules advisers must remember about Regulation S-P:

1. Advisers must provide clients with an initial and an annual notice of its privacy policies and practices.
2. Advisers must not disclose nonpublic information about their clients to nonaffiliated third parties unless the adviser has provided its clients with the notice.
3. Advisers must provide a method for clients to prevent the disclosure of their nonpublic personal information (i.e., the ability to "opt out").

❖ *What Must the Privacy Notice Contain?*

The notice must be clear and conspicuous (i.e., reasonably understandable). It must include:

1) categories of nonpublic information that the adviser collects;
2) categories of information that the adviser may disclose;
3) categories of affiliates and nonaffiliates with which the adviser shares the information;
4) the adviser's policies and practices for protecting the confidentiality and security of information;
5) an explanation of the individual's right to opt out of the disclosure, including an explanation as to how the individual may exercise the right; and
6) the adviser's policies with respect to protecting the confidentiality, security, and integrity of the information collected.

The SEC has adopted a model form that advisers may use. While the use of the form is by no means mandatory, it provides an adviser with a "safe harbor" for compliance with the rules. You can find the form at

http://www.sec.gov/divisions/marketreg/tmcompliance/modelprivacyform-secg.htm

❖ *What Is Considered a Nonaffiliated Third Party?*

The restrictions in the privacy rules apply to disclosure to nonaffiliated third parties of the adviser. Accordingly, an adviser may share with affiliates and a joint employee of the adviser and the third party. Also, disclosure is permitted in the course of rendering advisory services to the client (for example, with a broker or lawyer) with the client's consent or with a provider of services to the adviser (for example, a marketer), as long as the adviser entered into a contract with the service provider that provides that the information be kept confidential and prohibits the service provider from using the information outside the purpose for which it was revealed.

❖ *Who Are the Consumers and Customers Protected by the Privacy Rules?*

While Regulation S-P only applies to clients and investors who are natural persons, I nevertheless recommend that an adviser apply the same safeguards to entity clients and fund investors.

❖ *What Else Do I Need to Think About?*

States may have specific rules and regulations on how advisers must treat nonpublic personal information of their residents. They vary considerably, and you should consult with counsel regarding your particular circumstances.

■ **Disclosure** (Rules 203-1, 204(b)-1)

SEC and state-registered investment advisers have significant disclosure obligations. The most significant tool in this regard is Form ADV, which is used to register initially and, once registered, to update data about your advisory business. The newly created Form PF imposes additional disclosure obligations on advisers to private funds. Due to their importance, I dedicated separate chapters (chapters 7 and 9) to these forms, which I encourage you to read carefully.

■ **Proxy Voting** (Rule 206(4)-6)

In many instances, clients give advisers the authority to vote proxies on their behalf.

❖ *What Are the General Principles?*

An investment adviser who has proxy voting authority over client securities must vote them in the best interest of the client and not its own interest. Rule 206(4)-6 requires advisers with proxy voting authority to:

- adopt written policies and procedures that ensure that the adviser votes proxies in the best interest of the client and that they specifically address conflicts of interest that may arise and how they will be addressed; and
- describe the voting policies and procedures to the client, deliver a copy to the client, and disclose how clients may obtain information on how the adviser voted the proxies.

❖ *When Do the Proxy Voting Rules Apply?*

The rules apply to all advisers who have proxy voting authority whether the authority is explicit or implied, so it may apply even when the advisory contract is silent but the adviser has overall discretionary authority. I would recommend that, if you do not intend to vote proxies for your clients, you expressly include a clause to that effect in your advisory contract.

❖ *What Should Proxy Voting Policies and Procedures Contain?*

It is not sufficient for an adviser to merely state that it will vote proxies in the best interest of clients; rather, the adviser's policies and procedures must address the specifics as to how it will vote proxies and what factors the adviser will take into account when voting on particular matters. The policies and procedures must also discuss how the adviser intends to address any conflicts of interest.

■ **Record Keeping** (Rule 204-2)

Section 204 and Rule 204-2 require that SEC-registered advisers maintain and preserve books and records related to their business and make them available to SEC examiners for inspection.

❖ *What Kind of Records Must Be Kept?*

In general, the SEC requires an adviser to maintain two types of books and records: 1) typical accounting and other records, such as checkbooks and bank statements that any business would normally keep and 2) records the SEC believes necessary in light of the adviser's fiduciary duties, such as:

- A record of the personal securities transactions and holdings of the adviser and its employees and all other documents evidencing compliance with the adviser's code of ethics.
- A list of all persons who are current and former access persons (going back five years).
- Trade or order tickets and instructions from clients concerning the purchase and sale of securities.
- All communications received and copies of all written communications sent by the adviser relating to recommendations and advice to clients, the receipt and delivery of funds or securities, and the placing or executing of any order to purchase or sell any security.
- Copies of all newsletters, advertisements, newspaper articles, etc., sent to ten or more persons.
- Documents necessary to substantiate performance information contained in advertisements.
- Copies of powers of attorney.
- Copies of each written statement given to any client in compliance with the brochure rule and any document prepared in compliance with the requirements of Form ADV.
- Clients' acknowledgment of receipt of a solicitation agreement and the solicitor's statement.
- Documents substantiating performance advertising.
- All documents pertaining to the pay-to-play rule, including records regarding political contributions and advisory services to any government entity.

Each business is different, so an adviser may be required to maintain additional records based on its specific operations, for example, if it has custody of client assets.

❖ *How Long, How and Where Do I Need to Keep My Records?*

Generally, most books and records must be kept for five years. For the first two years, they must be kept in the adviser's offices; after two years, they are to be kept in an easily accessible location. If the adviser maintains original books and records somewhere other than its principal office and place of business (such as with a fund's administrator), it must be noted in its Form ADV.

Original books and records may be stored using either micrographic or electronic media, and the adviser should be able to produce it promptly (generally within twenty-four hours) upon request by SEC staff. To ease this process, an adviser should arrange and index electronic records in a way that permits easy location, access, and retrieval. Duplicate copies of advisory records should be stored in a location separate from the principal office in order to ensure business continuity in case of a disaster.

Performance-Based Fees (Rule 205-3)

Section 205(a)(1) of the Investment Advisers Act generally prohibits an investment adviser from entering into an investment advisory contract that varies with the adviser's success in managing the client's money. This means that an advisory contract may not contemplate a fee based on a share of capital gains on a client's funds or capital appreciation thereof.

There are a number of important exceptions to the prohibition on performance-based fees:

1) Advisers may base their fees on the amount of assets under management.
2) Advisers may charge a fulcrum fee, which is a fee for "big players" where the investment advisory contract involves registered investment companies or clients with over $1 million of assets. A valid fulcrum fee must be based on the asset value over a set period of time and must increase or decrease proportionally based on asset performance in relation to an index.
3) Advisers may charge performance-based fees to qualified clients. A qualified client is a client who:

- has at least $1 million under management immediately after entering into the advisory contract with the adviser;
- has in the adviser's reasonable belief a net worth (together, in the case of a natural person, with assets held jointly with a spouse, excluding the primary residence) of more than $2 million or is a qualified purchaser under the Investment Company Act (which has even higher wealth standards) at the time the contract is entered into;
- is an executive officer, director, trustee, general partner, and other employee of the adviser;
- is a fund that is not registered under the Investment Company Act but has only qualified purchaser investors (i.e., is exempted from Investment Company Act registration because of Section 3(c)(7) under that Act);
- is another type of fund but only if each investor in the fund is a qualified client with whom the adviser would be allowed to enter into a performance fee agreement individually; or
- is not a resident of the United States.

■ Solicitation Arrangements (Rule 206(4)-3)

An adviser is prohibited under Rule 206(4)-3 from paying a cash fee to a solicitor unless the arrangement meets a number of requirements. A solicitor is anyone who solicits clients for or refers clients to an investment adviser.

❖ *What Are the Requirements for the Solicitor Agreement?*

Generally, an agreement with a solicitor must be in writing and must describe the scope of the solicitor's activities and the compensation. In addition, the agreement must contain an undertaking by the solicitor that he or she will perform his/her duties under the agreement in a manner consistent with the adviser's instructions and the Advisers Act and require the solicitor to provide the potential client with a copy of the adviser's brochure (Part 2A of Form ADV) and a separate written disclosure statement at the time of the solicitation, which must describe the terms of the solicitation arrangement, including the compensation.

❖ *What Are the Other Obligations?*

The adviser must receive a signed and dated acknowledgment of receipt from the client. The adviser must also make a bona fide effort to ascertain that the solicitor has complied with the other terms of their agreement.

❖ *When Is a Solicitor Disqualified?*

An adviser cannot engage a solicitor who is disqualified. Reasons for disqualification include conviction of a felony or misdemeanor within the past ten years involving securities matters, bribery, perjury, burglary, or similar activities.

❖ *What Else Do I Have to Keep in Mind?*

The Advisers Act does not require a solicitor to register as an investment adviser as long as the solicitor's activities are strictly limited to making referrals. However, keep in mind that, depending on the circumstances, a solicitor may fall under the definition of a broker under the 34 Act and state laws and, if so, would need to be registered or exempt from registration as a broker-dealer. Many states also require that a solicitor be registered as an investment adviser representative with the state securities authorities.

■ Custody (Rule 206(4)-2)

If an adviser has custody of clients' funds or securities, it is required to maintain safeguards meant to protect these assets. Custody is defined as holding client funds or securities directly or indirectly, or having the authority to obtain possession of them. Examples for custody include:

- physical possession of funds or securities;

- an arrangement that allows the adviser to withdraw funds or securities, such as check-writing authority, or the ability to deduct advisory fees from client accounts; or
- any arrangement that gives the adviser or its personnel legal ownership of or access to client assets, such as the adviser's role as a trustee, or the general partner of a fund.

I dedicated an entire chapter to custody (chapter 11), which you should read if you are not sure whether you have custody or not and to learn what it entails if you do.

Advertising and Other Client Communications (Rule 206(4)-1)

Rule 206(4)-1 generally prohibits advisers from using any advertisement that contains any untrue statement of a material fact or that is otherwise misleading. All advertising is subject to this general rule and a number of specific prohibitions.

What Is an Advertisement?

Advertisement is defined broadly. It includes any notice, newsletter, letter, and e-mail, or any other written communication addressed to more than one person. It also refers to a notice or other announcement in any publication or done by radio or television that offers investment advisory services, including allcommunications through social media platforms (which I discuss separately below). Advertisements generally do not include written communications responding to an unsolicited request by a client.

What Are the Specific Prohibitions?

The specific prohibitions on adviser advertisements are:

1. using advertisements that contain testimonials;
2. performance advertising (i.e., past specific recommendations by the adviser, unless the advertisement satisfies a number of specific requirements);
3. representing that any graph, chart, or formula can, in and of itself, be used to determine which securities to buy or sell, unless it includes a prominent disclaimer; or
4. stating that any report, analysis, or service is free, unless it really is.

In addition, an adviser is prohibited from attaching phrases such as *RIA* or *Registered Investment Adviser* to its name in a manner that implies that it: 1) is or has been officially endorsed, sponsored, recommended, or approved by the SEC or any other governmental authority or 2) has specific professional competence, education, or special training.

❖ *Use of Testimonials*

An adviser is prohibited from using an advertisement that contains testimonials. Testimonials are defined as any statement by a former or present client that endorses the adviser or refers to the client's favorable investment experience with it. This prohibition is interpreted broadly. However, an adviser may include a partial client list in advertising materials, but only if:

1) it does not use performance-based data to determine which clients to include on the list;
2) each list includes a prominent disclaimer that it is not known whether the listed clients approve or disapprove of the adviser or the advisory services provided;
3) each list includes disclosure about the objective criteria used to determine which clients to include on the list; and
4) each client identified on the list has consented to being identified.

In addition, advisers may include in an advertisement a bona fide, unbiased third-party report or article.

❖ *Performance Advertising*

Advertisements that contain past performance of investments picked by the adviser – both actual performance and hypothetical or model results – must not be misleading. Cherry-picking (i.e., referring to profitable past recommendations while ignoring the unprofitable ones) is prohibited. Performance advertising is also misleading if it implies something about an adviser's competence or possible future investment results that would be unwarranted if the investor knew all the facts. To that end, performance advertisements must:

1) disclose the effect of material market or economic conditions on the performance results;
2) disclose whether or not, and to what extent, the results portrayed reflect the reinvestment of earnings;
3) if results are presented in comparison to an index, disclose all material facts relevant to the comparison; and
4) disclose any material conditions, objectives, or investment strategies used to obtain the results.

Advertisements cannot suggest or make claims about the potential for profit without also disclosing the possibility of loss. Model performance results must include a prominent discussion/disclaimer of the limitations inherent in them. As a general rule, performance results must always be presented net of fees and other expenses.

All communications that may be considered advertisements should be carefully vetted in accordance with an adviser's processes and procedures based on SEC guidance and underlying policy considerations. Performance-based communications need to contain an appropriate legend, which should be crafted with the help of experienced counsel.

■ Pay to Play (Rule 206(4)-5)

In 2010, the SEC adopted rule 206(4)-5 to address pay-to-play practices in which investment advisers make campaign contributions in exchange for contracts that would allow them to manage public pension plan assets and other government investment accounts. The rule applies to SEC-registered investment advisers, exempt reporting advisers, and foreign private advisers who provide, or are seeking to provide, investment advisory services to state or municipal government entities.

The pay-to-play rule contains three main prohibitions:

1) the two-year time-out;
2) the third party solicitor ban; and
3) the bundling ban.

❖ *Two-Year Time-Out*

Advisers are prohibited from receiving compensation for providing advice to a government entity within two years after a political contribution by the adviser or one of its covered associates has been made an official of the government entity and can influence the award of advisory business. Advisers may, however, provide advisory services to the government entity on a no-fee basis. The term *government entity* is limited to state and local entities; typically, pension plans are separate legal entities from state and local governments but have elected officials as board members. The term *covered associate* generally includes an adviser's executive officers, employees who solicit government entities (and their supervisors), and any Political Action Committee (PAC) controlled by the adviser.

The rule includes exceptions for *de minimis* contributions made by individual employees, generally in an amount up to $350 per official (per election) for whom an employee is entitled to vote and up to $150 per official (per election) for whom an employee is not entitled to vote. There is also an exception for a limited number of de minimis contributions that are discovered and returned within a certain time period. When a person becomes a covered associate (including when an existing employee is transferred or promoted), the adviser must look back into that person's contributions to determine if the time-out provisions of the rule apply. If the person is involved in soliciting clients, then the adviser must look as far as two years back. If the person is not involved in soliciting clients, then the adviser is only required to look at the contributions made in the last six months.

I would recommend circulating a questionnaire to all covered associates at least annually to determine what, if any, political contributions have been made. The same questionnaire should be completed by prospective employees that will become covered associates and existing employees that are expected to become covered associates to ensure compliance with the provisions of this rule.

❖ *Third-Party Solicitor Ban*

An adviser and its covered associates are prohibited from paying a third party to solicit government clients, unless such third party is a *regulated person* (i.e., a registered investment adviser that meets the requirements of the look-back or the bundling prohibitions, a registered municipal adviser, or a registered broker-dealer). I would recommend that you review your current third-party solicitors to make sure they can legally perform services for you under this rule.

This ban does not extend to payments made by the adviser to third parties that provide legal and accounting or other professional services as long as such third parties are not being paid by you (directly or indirectly) for communicating with the government entity for the purpose of obtaining or retaining investment advisory business for you.

❖ *Bundling Ban*

Rule 206(4)-5 prohibits an adviser and its covered associates from *bundling* contributions (i.e., coordinating or soliciting any person or PAC to make any contribution to an official of a government entity to which the adviser is providing or seeking to provide investment advisory services or any payment to a political party of a state or locality where the investment adviser is providing or seeking to provide investment advisory services to a government entity.

❖ *Catch-All Provision*

Rule 206(4)-5(d) prohibits acts done indirectly, which, if done directly, would violate the rule.

❖ *Covered Investment Pools*

Rule 206(4)-5 includes a provision that applies each of the prohibitions of the rule to an adviser that manages assets of a government entity through a covered investment pool. A *covered investment pool* is defined as 1) any investment company registered under the Investment Company Act that is an investment option of a plan or program of a government entity or 2) any company that would be an investment company under the Investment Company Act but for the exclusions from that definition provided by Section 3(c)(1), Section 3(c)(7) or Section 3(c)(11) of that act.

❖ *Record Keeping*

Advisers providing investment advisory services to government entities must keep a record of all political contributions made by it and its covered associates in the past five years (starting September 13, 2010). Those records should include: the names, titles, and business and home addresses of all covered associates; all government entities to which the adviser has provided investment advisory services or that are or were investors in any fund to which the adviser has provided investment advisory services; all contributions made by the adviser or any of its covered associates to an official of a government entity; all payments to a political party of a state or to a PAC; and the name and business address of each third-party solicitor to whom the adviser has made payments.

■ **Advisory Contracts** (Section 205)

An adviser's contract with clients does not have to be in writing, but Section 205 of the Advisers Act requires all contracts between an adviser and its clients to meet minimum requirements, such as an agreement on the fees and client consents to changes, as well as other provisions providing a certain degree of protection for the client.

❖ *Fees*

Advisers and clients are generally free to agree to the amount of compensation the adviser gets for its services and the method by which it will get paid, with the exception of performance fees, which are discussed in more detail above.

❖ *Assignment and Partnership Changes*

Each advisory contract must provide that it may not be assigned by the adviser to any other person without the prior consent of the client. In addition, if the advisory firm is a partnership, the contracts must provide that it will notify the other party to the contract of any change in the membership of such partnership within a reasonable time after such change.

❖ *Hedge and Indemnity Clauses*

An adviser violates the Advisers Act if the firm utilizes any legend or hedge clause or other provision that leads clients to believe they have waived any cause of action they might have under federal or state securities statutes. Depending upon the facts and circumstances, a hedge clause may be considered misleading, which renders the contract void.

There are a number of facts and circumstances that help determine if a hedge clause is misleading, such as whether or not:

- the client is sophisticated regarding legal matters;
- the hedge clause was highlighted by the advisor and explained in person to the client;
- enhanced disclosure was provided to explain situations where a client may still have a cause of action; and
- the client was assisted by a sophisticated intermediary.

As a rule of thumb, an adviser is likely to have violated its fiduciary duty if it used a hedge clause with an unsophisticated client without explaining its legal implications.

❖ *Termination Penalties*

Fee arrangements that may have the effect of penalizing a client for ending the advisory relationship are inconsistent with the adviser's fiduciary duties and probably violate Section 206. Accordingly, an adviser receiving its fee in advance should give a client terminating the advisory contract a *pro rata* refund of pre-paid fees (less reasonable expenses), unless the contract provides that the adviser is to receive a pre-determined amount upon termination for services already performed, and the practice is disclosed in the adviser's Form ADV.

■ **Antifraud Rule** (Rule 206(4)-8)

The antifraud rule is one of the core rules under the Advisers Act and the broadest among them. Under the antifraud rule, it is illegal to:

1. make untrue statements of material fact or omitting to state a material fact necessary for the statements not to be misleading to any fund investor or prospective fund investor; or
2. engage in any act, practice, or course of business that is fraudulent, deceptive, or manipulative with respect to any fund investor or prospective fund investor.

The standard for enforcement of the antifraud rules is negligence, and a violation does not require intent or knowledge of wrongdoing on the adviser's part. Accordingly, each adviser should review all of its marketing materials, offering documents, communications in social media, etc., for false or misleading statements or information, including biographical information and experience of management, information on and valuation of past returns, and policies regarding disclosure to some groups of fund investors.

Social Media

This chapter would not be complete without a few words on social media. Most advisory firms today have a presence on Twitter, LinkedIn, and Facebook, or similar platforms. Its personnel may be active on numerous platforms in a personal or professional capacity. As a general rule, advisers often forget, but always should keep in mind, that while social media is a relatively new phenomenon, all of the rules that apply to more traditional ways of communicating to potential and existing clients and operating an advisory business still apply. In the past few years, the SEC has issued alerts and guidance on this topic, which I would urge you to read. They can be found on the SEC's website at
http://www.sec.gov/investment/im-guidance-2014-04.pdf.

❖ *Policies and Procedures*

The first and cardinal rule is that every investment adviser should adopt policies and procedures regarding social media whether their firm has a presence on social media or not to ensure that its personnel understands what the firm's ground rules are. Once adopted, the policies and procedures need to be constantly monitored in the face of rapidly changing technology. While some investment advisers do have policies and procedures that specifically govern the use of social media, many firms have multiple overlapping sections in their compliance manual that apply to advertising, client communications, or electronic communications, generally, which may or may not address social media. This may cause confusion and many procedures may not be specific enough as to what types of social media are permitted and how they may be used. Instead, every adviser should take a holistic look at their set of relevant policies and procedures and make sure that they are consistent and concise.

The SEC uses a checklist of thirteen nonexhaustive factors every adviser should consider when evaluating the effectiveness of its policies regarding the use of social media:

1) Has the adviser adopted usage guidelines that specify or prohibit certain sites and appropriate and inappropriate use of those sites?
2) Has the adviser set content standards and restrictions (e.g., investment recommendations) to avoid fiduciary duty or other regulatory issues?
3) Is the adviser monitoring its own as well as third-party sites on which its employees participate?
4) How often does the adviser monitor such sites?
5) Does the adviser have a preapproval policy for content?
6) Has the adviser dedicated sufficient resources to monitor social media activity?
7) Has the adviser implemented criteria for the approval of the use of specific social media sites?
8) Has the adviser adopted employee training related to the use of social media?

9) Does the adviser require employees to certify that they understand and are in compliance with the firm's social media policy?

10) Is the adviser monitoring the functionality of each social media site used by employees to determine if content, including upgrades or modifications, creates compliance issues?

11) Has the adviser adopted policies and procedures limiting an employee's or solicitor's ability to use personal or third-party social media sites to conduct or solicit business?

12) Does the use of social media sites pose information security risks?

13) If the adviser is part of a larger financial services or corporate entity, has it enforced usage guidelines for an enterprise-wide social media site that would not result in Advisers Act violations?

❖ *Third-Party Content*

Some firms limit third-party postings to authorized users and prohibit postings by the general public. Other firms allow third-party postings but restrict interaction by firm personnel with third parties. If an investment adviser allows third parties to make postings on its social media site (by, for example, posting messages, forwarding links, or posting articles), the investment adviser should consider implementing appropriate policies and procedures and instituting reasonable safeguards to avoid a violation of the securities laws. Depending on the facts and circumstances, the SEC may view certain third-party content as a prohibited testimonial (such as the "like" feature on an adviser's social media site if, for example, the "like" relates to a third party's experience with the adviser as a client).

❖ *Record Keeping*

Communications made on social media sites, depending upon the content of those communications, are subject to record-keeping obligations pursuant to Rule 204-2 under the Advisers Act. Investment advisers should consider the following when formulating their retention and record-keeping policies and procedures: if a social media communication is a required record and, if so, how long it must be retained; the form in which a social media communication is being retained; whether to conduct employee training or not; how to arrange or index social media communications that are required records; whether or not to conduct periodic test checking for compliance; and whether to employ third parties to retain social media communications that are required records or not.

■ Self-Dealing – Brokerage Arrangements and Client Transactions (Section 206(3))

The allocation and execution of trades on behalf of a client have always been sources of a multitude of compliance issues for registered investment advisers. Frequent issues involve the best execution of trades or how to allocate trades fairly between clients or how to deal with trades where the adviser is involved in both sides of the transaction. The set of issues and the SEC's approach to them are deeply rooted within the antifraud provisions of the Advisers Act and are one of the SEC's perennial favorites for review.

❖ *Best Execution*

As fiduciaries, advisers are required to provide or to select brokers who provide the best execution for client transactions. Best execution refers to the best qualitative execution of securities transactions for clients, while taking into consideration the full range and quality of a broker's services, and not necessarily simply the best price. Factors include the broker's execution capability, commission rate, financial responsibility, responsiveness to the adviser, and the value of any research services provided.

❖ *Principal Transactions and Agency Cross Transactions*

Section 206(3) of the Advisers Act prohibits an investment adviser from knowingly acting as a principal in any securities transaction with a client without first disclosing in writing to the client the capacity in which the adviser is acting and obtaining the client's written consent to the transaction. This prohibition also applies where an affiliate or controlling person of the adviser is acting as a principal. In the private fund context, if the adviser (and/or its controlling persons) owns more than 25 percent of a fund that is a counterparty to the client in a transaction, the transaction may be treated as a principal transaction and subject to Section 206(3). Blanket preapproval of transactions involving principals does not suffice. However, advisers may seek preapproval of agency cross transactions, where the adviser or its affiliate (typically an affiliated broker-dealer) effects transactions between one of its advisory clients and a third party and receives compensation as agent to the third party. For agency cross transactions, specific reporting is mandated by Rule 206(3)-2.

❖ *Allocation of Securities Transactions*

Another set of issues arises from the allocation of trades where advisers buy and sell the same securities for different clients, or refrain from doing so. An adviser must allocate securities and investment recommendations among clients in a fair and equitable manner. To comply, registered advisers must adopt written policies and procedures that address investment-opportunity allocations among clients. At a minimum, advisers should have a robust policy in place and provide clients with complete and accurate disclosure of the policy. Regardless of the allocation policy adopted, it should be applied on a consistent basis. The SEC's staff often scrutinizes trade allocation practices during examinations because of the potential for abuse of clients.

❖ *Trade Aggregation*

The SEC recognizes that aggregation of trades for multiple client accounts may be beneficial to clients in various circumstances (e.g., by resulting in lower brokerage commissions). Advisers should have a policy regarding trade aggregation and adhere to it religiously. At the very least, when aggregating client trades an investment adviser must fully disclose its aggregation policies in Form ADV and must aggregate the trades in a fair, equitable, and consistent manner.

❖ *Trade Errors*

Investment advisers are required to correct trade errors that arise in the course of managing client assets in a manner that is consistent with their fiduciary obligations to clients. An adviser should have a written policy addressing trade errors and adhere to it religiously.

❖ *Soft Dollar Arrangements*

Soft dollar arrangements are arrangements under which an adviser receives products or services from a broker other than the execution of securities transactions in exchange for client-brokerage transactions. Not surprisingly, soft dollar arrangements are a source for conflicts of interest in meeting an adviser's obligation of best execution. They are also invariably scrutinized by the SEC. Section 28(e) of the 34 Act creates a safe harbor that allows an adviser to pay more than the lowest availa ble commission if the adviser determines in good faith that such amount of commission was reasonable in relation to the value of the brokerage and research services provided by the broker.

Under the soft dollar safe harbor, an adviser may pay commissions to a broker that are higher than those of competitors, as long as the services provided by the broker-dealer:

1. are limited to "research" or "brokerage,"
2. constitute lawful and appropriate assistance to advisers in the performance of rendering investment advice, and
3. the adviser determines in good faith that the commission services are reasonable in light of the value of the brokerage and research services received.

Typical products and services within the safe harbor consists of research reports, market data, discussions with research analysts, meeting with executives, software for securities analysis, and publications. Products and services outside the safe harbor include computer hardware, telephone lines, peripherals, salaries, rent, travel, entertainment and meals, accounting software, record keeping, client reporting, and other administrative functions, and marketing seminars and other marketing costs.

Soft dollar arrangements that fall outside the safe harbor are not prohibited; however, they will come under greater scrutiny from regulators and clients. Advisers should carefully consider best execution and reasonableness of the commissions paid by clients and create a record of the analysis. Moreover, while all soft dollar arrangements must be disclosed in Form ADV, it is even more important to also disclose on the form all details regarding types of arrangements outside the safe harbor. Answers to questions regarding the arrangement and offering of services and/or products and the results they produce should be disclosed to clients in the Form ADV or disclosure brochure.

■ Wrap Fee Programs (Rule 204-3(d))

Rule 204-3(d) under the Advisers Act requires a sponsor of a wrap fee program to prepare a wrap fee brochure that provides in narrative form a full explanation of the program and its sponsor and to deliver the wrap fee brochure to wrap fee clients. A *wrap fee program* is a program under which a sponsor provides investment advisory and brokerage execution services for a single "wrapped" fee that is not based on the transactions in a client's account. An investment advisory program under which all clients pay traditional, transaction-based commissions is not a wrap fee program. Similarly, a program under which client assets are allocated among mutual funds is not a wrap fee program because normally there is no payment for brokerage execution.

Schedule H to Form ADV sets forth the information required in the wrap fee brochure. The wrap fee brochure must be prepared by the sponsor of the wrap fee program (i.e., the person that, for a portion of the fee, sponsors, organizes, or administers the program or recommends portfolio managers under the program). Some wrap fee programs will have more than one sponsor, in which case only one of the sponsors, as selected by the sponsors, needs to prepare the wrap fee brochure. An investment adviser providing portfolio management services to wrap fee clients is not a sponsor unless it performs other duties that would cause it to fall within the definition.

Advisers who sponsor wrap fee programs should seek experienced counsel to make sure that potential Investment Company Act issues are addressed.

■ SEC Examinations (Section 204)

I could not end this book without writing a few words on SEC examinations. They are not Armageddon. My clients have been through more than just a few; some of them were more contentious than others, so trust me. The fact is that an adviser's books and records are subject to examination by the SEC staff. The main purpose of these examinations is to determine if the firm complies with securities laws adheres to the disclosures it has provided to its clients, and maintains appropriate compliance programs. The examinations also provide the SEC and its staff with information about the effectiveness of securities rules and laws and the securities industry's compliance efforts.

In general, there are three types of examinations:

1) "routine" examinations, where an adviser is selected for examination randomly or on risk- or time-based criteria (although there have been indications that the SEC will begin to rely more on tips, complaints, and referrals in selecting investment advisers for routine examinations);
2) "for cause" examinations, where information suggests that the adviser might have been involved in a violation of the federal securities laws; and
3) "sweep" examinations, where a larger demographic of advisers is simultaneously examined to investigate particular industry practices with select follow-up examinations.

Notice of inspection is typically given anywhere from a few days to a few weeks in advance. The staff may arrive unannounced when conducting "for cause" examinations, an adviser's first examination, an examination of a sales office, or focused examinations. Exams typically include the SEC visiting the adviser's office and interviewing its staff. An adviser should have a dedicated space for the SEC to work, where they can review documents and interview the adviser's staff with minimal disruption to the business.

Routine exams are preceded or accompanied by a letter outlining the books and records to be produced for review by examiners on or by a specified date. The request for documents may be extensive. In conducting its examinations, the SEC staff typically looks for the "output" of the policies and procedures. For example, if the procedures require that an internal committee meet quarterly to review your brokerage transactions for compliance with soft dollar policies, the SEC staff will likely request to review the minutes of these meetings. The SEC staff has gone so far as to say that it would prefer to see how an adviser identifies and resolves a breach of policies and procedures rather than to see that it has not identified any breaches at all. While the duration of the examination depends on the size of the business and the scope of the examination, examinations typically average between eight to ten business days on the premises with a view toward completion within ninety days. At the conclusion of its examination work, the staff will generally provide a preview of its conclusions. This may occur in person or, on occasion, by telephone. Sometimes these previews result in opportunities to correct misunderstandings by the staff. If, as occurs in most examinations, the staff identifies an issue, it will be noted in a deficiency letter to which the adviser is requested to respond, typically within thirty days.

Responses should include the corrective measures the adviser has taken in response to the deficiency. The response to requests and the attitude of an adviser's personnel may affect the staff's assessment of whether or not it has a "culture of compliance" and the strength of the compliance regime. Deficiencies discovered during the exam will generally be the first items reviewed in subsequent exams. Where significant violations are cited in the deficiency letter, a follow-up inspection within one year is likely.

Chapter 12 **Key Take-Aways**

Each investment adviser is a fiduciary and owes its clients a duty of care and loyalty. The fiduciary responsibility is at the core of the adviser/client relationship and should form the underpinning for all aspects of how a firm conducts its business.

While the Advisers Act contains a number of specific requirements and prohibitions, it is by nature a principles-based body of law with one of its main principles being that of comprehensive disclosure of all material facts relevant to the client, and, most importantly, the conflicts of interest that the adviser is exposed to.

No client/adviser relationship is entirely free of conflicts of interest. Advisers should avoid them or eliminate them. Where this is not possible, advisers should disclose conflicts of interest fully in their Form ADV and other communications.

The law, as well as SEC guidance and interpretations, is ever evolving. Advisers should sign up for the SEC's electronic updates, Twitter feeds, etc., on the SEC's website, Investment Management Division, to make it easier to stay up to date with new developments and SEC priorities.

Appendixes

Form ADV

OMB APPROVAL	
OMB Number:	3235-0049
Expires:	October 31, 2014
Estimated average burden hours per response	10.50

FORM ADV (Paper Version)

- **UNIFORM APPLICATION FOR INVESTMENT ADVISER REGISTRATION AND**
- **REPORT FORM BY EXEMPT REPORTING ADVISERS**

Form ADV: General Instructions

Read these instructions carefully before filing Form ADV. Failure to follow these instructions, properly complete the form, or pay all required fees may result in your application or report being delayed or rejected.

In these instructions and in Form ADV, "you" means the investment adviser (i.e., the advisory firm). If you are a "separately identifiable department or division" (SID) of a bank, "you" means the SID, rather than your bank, unless the instructions or the form provide otherwise. Terms that appear in *italics* are defined in the Glossary of Terms to Form ADV.

Special One-Time Dodd-Frank Transition Filing for SEC-Registered Advisers:

- Form ADV amendment: If you are a mid-sized adviser registered with us on July 21, 2011 you must maintain your SEC registration and comply with the Advisers Act until January 1, 2012, unless you file a "full withdrawal" on Form ADV-W to withdraw from registration in all of the jurisdictions with which you are registered (or have an application for registration pending). See Advisers Act sections 203 and 203A(a)(2); SEC rule 203A-5(a). For example, you may file Form ADV-W and withdraw your registration with us and any *state securities authorities* before January 1, 2012 because you are exempt from registration under section 203 of the Act and state securities laws or are no longer in business, but you may not switch to state registration until after January 1, 2012.

  If you are registered or have an application for registration pending with the SEC on January 1, 2012, you must file an amendment to Form ADV no later than March 30, 2012. File an *annual updating amendment* if your annual amendment is due during this period, or file an other-than-annual amendment. See SEC rule 204-1. You must update your responses to all items and corresponding sections of Schedules A, B, C and D, including the reporting of your regulatory assets under management determined within 90 days of the filing. See SEC rule 203A-5(b). If you are no longer eligible for Commission registration, you must mark Item 2.A.(13) of Form ADV, Part 1A. You should amend your *brochure* if any information has become materially inaccurate. See Form ADV, Part 2A, Instructions 4 and 6.

- Form ADV-W filing: If you are no longer eligible for Commission registration, you must withdraw your Commission registration by filing Form ADV-W no later than June 28, 2012. See SEC rule 203A-5(c)(1). You should consult state law or

SEC 1707 (09-11)
File 1 of 4

the *state securities authority* for the states in which you are "doing business" as soon as possible to determine if you are required to register in these states and to begin the registration process. See General Instruction 1. Until you file your Form ADV-W with the SEC, you will remain subject to SEC regulation, and you also will be subject to regulation in any states where you register. See SEC rule 203A-1(b)(2).

Failure to amend your Form ADV or file Form ADV-W, as required by this instruction, is a violation of SEC rules and could lead to your registration being revoked.

1. Where can I get more information on Form ADV, electronic filing, and the IARD?

The SEC provides information about its rules and the Advisers Act on its website: <http://www.sec.gov/iard>.

NASAA provides information about state investment adviser laws and state rules, and how to contact a *state securities authority*, on its website: <http://www.nasaa.org>.

FINRA provides information about the IARD and electronic filing on the IARD website: <http://www.iard.com>.

2. What is Form ADV used for?

Investment advisers use Form ADV to:

- Register with the Securities and Exchange Commission
- Register with one or more *state securities authorities*
- Amend those registrations;

- Report to the SEC as an *exempt reporting adviser*
- Report to one or more *state securities authorities* as an *exempt reporting adviser*
- Amend those reports; and
- Submit a final report as an *exempt reporting adviser*

3. How is Form ADV organized?

Form ADV contains four parts:

- Part 1A asks a number of questions about you, your business practices, the *persons* who own and *control* you, and the *persons* who provide investment advice on your behalf.
  - o All advisers registering with the SEC or any of the *state securities authorities* must complete Part 1A.
  - o *Exempt reporting advisers* (that are not also registering with any *state securities authority*) must complete only the following Items of Part 1A: 1, 2, 3, 6, 7, 10, and 11, as well as corresponding schedules. *Exempt reporting advisers* that are registering with any *state securities authority* must complete all of Form ADV.

Part 1A also contains several supplemental schedules. The items of Part 1A let you know which schedules you must complete.

- Schedule A asks for information about your direct owners and executive officers.
- Schedule B asks for information about your indirect owners.
- Schedule C is used by paper filers to update the information required by Schedules A and B (see Instruction 16).
- Schedule D asks for additional information for certain items in Part 1A.
- Disclosure Reporting Pages (or DRPs) are schedules that ask for details about disciplinary events involving you or your *advisory affiliates*.

- Part 1B asks additional questions required by *state securities authorities*. Part 1B contains three additional DRPs. If you are applying for SEC registration or are registered only with the SEC, you do not have to complete Part 1B. (If you are filing electronically and you do not have to complete Part 1B, you will not see Part 1B.)

- Part 2A requires advisers to create narrative *brochures* containing information about the advisory firm. The requirements in Part 2A apply to all investment advisers registered with or applying for registration with the SEC, but do not apply to *exempt reporting advisers*.

- Part 2B requires advisers to create *brochure supplements* containing information about certain *supervised persons*. The requirements in Part 2B apply to all investment advisers registered with or applying for registration with the SEC, but do not apply to *exempt reporting advisers*.

4. When am I required to update my Form ADV?

- SEC- and State-Registered Advisers:

  - Annual updating amendments: You must amend your Form ADV each year by filing an *annual updating amendment* within 90 days after the end of your fiscal year. When you submit your *annual updating amendment*, you must update your responses to all items, including corresponding sections of Schedules A, B, C, and D. You must submit your summary of material changes required by Item 2 of Part 2A either in the *brochure* (cover page or the page immediately thereafter) or as an exhibit to your *brochure*.

  - Other-than-annual amendments: In addition to your *annual updating amendment*, if you are registered with the SEC or a *state securities authority*, you must amend your Form ADV, including corresponding sections of Schedules A, B, C, and D, by filing additional amendments (other-than-annual amendments) promptly if:

    - information you provided in response to Items 1, 3, 9 (except 9.A.(2), 9.B.(2), 9.E., and 9.F.), or 11 of Part 1A or Items 1, 2.A. through 2.F., or 2.I. of Part 1B becomes inaccurate in any way;

- information you provided in response to Items 4, 8, or 10 of Part 1A or Item 2.G. of Part 1B becomes materially inaccurate; or
- information you provided in your *brochure* becomes materially inaccurate (see note below for exceptions)

Notes: Part 1: If you are submitting an other-than-annual amendment, you are not required to update your responses to Items 2, 5, 6, 7, 9.A.(2), 9.B.(2), 9.E., 9.F., or 12 of Part 1A or Items 2.H. or 2.J. of Part 1B even if your responses to those items have become inaccurate.

Part 2: You must amend your *brochure supplements* (see Form ADV, Part 2B) promptly if any information in them becomes materially inaccurate. If you are submitting an other-than-annual amendment to your *brochure*, you are not required to update your summary of material changes as required by Item 2. You are not required to update your *brochure* between annual amendments solely because the amount of *client* assets you manage has changed or because your fee schedule has changed. However, if you are updating your *brochure* for a separate reason in between annual amendments, and the amount of *client* assets you manage listed in response to Item 4.E or your fee schedule listed in response to Item 5.A has become materially inaccurate, you should update that item(s) as part of the interim amendment.

- If you are an SEC-registered adviser, you are required to file your *brochure* amendments electronically through IARD. You are not required to file amendments to your *brochure supplements* with the SEC, but you must maintain a copy of them in your files.
- If you are a state-registered adviser, you are required to file your *brochure* amendments and *brochure supplement* amendments with the appropriate *state securities authorities* through IARD.

- Exempt reporting advisers:
  - Annual Updating Amendments: You must amend your Form ADV each year by filing an *annual updating amendment* within 90 days after the end of your fiscal year. When you submit your *annual updating amendment*, you must update your responses to all required items, including corresponding sections of Schedules A, B, C and D.
  - Other-than-Annual Amendments: In addition to your *annual updating amendment*, you must amend your Form ADV by filing additional amendments (other-than-annual amendments) promptly if:
    - information you provided in response to Items 1, 3, or 11 becomes inaccurate in any way; or

- information you provided in response to Item 10 becomes materially inaccurate.

Failure to update your Form ADV, as required by this instruction, is a violation of SEC rules or similar state rules and could lead to your registration being revoked.

5. Part 2 of Form ADV was amended recently. When do I have to comply with the new requirements?

If you are applying for registration with the SEC: As of January 1, 2011, every application for registration must include a narrative *brochure* prepared in accordance with the requirements of (amended) Part 2A of Form ADV. See SEC rule 203-1. The SEC will no longer accept any application that does not include a *brochure*(s) that satisfies the requirements of (amended) Part 2 of Form ADV.

If you already are registered with the SEC: Until you file your first *annual updating amendment* for your fiscal year that ended on or after December 31, 2010, you may (but are not required to) submit a narrative *brochure* that meets the requirements of (amended) Part 2A of Form ADV. If you do not do this, you must continue to comply with the requirements for preparing, delivering, and offering "old" Part II of Form ADV. Your first *annual updating amendment* must contain a narrative *brochure* that meets the requirements of (amended) Part 2A of Form ADV.

Note: Until you are required to meet the requirements of (amended) Part 2, you can satisfy the requirements related to "old" Part II by updating the information in your "old" Part II whenever it becomes materially inaccurate. You must deliver "old" Part II or a *brochure* containing at least the information contained in "old" Part II to prospective *clients* and annually offer it to current *clients*. You are not required to file "old" Part II with the SEC, but you must keep a copy in your files, and provide it to the SEC staff upon request.

If you are applying for registration or are registered with one or more *state securities authorities*, contact the appropriate *state securities authorities* or check <http://www.nasaa.org> for more information about the implementation deadline for the amended Part 2.

6. Where do I sign my Form ADV application or amendment?

You must sign the appropriate Execution Page. There are three Execution Pages at the end of the form. Your initial application, your initial report (in the case of an *exempt reporting adviser*), and all amendments to Form ADV must include at least one Execution Page.

- If you are applying for or are amending your SEC registration, or if you are reporting as an *exempt reporting adviser* or amending your report, you must sign and submit either a:
  - Domestic Investment Adviser Execution Page, if you (the advisory firm) are a resident of the United States; or

  - *Non-Resident* Investment Adviser Execution Page, if you (the advisory firm) are not a resident of the United States.

- If you are applying for or are amending your registration with a *state securities authority*, you must sign and submit the State-Registered Investment Adviser Execution Page.

7. Who must sign my Form ADV or amendment?

The individual who signs the form depends upon your form of organization:

- For a sole proprietorship, the sole proprietor.
- For a partnership, a general partner.
- For a corporation, an authorized principal officer.
- For a "separately identifiable department or division" (SID) of a bank, a principal officer of your bank who is directly engaged in the management, direction, or supervision of your investment advisory activities.
- For all others, an authorized individual who participates in managing or directing your affairs.

The signature does not have to be notarized, and in the case of an electronic filing, should be a typed name.

8. How do I file my Form ADV?

Complete Form ADV electronically using the Investment Adviser Registration Depository (IARD) if:

- You are filing with the SEC (and submitting *notice filings* to any of the *state securities authorities*), or

- You are filing with a *state securities authority* that requires or permits advisers to submit Form ADV through the IARD.

  Note: SEC rules require advisers that are registered or applying for registration with the SEC, or that are reporting to the SEC as an *exempt reporting adviser*, to file electronically through the IARD system. See SEC rules 203-1 and 204-4.

To file electronically, go to the IARD website (<www.iard.com>), which contains detailed instructions for advisers to follow when filing through the IARD.

Complete Form ADV (Paper Version) on paper if:

- You are filing with the SEC or a *state securities authority* that requires electronic filing, but you have been granted a continuing hardship exemption. Hardship exemptions are described in Instruction 17.

- You are filing with a *state securities authority* that permits (but does not require) electronic filing and you do not file electronically.

9. How do I get started filing electronically?

First, obtain a copy of the IARD Entitlement Package from the following website: <http://www.iard.com/GetStarted.asp>. Second, request access to the IARD system for your firm by completing and submitting the IARD Entitlement Package. The IARD Entitlement Package must be submitted on paper. Mail the forms to: FINRA Entitlement Group, P.O. Box 9495, Gaithersburg, MD 20898-9495.

When FINRA receives your Entitlement Package, they will assign a *CRD* number (identification number for your firm) and a user I.D. code and password (identification number and system password for the individual(s) who will submit Form ADV filings for your firm). Your firm may request an I.D. code and password for more than one individual. FINRA also will create a financial account for you from which the IARD will deduct filing fees and any state fees you are required to pay. If you already have a *CRD* account with FINRA, it will also serve as your IARD account; a separate account will not be established.

Once you receive your *CRD* number, user I.D. code and password, and you have funded your account, you are ready to file electronically.

Questions regarding the Entitlement Process should be addressed to FINRA at 240.386.4848.

10. If I am applying for registration with the SEC, or amending my SEC registration, how do I make *notice filings* with the *state securities authorities*?

If you are applying for registration with the SEC or are amending your SEC registration, one or more *state securities authorities* may require you to provide them with copies of your SEC filings. We call these filings "*notice filings*." Your *notice filings* will be sent electronically to the states that you check on Item 2.C. of Part 1A. The *state securities authorities* to which you send *notice filings* may charge fees, which will be deducted from the account you establish with FINRA. To determine which *state securities authorities* require SEC-registered advisers to submit *notice filings* and to pay fees, consult the relevant state investment adviser law or *state securities authority*. See General Instruction 1.

If you are granted a continuing hardship exemption to file Form ADV on paper, FINRA will enter your filing into the IARD and your *notice filings* will be sent electronically to the *state securities authorities* that you check on Item 2.C. of Part 1A.

11. I am registered with a state. When must I switch to SEC registration?

If at the time of your *annual updating amendment* you meet at least one of the requirements for SEC registration in Item 2.A.(1) to (12) of Part 1A, you must register with the SEC within 90 days after you file the *annual updating amendment*. Once you register with the SEC, you are subject to SEC regulation, regardless of whether you remain registered with one or more states. See SEC rule 203A-1(b)(2). Each of your *investment adviser representatives*, however, may be subject to registration in those states in which the representative has a place of business. See Advisers Act section 203A(b)(1); SEC rule 203A-3(a). For additional information, consult the investment adviser laws or the *state securities authority* for the particular state in which you are "doing business." See General Instruction 1.

12. I am registered with the SEC. When must I switch to registration with a *state securities authority*?

If you check box 13 in Item 2.A. of Part 1A to report on your *annual updating amendment* that you are no longer eligible to register with the SEC, you must withdraw from SEC registration within 180 days after the end of your fiscal year by filing Form ADV-W. See SEC rule 203A-1(b)(2). You should consult state law or the *state securities authority* for the states in which you are "doing business" to determine if you are required to register in these states. See General Instruction 1. Until you file your Form ADV-W with the SEC, you will remain subject to SEC regulation, and you also will be subject to regulation in any states where you register. See SEC rule 203A-1(b)(2).

13. I am an *exempt reporting adviser*. When must I submit my first report on Form ADV?

- <u>All exempt reporting advisers:</u>
  You must submit your initial Form ADV filing within 60 days of relying on the exemption from registration under either section 203(l) of the Advisers Act as an adviser solely to one or more venture capital funds or section 203(m) of the Advisers Act because you act solely as an adviser to private funds and have assets under management in the United States of less than $150 million.

- <u>Additional instruction for advisers switching from being registered to being exempt reporting advisers:</u>
  If you are currently registered as an investment adviser (or have an application for registration pending) with the SEC or with a *state securities authority*, you must file a Form ADV-W to withdraw from registration in the jurisdictions where you are switching. You must submit the Form ADV-W <u>before</u> submitting your first report as an exempt reporting adviser.

14. I am an *exempt reporting adviser*. Is it possible that I might be required to also register with or submit a report to a *state securities authority*?

Yes, you may be required to register with or submit a report to one or more *state securities authorities*. If you are required to register with one or more *state securities authorities*, you must complete all of Form ADV. See General Instruction 3. If you are required to submit a report to one or more *state securities authorities*, check the box(es) in Item 2.C. of Part 1A next to the state(s) you would like to receive the report. Each of your *investment adviser representatives* may also be subject to registration requirements. For additional information about the requirements that may apply to you, consult the investment adviser laws or the *state securities authority* for the particular state in which you are "doing business." See General Instruction 1.

15. What do I do if I no longer meet the definition of an "*exempt reporting adviser*"?

- Advisers Switching to SEC Registration:

  - You may no longer be an *exempt reporting adviser* and may be required to register with the SEC if you wish to continue doing business as an investment adviser. For example, you may be relying on section 203(l) and wish to accept a *client* that is not a venture capital fund as defined in SEC rule 203(l)-1, or you may have been relying on SEC rule 203(m)-1 and reported in Section 2.B. of Schedule D to your *annual updating amendment* that you have *private fund* assets of $150 million or more.

    - If you are relying on section 203(l), unless you qualify for another exemption, you would violate the Advisers Act's registration requirement if you accept a *client* that is not a venture capital fund as defined in SEC rule 203(l)-1 before the SEC approves your application for registration. You must submit your final report as an *exempt reporting adviser* and apply for SEC registration in the same filing.

    - If you were relying on SEC rule 203(m)-1 and you reported in Section 2.B. of Schedule D to your *annual updating amendment* that you have *private fund* assets of $150 million or more, you must register with the SEC unless you qualify for another exemption. If you have complied with all SEC reporting requirements applicable to an *exempt reporting adviser* as such, you have up to 90 days after filing your *annual updating amendment* to apply for SEC registration, and you may continue doing business as a *private fund* adviser during this time. You must submit your final report as an *exempt reporting adviser* and apply for SEC registration in the same filing. Unless you qualify for another exemption, you would violate the Advisers Act's registration requirement if you accept a *client* that is not a *private fund* during this transition period before the SEC approves your application for registration, and you must comply with all SEC reporting requirements applicable to an *exempt reporting adviser* as such during this 90-day transition period. If you have not complied with all SEC reporting requirements applicable to an *exempt reporting adviser* as such, this 90-day transition period is not available to you. Therefore, if the transition period is not available to you, and you do not qualify for another exemption, your application for registration must be approved by the SEC before you meet or exceed SEC rule 203(m)-1's $150 million asset threshold.

- You will be deemed in compliance with the Form ADV filing and reporting requirements until the SEC approves or denies your application. If your application is approved, you will be able to continue business as a registered adviser.

- If you register with the SEC, you may be subject to state *notice filing* requirements. To determine these requirements, consult the investment adviser laws or the *state securities authority* for the particular state in which you are "doing business." See General Instruction 1.

Note: If you are relying on SEC rule 203(m)-1 and you accept a *client* that is not a *private fund*, you will lose the exemption provided by SEC rule 203(m)-1 immediately. To avoid this result, you should apply for SEC registration in advance so that the SEC has approved your registration before you accept a *client* that is not a *private fund.*

The 90-day transition period described above also applies to investment advisers with their *principal offices and places of business* outside of the United States with respect to their *clients* who are *United States persons* (*e.g.*, the adviser would not be eligible for the 90-day transition period if it accepted a *client* that is a *United States person* and is not a *private fund*).

- Advisers Not Switching to SEC Registration:

  - You may no longer be an *exempt reporting adviser* but may not be required to register with the SEC or may be prohibited from doing so. For example, you may cease to do business as an investment adviser, become eligible for an exemption that does not require reporting, or be ineligible for SEC registration. In this case, you must submit a final report as an *exempt reporting adviser* to update only Item 1 of Part 1A of Form ADV.

  - You may be subject to state registration requirements. To determine these requirements, consult the investment adviser laws or the *state securities authority* for the particular state in which you are "doing business." See General Instruction 1.

16. Are there filing fees?

Yes. These fees go to support and maintain the IARD. The IARD filing fees are in addition to any registration or other fee that may be required by state law. You must pay an IARD filing fee for your initial application, your initial report, and each *annual updating amendment*. There is no filing fee for an other-than-annual amendment, a final report as an *exempt reporting adviser*, or Form ADV-W. The IARD filing fee schedule is published at <http://www.sec.gov/iard>; <http://www.nasaa.org>; and <http://www.iard.com>.

If you are submitting a paper filing under a continuing hardship exemption (see Instruction 17), you are required to pay an additional fee. The amount of the additional fee depends on whether you are filing Form ADV or Form ADV-W. (There is no additional fee for filings made on Form ADV-W.) The hardship filing fee schedule is available by contacting FINRA at 240.386.4848.

17. What if I am not able to file electronically?

If you are required to file electronically but cannot do so, you may be eligible for one of two types of hardship exemptions from the electronic filing requirements.

- A **temporary hardship exemption** is available if you file electronically, but you encounter unexpected difficulties that prevent you from making a timely filing with the IARD, such as a computer malfunction or electrical outage. This exemption does not permit you to file on paper; instead, it extends the deadline for an electronic filing for seven business days. See SEC rules 203-3(a) and 204-4(e).

- A **continuing hardship exemption** may be granted if you are a small business and you can demonstrate that filing electronically would impose an undue hardship. You are a small business, and may be eligible for a continuing hardship exemption, if you are required to answer Item 12 of Part 1A (because you have assets under management of less than $25 million) and you are able to respond "no" to each question in Item 12. See SEC rule 0-7.

  If you have been granted a continuing hardship exemption, you must complete and submit the paper version of Form ADV to FINRA. FINRA will enter your responses into the IARD. As discussed in General Instruction 16, FINRA will charge you a fee to reimburse it for the expense of data entry.

18. I am eligible to file on paper. How do I make a paper filing?

When filing on paper, you must:

- Type all of your responses.
- Include your name (the same name you provide in response to Item 1.A. of Part 1A) and the date on every page.
- If you are amending your Form ADV:
  - complete page 1 and circle the number of any item for which you are changing your response.
  - include your SEC 801-number (if you have one), or your 802-number (if you have one), and your CRD number (if you have one) on every page.
  - complete the amended item in full and circle the number of the item for which you are changing your response.
  - to amend Schedule A or Schedule B, complete and submit Schedule C.

Where you submit your paper filing depends on why you are eligible to file on paper:

- If you are filing on paper because you have been granted a continuing hardship exemption, submit one manually signed Form ADV and one copy to: IARD Document Processing, FINRA, P.O. Box 9495, Gaithersburg, MD 20898-9495.

  If you complete Form ADV on paper and submit it to FINRA but you do not have a continuing hardship exemption, the submission will be returned to you.

- If you are filing on paper because a state in which you are registered or in which you are applying for registration allows you to submit paper instead of electronic filings, submit one manually signed Form ADV and one copy to the appropriate *state securities authorities*.

19. Who is required to file Form ADV-NR?

Every *non-resident* general partner and *managing agent* of all SEC-registered advisers and *exempt reporting advisers*, whether or not the adviser is resident in the United States, must file Form ADV-NR in connection with the adviser's initial application or report. A general partner or *managing agent* of an SEC-registered adviser or *exempt reporting adviser* who becomes a *non-resident* after the adviser's initial application or report has been submitted must file Form ADV-NR within 30 days. Form ADV-NR must be filed on paper (it cannot be filed electronically).

Submit Form ADV-NR to the SEC at the following address:

> Securities and Exchange Commission, 100 F Street, NE, Washington, DC 20549; Attn: Branch of Registrations and Examinations.

Failure to file Form ADV-NR promptly may delay SEC consideration of your initial application.

Federal Information Law and Requirements

Sections 203 and 204 of the Advisers Act [15 U.S.C. §§ 80b-3 and 80b-4] authorize the SEC to collect the information required by Form ADV. The SEC collects the information for regulatory purposes, such as deciding whether to grant registration. Filing Form ADV is mandatory for advisers who are required to register with the SEC and for *exempt reporting advisers*. The SEC maintains the information submitted on this form and makes it publicly available. The SEC may return forms that do not include required information. Intentional misstatements or omissions constitute federal criminal violations under 18 U.S.C. § 1001 and 15 U.S.C. § 80b-17.

SEC's Collection of Information

An agency may not conduct or sponsor, and a person is not required to respond to, a collection of information unless it displays a currently valid control number. The Advisers Act authorizes the

SEC to collect the information on Form ADV from investment advisers. See 15 U.S.C. §§ 80b-3 and 80b-4. Filing the form is mandatory.

The form enables the SEC to register investment advisers and to obtain information from and about *exempt reporting advisers*. Every applicant for registration with the SEC as an adviser, and every *exempt reporting adviser*, must file the form. See 17 C.F.R. § 275.203-1 and 204-4. By accepting a form, however, the SEC does not make a finding that it has been completed or submitted correctly. The form is filed annually by every adviser, no later than 90 days after the end of its fiscal year, to amend its registration or its report. It is also filed promptly during the year to reflect material changes. See 17 C.F.R. § 275.204-1. The SEC maintains the information on the form and makes it publicly available through the IARD.

Anyone may send the SEC comments on the accuracy of the burden estimate on page 1 of the form, as well as suggestions for reducing the burden. The Office of Management and Budget has reviewed this collection of information under 44 U.S.C. § 3507.

The information contained in the form is part of a system of records subject to the Privacy Act of 1974, as amended. The SEC has published in the Federal Register the Privacy Act System of Records Notice for these records.

FORM ADV (Paper Version)

- **UNIFORM APPLICATION FOR INVESTMENT ADVISER REGISTRATION AND**
- **REPORT BY EXEMPT REPORTING ADVISERS**

Form ADV: Instructions for Part 1A

These instructions explain how to complete certain items in Part 1A of Form ADV.

1. Item 1: Identifying Information

a. **Separately Identifiable Department or Division of a Bank.** If you are a "separately identifiable department or division" (SID) of a bank, answer Item 1.A. with the full legal name of your bank, and answer Item 1.B. with your own name (the name of the department or division) and all names under which you conduct your advisory business. In addition, your *principal office and place of business* in Item 1.F. should be the principal office at which you conduct your advisory business. In response to Item 1.I., the website addresses you list on Schedule D should be sites that provide information about your own activities, rather than general information about your bank.

b. **Item 1.O.: Assets.** For purposes of Item 1.O. only, "assets" refers to your total assets, rather than the assets you manage on behalf of clients. Determine your total assets using the total assets shown on the balance sheet for your most recent fiscal year end.

2. Item 2: SEC Registration and SEC Report by *Exempt Reporting Advisers*

If you are registered or applying for registration with the SEC, you must indicate in Item 2.A. why you are eligible to register with the SEC by checking at least one of the boxes.

a. **Item 2.A.(1): Adviser with Regulatory Assets Under Management of $100 Million or More.** You may check box 1 only if your response to Item 5.F.(2)(c) is $100 million or more, or you are filing an *annual updating amendment* with the SEC and your response to Item 5.F.(2)(c) is $90 million or more. While you may register with the SEC if your regulatory assets under management are at least $100 million but less than $110 million, you must register with the SEC if your regulatory assets under management are $110 million or more. If you are a SEC-registered adviser, you may remain registered with the SEC if your regulatory assets under management are $90 million or more. See SEC rule 203A-1(a). Part 1A Instruction 5.b. explains how to calculate your regulatory assets under management.

If you are a state-registered adviser and you report on your *annual updating amendment* that your regulatory assets under management increased to $100 million or more, you may register with the SEC. If your regulatory assets under management increased to $110 million or more, you must register with the SEC within 90 days after you file that *annual updating amendment.* See SEC rule 203A-1(b)(1) and Form ADV General Instruction 11.

SEC 1707 (09-11)
File 1 of 4

b. **Item 2.A.(2): Mid-Sized Adviser.** You may check box 2 only if your response to Item 5.F(2)(c) is $25 million or more but less than $100 million, and you satisfy one of the requirements below. Part 1A Instruction 5.b. explains how to calculate your regulatory assets under management.

You must register with the SEC if you meet at least one of the following requirements:

- You are not required to be registered as an investment adviser with the *state securities authority* of the state where you maintain your *principal office and place of business* pursuant to that state's investment adviser laws. If you are exempt from registration with that state or are excluded from the definition of investment adviser in that state, you must register with the SEC. You should consult the investment adviser laws or the *state securities authority* for the particular state in which you maintain your *principal office and place of business* to determine if you are required to register in that state. See General Instruction 1.

- You are not subject to examination by the *state securities authority* of the state where you maintain your *principal office and place of business*. To determine whether such *state securities authority* does not conduct such examinations, see: http://www.sec.gov/divisions/investment/midsizedadviserinfo.htm.

See section 203A(a)(2) of the Advisers Act.

c. **Item 2.A.(5): Adviser to an Investment Company.** You may check box 5 only if you currently provide advisory services under an investment advisory contract to an investment company registered under the Investment Company Act of 1940 and the investment company is operational (i.e., has assets and shareholders, other than just the organizing shareholders). See sections 203A(a)(1)(B) and 203A(a)(2)(A) of the Advisers Act. Advising investors about the merits of investing in mutual funds or recommending **particular mutual funds does not make you eligible to check this box.**

d. **Item 2.A.(6): Adviser to a Business Development Company. You may check box 6 only** if your response to Item 5.F.(2)(c) is $25 million or more of regulatory assets under management, and you currently provide advisory services under an investment advisory contract to a company that has elected to be a business development company pursuant to section 54 of the Investment Company Act of 1940, that has not withdrawn the election, and that is operational (i.e., has assets and shareholders, other than just the organizing shareholders). See section 203A(a)(2)(A) of the Advisers Act. Part 1A Instruction 5.b. explains how to calculate your regulatory assets under management.

e. **Item 2.A.(7): Pension Consultant.** You may check box 7 only if you are eligible for the pension consultant exemption from the prohibition on SEC registration.

- You are eligible for this exemption if you provided investment advice to employee benefit plans, governmental plans, or church plans with respect to assets having an aggregate value of $200 million or more during the 12-month period that ended within 90 days of filing this Form ADV. You are not eligible for this exemption if you only advise plan participants on allocating their investments within their pension plans. See SEC rule 203A-2(a).

- To calculate the value of assets for purposes of this exemption, aggregate the assets of the plans for which you provided advisory services at the end of the 12-month period. If you provided advisory services to other plans during the 12-month period, but your employment or contract terminated before the end of the 12-month period, you also may include the value of those assets.

f. **Item 2.A.(8): Related Adviser.** You may check box 8 only if you are eligible for the related adviser exemption from the prohibition on SEC registration. See SEC rule 203A-2(b). You are eligible for this exemption if you *control*, are *controlled* by, or are under common *control* with an investment adviser that is registered with the SEC, and you have the same *principal office and place of business* as that other investment adviser. Note that you may not rely on the SEC registration of an Internet adviser under rule 203A-2(e) in establishing eligibility for this exemption. See SEC rule 203A-2(e)(1)(iii). If you check box 8, you also must complete Section 2.A.(8) of Schedule D.

g. **Item 2.A.(9): Newly-Formed Adviser.** You may check box 9 only if you are eligible for the newly-formed-adviser exemption from the prohibition on SEC registration. See SEC rule 203A-2(c). You are eligible for this exemption if:

- immediately before you file your application for registration with the SEC, you were not registered or required to be registered with the SEC or a *state securities authority;* and

- at the time of your formation, you have a reasonable expectation that within 120 days of registration you will be eligible for SEC registration.

If you check box 9, you also must complete Section 2.A.(9) of Schedule D.

You must file an amendment to Part 1A of your Form ADV that updates your response to Item 2.A. within 120 days after the SEC declares your registration effective. You may not check box 9 on your amendment; since this exemption is available only if you are not registered, you may not "re-rely" on this exemption. If you indicate on that amendment (by checking box 13) that you are not eligible to register with the SEC, you also must file a Form ADV-W to withdraw your SEC registration no later than 120 days after your registration was declared effective. You should contact the appropriate *state securities authority* to determine how long it may take to become state-registered sufficiently in advance of when you are required to file Form ADV-W to withdraw from SEC registration.

Note: If you expect to be eligible for SEC registration because of the amount of your regulatory assets under management, that amount must be $100 million or more no later than 120 days after your registration is declared effective.

h. **Item 2.A.(10): Multi-State Adviser.** You may check box 10 only if you are eligible for the multi-state adviser exemption from the prohibition on SEC registration. See SEC rule 203A-2(d). You are eligible for this exemption if you are required to register as an investment adviser with the *state securities authorities* of 15 or more states. If you check box 10, you must complete Section 2.A.(10) of Schedule D. You must complete Section 2.A.(10) of Schedule D in each *annual updating amendment* you submit.

   If you check box 10, you also must:
   - create and maintain a list of the *states* in which, but for this exemption, you would be required to register;
   - update this list each time you submit an *annual updating amendment* in which you continue to represent that you are eligible for this exemption; and
   - maintain the list in an easily accessible place for a period of not less than five years from each date on which you indicate that you are eligible for the exemption.

   If, at the time you file your *annual updating amendment*, you are required to register in less than 15 *states* and you are not otherwise eligible to register with the SEC, you must check box 13 in Item 2.A. You also must file a Form ADV-W to withdraw your SEC registration. See Part 1A Instruction 2.j.

i. **Item 2.A.(11): Internet Adviser**. You may check box 11 only if you are eligible for the Internet adviser exemption from the prohibition on SEC registration. See SEC rule 203A-2(e). You are eligible for this exemption if:

   - you provide investment advice to your *clients* through an interactive website. An interactive website means a website in which computer software-based models or applications provide investment advice based on personal information each *client* submits through the website. Other forms of online or Internet investment advice do not qualify for this exemption;

   - you provide investment advice to all of your *clients* exclusively through the interactive website, except that you may provide investment advice to fewer than 15 *clients* through other means during the previous 12 months; and

   - you maintain a record demonstrating that you provide investment advice to your *clients* exclusively through an interactive website in accordance with these limits.

j. **Item 2.A.(13): Adviser No Longer Eligible to Remain Registered with the SEC.** You must check box 13 if:

   - you are registered with the SEC;
   - you are filing an *annual updating amendment* to Form ADV in which you indicate in response to Item 5.F.(2)(c) that you have regulatory assets under management of less than $90 million; and

- you are not eligible to check any other box (other than box 13) in Item 2.A. (and are therefore no longer eligible to remain registered with the SEC).

You must withdraw from SEC registration within 180 days after the end of your fiscal year by filing Form ADV-W. Until you file your Form ADV-W, you will remain subject to SEC regulation, and you also will be subject to regulation in the *states* in which you register. See SEC rule 203A-1(b)(2).

k. **Item 2.B.: Reporting by *Exempt Reporting Advisers*.** You may check box 2.B.(1) only if you qualify for the exemption from SEC registration as an adviser solely to one or more venture capital funds. See SEC rule 203(l)-1. You may check box 2.B.(2) only if you qualify for the exemption from SEC registration because you act solely as an adviser to *private funds* and have assets under management in the United States of less than $150 million. See SEC rule 203(m)-1. You may check both boxes to indicate that you qualify for both exemptions. You should check box 2.B.(3) if you act solely as an adviser to *private funds* but you are no longer eligible to check box 2.B.(2) because you have assets under management in the United States of $150 million or more. If you check box 2.B.(2) or (3), you also must complete Section 2.B. of Schedule D.

3. Item 3: Form of Organization

If you are a "separately identifiable department or division" (SID) of a bank, answer Item 3.A. by checking "other." In the space provided, specify that you are a "SID of" and indicate the form of organization of your bank. Answer Items 3.B. and 3.C. with information about your bank.

4. Item 4: Successions

a. **Succession of an SEC-Registered Adviser.** If you (1) have taken over the business of an investment adviser or (2) have changed your structure or legal status (e.g., form of organization or state of incorporation), a new organization has been created, which has registration obligations under the Advisers Act. There are different ways to fulfill these obligations. You may rely on the registration provisions discussed in the General Instructions, or you may be able to rely on special registration provisions for "successors" to SEC-registered advisers, which may ease the transition to the successor adviser's registration.

To determine if you may rely on these provisions, review "Registration of Successors to Broker-Dealers and Investment Advisers," Investment Advisers Act Release No. 1357 (Dec. 28, 1992). If you have taken over an adviser, follow Part 1A Instruction 4.a(1), Succession by Application. If you have changed your structure or legal status, follow Part 1A Instruction 4.a(2), Succession by Amendment. If either (1) you are a "separately identifiable department or division" (SID) of a bank that is currently registered as an investment adviser, and you are taking over your bank's advisory business; or (2) you are a SID currently registered as an investment adviser, and your bank is taking over your advisory business, then follow Part 1A Instruction 4.a(1), Succession by Application.

(1) **Succession by Application.** If you are not registered with the SEC as an adviser, and you are acquiring or assuming substantially all of the assets and liabilities of the advisory business of an SEC-registered adviser, file a new application for registration on Form ADV. You will receive new registration numbers. You must file the new application within 30 days after the succession. On the application, make sure you check "yes" to Item 4.A., enter the date of the succession in Item 4.B., and complete Section 4 of Schedule D.

Until the SEC declares your new registration effective, you may rely on the registration of the adviser you are acquiring, but only if the adviser you are acquiring is no longer conducting advisory activities. Once your new registration is effective, a Form ADV-W must be filed with the SEC to withdraw the registration of the acquired adviser.

(2) **Succession by Amendment.** If you are a new investment adviser formed solely as a result of a change in form of organization, a reorganization, or a change in the composition of a partnership, and there has been no practical change in *control* or management, you may amend the registration of the registered investment adviser to reflect these changes rather than file a new application. You will keep the same registration numbers, and you should not file a Form ADV-W. On the amendment, make sure you check "yes" to Item 4.A., enter the date of the succession in Item 4.B., and complete Section 4 of Schedule D. You must submit the amendment within 30 days after the change or reorganization.

b. **Succession of a State-Registered Adviser.** If you (1) have taken over the business of an investment adviser or (2) have changed your structure or legal status (e.g., form of organization or state of incorporation), a new organization has been created, which has registration obligations under state investment adviser laws. There may be different ways to fulfill these obligations. You should contact each state in which you are registered to determine that state's requirements for successor registration. See Form ADV General Instruction 1.

5. Item 5: Information About Your Advisory Business

a. **Newly-Formed Advisers:** Several questions in Item 5 that ask about your advisory business assume that you have been operating your advisory business for some time. Your response to these questions should reflect your current advisory business (i.e., at the time you file your Form ADV), with the following exceptions:

- base your response to Item 5.E. on the types of compensation you expect to accept;
- base your response to Item 5.G. and Item 5.J. on the types of advisory services you expect to provide during the next year; and
- skip Item 5.H.

b. **Item 5.F: Calculating Your Regulatory Assets Under Management.** In determining the amount of your regulatory assets under management, include the securities portfolios for which you provide continuous and regular supervisory or management services as of the date of filing this Form ADV.

(1) **Securities Portfolios**. An account is a securities portfolio if at least 50% of the total value of the account consists of securities. For purposes of this 50% test, you may treat cash and cash equivalents (i.e., bank deposits, certificates of deposit, bankers acceptances, and similar bank instruments) as securities. You must include securities portfolios that are:

(a) your family or proprietary accounts;

(b) accounts for which you receive no compensation for your services; and

(c) accounts of *clients* who are not *United States persons*.

For purposes of this definition, treat all of the assets of a *private fund* as a securities portfolio, regardless of the nature of such assets. For accounts of *private funds*, moreover, include in the securities portfolio any uncalled commitment pursuant to which a *person* is obligated to acquire an interest in, or make a capital contribution to, the *private fund*.

(2) **Value of Portfolio**. Include the entire value of each securities portfolio for which you provide continuous and regular supervisory or management services. If you provide continuous and regular supervisory or management services for only a portion of a securities portfolio, include as regulatory assets under management only that portion of the securities portfolio for which you provide such services. Exclude, for example, the portion of an account:

(a) under management by another *person*; or

(b) that consists of real estate or businesses whose operations you "manage" on behalf of a *client* but not as an investment.

Do not deduct any outstanding indebtedness or other accrued but unpaid liabilities.

(3) **Continuous and Regular Supervisory or Management Services.**

General Criteria. You provide continuous and regular supervisory or management services with respect to an account if:

(a) you have *discretionary authority* over and provide ongoing supervisory or management services with respect to the account; or

(b) you do not have *discretionary authority* over the account, but you have ongoing responsibility to select or make recommendations, based upon the needs of the *client*, as to specific securities or other investments the account may purchase or sell and, if such recommendations are accepted by the *client*, you are responsible for arranging or effecting the purchase or sale.

Factors. You should consider the following factors in evaluating whether you provide continuous and regular supervisory or management services to an account.

(a) **Terms of the advisory contract.** If you agree in an advisory contract to provide ongoing management services, this suggests that you provide these services for the account. Other provisions in the contract, or your actual management practices, however, may suggest otherwise.

(b) **Form of compensation.** If you are compensated based on the average value of the *client's* assets you manage over a specified period of time, that suggests that you provide continuous and regular supervisory or management services for the account. If you receive compensation in a manner similar to either of the following, that suggests you do not provide continuous and regular supervisory or management services for the account --

(i) you are compensated based upon the time spent with a *client* during a *client* visit; or

(ii) you are paid a retainer based on a percentage of assets covered by a financial plan.

(c) **Management practices.** The extent to which you actively manage assets or provide advice bears on whether the services you provide are continuous and regular supervisory or management services. The fact that you make infrequent trades (e.g., based on a "buy and hold" strategy) does not mean your services are not "continuous and regular."

Examples. You may provide continuous and regular supervisory or management services for an account if you:

(a) have *discretionary authority* to allocate *client* assets among various mutual funds;

(b) do not have *discretionary authority*, but provide the same allocation services, and satisfy the criteria set forth in Instruction 5.b.(3);

(c) allocate assets among other managers (a "manager of managers"), but only if you have *discretionary authority* to hire and fire managers and reallocate assets among them; or

(d) you are a broker-dealer and treat the account as a brokerage account, but only if you have *discretionary authority* over the account.

You do not provide continuous and regular supervisory or management services for an account if you:

(a) provide market timing recommendations (i.e., to buy or sell), but have no ongoing management responsibilities;

(b) provide only *impersonal investment advice* (e.g., market newsletters);

(c) make an initial asset allocation, without continuous and regular monitoring and reallocation; or

(d) provide advice on an intermittent or periodic basis (such as upon *client* request, in response to a market event, or on a specific date (e.g., the account is reviewed and adjusted quarterly)).

(4) **Value of Regulatory Assets Under Management**. Determine your regulatory assets under management based on the current market value of the assets as determined within 90 days prior to the date of filing this Form ADV. Determine market value using the same method you used to report account values to *clients* or to calculate fees for investment advisory services.

In the case of a *private fund*, determine the current market value (or fair value) of the *private fund*'s assets and the contractual amount of any uncalled commitment pursuant to which a person is obligated to acquire an interest in, or make a capital contribution to, the *private fund*.

(5) **Example.** This is an example of the method of determining whether an account of a *client* other than a *private fund* may be included as regulatory assets under management.

The *client's* portfolio consists of the following:

$ 6,000,000	stocks and bonds
$ 1,000,000	cash and cash equivalents
$ 3,000,000	non-securities (collectibles, commodities, real estate, etc.)
$10,000,000	Total Assets

First, is the account a securities portfolio? The account is a securities portfolio because securities as well as cash and cash equivalents (which you have chosen to include as securities) ($6,000,000 + $1,000,000 = $7,000,000) comprise at least 50% of the value of the account (here, 70%). (See Instruction 5.b(1)).

Second, does the account receive continuous and regular supervisory or management services? The entire account is managed on a *discretionary* basis and is provided ongoing supervisory and management services, and therefore receives continuous and regular supervisory or management services. (See Instruction 5.b.(3)).

Third, what is the entire value of the account? The entire value of the account ($10,000,000) is included in the calculation of the adviser's total regulatory assets under management.

6. Item 7: Financial Industry Affiliations and Private Fund Reporting

Item 7.B. and Section 7.B. of Schedule D ask questions about the *private funds* that you advise. You are required to complete a Section 7.B.(1) of Schedule D for each *private fund* that you advise, except in certain circumstances described under Item 7.B. and below.

a. If your *principal office and place of business* is outside the United States, for purposes of Item 7 and Section 7.B. of Schedule D you may disregard any *private fund* that, during your last fiscal year, was not a *United States person*, was not offered in the United States, and was not beneficially owned by any *United States person.*

b. When filing Section 7.B.(1) of Schedule D for a *private fund*, you must acquire an identification number for the fund by logging onto the IARD website and using the private fund identification number generator. You must continue to use the same identification number whenever you amend Section 7.B.(1) for that fund. If you file a Section 7.B.(1) for a *private fund* for which an identification number has already been acquired by another adviser, you must not acquire a new identification number, but must instead utilize the existing number. If you choose to complete a single Section 7.B.(1) for a master-feeder arrangement under instruction 6.d. below, you must acquire an identification number also for each feeder fund.

c. If any *private fund* has issued two or more series (or classes) of equity interests whose values are determined with respect to separate portfolios of securities and other assets, then each such series (or class) should be regarded as a separate *private fund.* In Section 7.B.(1) and 7.B.(2) of Schedule D, next to the name of the *private fund*, list the name and identification number of the specific series (or class) for which you are filing the sections. This only applies with respect to series (or classes) that you manage as if they were separate funds and not a fund's side pockets or similar arrangements.

d. In the case of a master-feeder arrangement (see questions 6-7 of Section 7.B.(1) of Schedule D), instead of completing a Section 7.B.(1) for each of the master fund and each feeder fund, you may complete a single Section 7.B.(1) for the master-feeder arrangement under the name of the master fund if the answers to questions 8, 10, 21 and 23 through 28 are the same for all of the feeder funds (or, in the case of questions 24 and 25, if the feeder funds do not use a prime broker or custodian). If you choose to complete a single Section 7.B.(1), you should disregard the feeder funds, except for the following:

   (1) **Question 11**: State the gross assets for the master-feeder arrangement as a whole.

   (2) **Question 12**: List the lowest minimum investment commitment applicable to any of the master fund and the feeder funds.

   (3) **Questions 13-16**: Answer by aggregating all investors in the master-feeder arrangement (but do not count the feeder funds themselves as investors).

   (4) **Questions 19-20**: For purposes of these questions, the *private fund* means any of the master fund or the feeder funds. In answering the questions, moreover, disregard the feeder funds' investment in the master fund.

(5) **Question 22**: List all of the Form D SEC file numbers of any of the master fund and feeder funds.

e. Additional Instructions:

(1) **Question 9: Investment in Registered Investment Companies:** For purposes of this question, disregard any open-end management investment company regulated as a money market fund under rule 2a-7 under the Investment Company Act if the *private fund* invests in such a company in reliance on rule 12d1-1 under the same Act.

(2) **Question 10: Type of *Private Fund*:** For purposes of this question, the following definitions apply:

"Hedge fund" means any *private fund* (other than a securitized asset fund):

(a) with respect to which one or more investment advisers (or *related persons* of investment advisers) may be paid a performance fee or allocation calculated by taking into account unrealized gains (other than a fee or allocation the calculation of which may take into account unrealized gains solely for the purpose of reducing such fee or allocation to reflect net unrealized losses);

(b) that may borrow an amount in excess of one-half of its net asset value (including any committed capital) or may have gross notional exposure in excess of twice its net asset value (including any committed capital); or

(c) that may sell securities or other assets short or enter into similar transactions (other than for the purpose of hedging currency exposure or managing duration).

A commodity pool is categorized as a hedge fund solely for purposes of this question. For purposes of this definition, do not net long and short positions. Include any borrowings or notional exposure of another person that are guaranteed by the *private fund* or that the *private fund* may otherwise be obligated to satisfy.

"Liquidity fund" means any *private fund* that seeks to generate income by investing in a portfolio of short-term obligations in order to maintain a stable net asset value per unit or minimize principal volatility for investors.

"Private equity fund" means any *private fund* that is not a hedge fund, liquidity fund, real estate fund, securitized asset fund, or venture capital fund and does not provide investors with redemption rights in the ordinary course.

"Real estate fund" means any *private fund* that is not a hedge fund, that does not provide investors with redemption rights in the ordinary course, and that invests primarily in real estate and real estate related assets.

"Securitized asset fund" means any *private fund* whose primary purpose is to issue asset backed securities and whose investors are primarily debt-holders.

"Venture capital fund" means any *private fund* meeting the definition of venture capital fund in rule 203(l)-1 under the Advisers Act.

"Other *private fund*" means any *private fund* that is not a hedge fund, liquidity fund, private equity fund, real estate fund, securitized asset fund, or venture capital fund.

(3) **Question 11: Gross Assets.** Report the assets of the *private fund* that you would include in calculating your regulatory assets under management according to instruction 5.b above.

(4) **Questions 19-20: Other clients' investments:** For purposes of these questions, disregard any feeder fund's investment in its master fund. (*See* questions 6-7 for the definition of "master fund" and "feeder fund.")

7. Item 10: *Control Persons*

If you are a "separately identifiable department or division" (SID) of a bank, identify on Schedule A your bank's executive officers who are directly engaged in managing, directing, or supervising your investment advisory activities, and list any other *persons* designated by your bank's board of directors as responsible for the day-to-day conduct of your investment advisory activities, including supervising *employees* performing investment advisory activities.

8. Additional Information.

If you believe your response to an item in Form ADV Part 1A requires further explanation, or if you wish to provide additional information, you may do so on Schedule D, in the Miscellaneous section. Completion of this section is optional.

GLOSSARY OF TERMS

1. **Advisory Affiliate:** Your advisory affiliates are (1) all of your officers, partners, or directors (or any ***person*** performing similar functions); (2) all ***persons*** directly or indirectly ***controlling*** or ***controlled*** by you; and (3) all of your current ***employees*** (other than ***employees*** performing only clerical, administrative, support or similar functions).

   If you are a "separately identifiable department or division" (SID) of a bank, your ***advisory affiliates*** are: (1) all of your bank's ***employees*** who perform your investment advisory activities (other than clerical or administrative ***employees***); (2) all ***persons*** designated by your bank's board of directors as responsible for the day-to-day conduct of your investment advisory activities (including supervising the ***employees*** who perform investment advisory activities); (3) all ***persons*** who directly or indirectly ***control*** your bank, and all ***persons*** whom you ***control*** in connection with your investment advisory activities; and (4) all other ***persons*** who directly manage any of your investment advisory activities (including directing, supervising or performing your advisory activities), all ***persons*** who directly or indirectly ***control*** those management functions, and all ***persons*** whom you ***control*** in connection with those management functions. *[Used in: Part 1A, Items 7, 11, DRPs; Part 1B, Item 2]*

2. **Annual Updating Amendment:** Within 90 days after your firm's fiscal year end, your firm must file an "annual updating amendment," which is an amendment to your firm's Form ADV that reaffirms the eligibility information contained in Item 2 of Part 1A and updates the responses to any other item for which the information is no longer accurate. *[Used in: General Instructions; Part 1A Instructions, Introductory Text, Item 2; Part 2A, Instructions, Appendix 1 Instructions; Part 2B, Instructions]*

3. **Brochure:** A written disclosure statement that you must provide to ***clients*** and prospective ***clients***. See SEC rule 204-3; Form ADV, Part 2A. *[Used in: General Instructions; Used throughout Part 2]*

4. **Brochure Supplement:** A written disclosure statement containing information about certain of your ***supervised persons*** that your firm is required by Part 2B of Form ADV to provide to ***clients*** and prospective ***clients***. See SEC rule 204-3; Form ADV, Part 2B. *[Used in: General Instructions; Used throughout Part 2]*

5. **Charged:** Being accused of a crime in a formal complaint, information, or indictment (or equivalent formal charge). *[Used in: Part 1A, Item 11; DRPs]*

6. **Client:** Any of your firm's investment advisory clients. This term includes clients from which your firm receives no compensation, such as family members of your supervised persons. If your firm also provides other services (*e.g.*, accounting services), this term does not include clients that are not investment advisory clients. *[Used throughout Form ADV and Form ADV-W]*

7. **Control:** The power, directly or indirectly, to direct the management or policies of a ***person***, whether through ownership of securities, by contract, or otherwise.

    - Each of your firm's officers, partners, or directors exercising executive responsibility (or ***persons*** having similar status or functions) is presumed to control your firm.

    - A ***person*** is presumed to control a corporation if the ***person***: (i) directly or indirectly has the right to vote 25 percent or more of a class of the corporation's voting securities; or (ii) has the power to sell or direct the sale of 25 percent or more of a class of the corporation's voting securities.

    - A ***person*** is presumed to control a partnership if the ***person*** has the right to receive upon dissolution, or has contributed, 25 percent or more of the capital of the partnership.

    - A ***person*** is presumed to control a limited liability company ("LLC") if the ***person***: (i) directly or indirectly has the right to vote 25 percent or more of a class of the interests of the LLC; (ii) has the right to receive upon dissolution, or has contributed, 25 percent or more of the capital of the LLC; or (iii) is an elected manager of the LLC.

    - A ***person*** is presumed to control a trust if the ***person*** is a trustee or ***managing agent*** of the trust.

    [Used in: General Instructions; Part 1A, Instructions, Items 2, 7, 10, 11, 12, Schedules A, B, C, D; DRPs]

8. **Custody:** Holding, directly or indirectly, client funds or securities, or having any authority to obtain possession of them. You have custody if a ***related person*** holds, directly or indirectly, client funds or securities, or has any authority to obtain possession of them, in connection with advisory services you provide to clients. Custody includes:

    - Possession of client funds or securities (but not of checks drawn by clients and made payable to third parties) unless you receive them inadvertently and you return them to the sender promptly, but in any case within three business days of receiving them;

    - Any arrangement (including a general power of attorney) under which you are authorized or permitted to withdraw client funds or securities maintained with a custodian upon your instruction to the custodian; and

    - Any capacity (such as general partner of a limited partnership, managing member of a limited liability company or a comparable position for another type of pooled investment vehicle, or trustee of a trust) that gives you or your supervised person legal ownership of or access to client funds or securities. *[Used in: Part 1A, Item 9; Part 1B, Instructions, Item 2; Part 2A, Items 15, 18]*

9. **Discretionary Authority or Discretionary Basis:** Your firm has discretionary authority or manages assets on a discretionary basis if it has the authority to decide which securities to purchase and sell for the ***client***. Your firm also has discretionary authority if it has the authority to decide which investment advisers to retain on behalf of the ***client***. *[Used in: Part 1A, Instructions, Item 8; Part 1B, Instructions; Part 2A, Items 4, 16, 18; Part 2B, Instructions]*

10. **Employee:** This term includes an independent contractor who performs advisory functions on your behalf. *[Used in: Part 1A, Instructions, Items 1, 5, 11; Part 2B, Instructions]*

11. **Enjoined:** This term includes being subject to a mandatory injunction, prohibitory injunction, preliminary injunction, or a temporary restraining ***order***. *[Used in: Part 1A, Item 11; DRPs]*

12. **Exempt Reporting Adviser:** An investment adviser that qualifies for the exemption from registration under section 203(l) of the Advisers Act because it is an adviser solely to one or more venture capital funds, or under rule 203(m)-1 of the Advisers Act because it is an adviser solely to ***private funds*** and has assets under management in the United States of less than $150 million. *[Used in: Throughout Part 1A; General Instructions; Form ADV-H; Form ADV-NR]*

13. **Felony:** For jurisdictions that do not differentiate between a felony and a ***misdemeanor***, a felony is an offense punishable by a sentence of at least one year imprisonment and/or a fine of at least $1,000. The term also includes a general court martial. *[Used in: Part 1A, Item 11; DRPs; Part 2A, Item 9; Part 2B, Item 3]*

14. **FINRA CRD** or **CRD:** The Web Central Registration Depository ("CRD") system operated by FINRA for the registration of broker-dealers and broker-dealer representatives. *[Used in: General Instructions, Part 1A, Item 1, Schedules A, B, C, D, DRPs; Form ADV-W, Item 1]*

15. **Foreign Financial Regulatory Authority:** This term includes (1) a foreign securities authority; (2) another governmental body or foreign equivalent of a ***self-regulatory organization*** empowered by a foreign government to administer or enforce its laws relating to the regulation of ***investment-related*** activities; and (3) a foreign membership organization, a function of which is to regulate the participation of its members in the activities listed above. *[Used in: Part 1A, Items 1, 11; DRPs; Part 2A, Item 9; Part 2B, Item 3]*

16. **Found:** This term includes adverse final actions, including consent decrees in which the respondent has neither admitted nor denied the findings, but does not include agreements, deficiency letters, examination reports, memoranda of understanding, letters of caution, admonishments, and similar informal resolutions of matters. *[Used in: Part 1A, Item 11; Part 1B, Item 2; Part 2A, Item 9; Part 2B, Item 3]*

17. **Government Entity:** Any state or political subdivision of a state, including (i) any agency, authority, or instrumentality of the state or political subdivision; (ii) a plan or pool of assets ***controlled*** by the state or political subdivision or any agency, authority, or instrumentality thereof; and (iii) any officer, agent, or employee of the state or political subdivision or any agency, authority, or instrumentality thereof, acting in their official capacity. *[Used in: Part 1A, Item 5]*

18. **High Net Worth Individual:** An individual who is a "qualified client" under rule 205-3 of the Advisers Act or who is a "qualified purchaser" as defined in section 2(a)(51)(A) of the Investment Company Act of 1940. *[Used in: Part 1A, Item 5; Schedule D]*

19. **Home State:** If your firm is registered with a ***state securities authority***, your firm's "home state" is the state where it maintains its ***principal office and place of business***. *[Used in: Part 1B, Instructions]*

20. **Impersonal Investment Advice:** Investment advisory services that do not purport to meet the objectives or needs of specific individuals or accounts. *[Used in: Part 1A, Instructions; Part 2A, Instructions; Part 2B, Instructions]*

21. **Independent Public Accountant:** A public accountant that meets the standards of independence described in rule 2-01(b) and (c) of Regulation S-X (17 CFR 210.2-01(b) and (c)). *[Used in: Item 9; Schedule D]*

22. **Investment Adviser Representative:** *Any of your firm's* ***supervised persons*** *(except* those that provide only ***impersonal investment advice***) is an investment adviser representative, if --

    - the ***supervised person*** regularly solicits, meets with, or otherwise communicates with your firm's ***clients***,
    - the ***supervised person*** has more than five ***clients*** who are natural persons and not ***high net worth individuals***, and
    - more than ten percent of the ***supervised person's*** clients are natural persons and not ***high net worth individuals.***

    NOTE: If your firm is registered with the ***state securities authorities*** and not the SEC, your firm may be subject to a different state definition of "investment adviser representative." Investment adviser representatives of SEC-registered advisers may be required to register in each state in which they have a place of business.

    [Used in: General Instructions; Part 1A, Item 7; Part 2B, Item 1]

23. **Investment-Related:** Activities that pertain to securities, commodities, banking, insurance, or real estate (including, but not limited to, acting as or being associated with an investment adviser, broker-dealer, municipal securities dealer, government securities broker or dealer, issuer, investment company, futures sponsor, bank, or savings association). *[Used in: Part 1A, Items, 7, 11, DRPs; Part 1B, Item 2; Part 2A, Items 9 and 19; Part 2B, Items 3, 4 and 7]*

24. **Involved:** Engaging in any act or omission, aiding, abetting, counseling, commanding, inducing, conspiring with or failing reasonably to supervise another in doing an act. *[Used in: Part 1A, Item 11; Part 2A, Items 9 and 19; Part 2B, Items 3 and 7]*

25. **Legal Entity Identifier:** A "legal entity identifier" assigned by or on behalf of an internationally recognized standards setting body and required for reporting purposes by the U.S. Department of the Treasury's Office of Financial Research or a financial regulator.

26. **Management Persons:** Anyone with the power to exercise, directly or indirectly, a ***controlling*** influence over your firm's management or policies, or to determine the general investment advice given to the ***clients*** of your firm.

    Generally, all of the following are management persons:

    - Your firm's principal executive officers, such as your chief executive officer, chief financial officer, chief operations officer, chief legal officer, and chief compliance officer; your directors, general partners, or trustees; and other individuals with similar status or performing similar functions;

    - The members of your firm's investment committee or group that determines general investment advice to be given to ***clients***; and

    - If your firm does not have an investment committee or group, the individuals who determine general investment advice provided to ***clients*** (if there are more than five people, you may limit your firm's response to their supervisors).

    [Used in: Part 1B, Item 2; Part 2A, Items 9, 10 and 19]

27. **Managing Agent:** A managing agent of an investment adviser is any ***person***, including a trustee, who directs or manages (or who participates in directing or managing) the affairs of any unincorporated organization or association that is not a partnership. *[Used in: General Instructions; Form ADV-NR; Form ADV-W, Item 8]*

28. **Minor Rule Violation:** A violation of a ***self-regulatory organization*** rule that has been designated as "minor" pursuant to a plan approved by the SEC. A rule violation may be designated as "minor" under a plan if the sanction imposed consists of a fine of $2,500 or less,

and if the sanctioned ***person*** does not contest the fine. (Check with the appropriate ***self-regulatory organization*** to determine if a particular rule violation has been designated as "minor" for these purposes.) *[Used in: Part 1A, Item 11]*

29. **Misdemeanor:** For jurisdictions that do not differentiate between a ***felony*** and a misdemeanor, a misdemeanor is an offense punishable by a sentence of less than one year imprisonment and/or a fine of less than $1,000. The term also includes a special court martial. *[Used in: Part 1A, Item 11; DRPs; Part 2A, Item 9; Part 2B, Item 3]*

30. **Non-Resident:** (a) an individual who resides in any place not subject to the jurisdiction of the United States; (b) a corporation incorporated in or that has its ***principal office and place of business*** in any place not subject to the jurisdiction of the United States; and (c) a partnership or other unincorporated organization or association that is formed in or has its ***principal office and place of business*** in any place not subject to the jurisdiction of the United States. *[Used in: General Instructions; Form ADV-NR]*

31. **Notice Filing:** SEC-registered advisers may have to provide ***state securities authorities*** with copies of documents that are filed with the SEC. These filings are referred to as "notice filings." *[Used in: General Instructions; Part 1A, Item 2; Execution Page(s); Form ADV-W]*

32. **Order:** A written directive issued pursuant to statutory authority and procedures, including an order of denial, exemption, suspension, or revocation. Unless included in an order, this term does not include special stipulations, undertakings, or agreements relating to payments, limitations on activity or other restrictions. *[Used in: Part 1A, Items 2 and 11; Schedule D; DRPs; Part 2A, Item 9; Part 2B, Item 3]*

33. **Performance-Based Fee:** An investment advisory fee based on a share of capital gains on, or capital appreciation of, ***client*** assets. A fee that is based upon a percentage of assets that you manage is not a performance-based fee. *[Used in: Part 1A, Item 5; Part 2A, Items 6 and 19]*

34. **Person:** A natural person (an individual) or a company. A company includes any partnership, corporation, trust, limited liability company ("LLC"), limited liability partnership ("LLP"), sole proprietorship, or other organization. *[Used throughout Form ADV and Form ADV-W]*

35. **Principal Office and Place of Business:** Your firm's executive office from which your firm's officers, partners, or managers direct, ***control***, and coordinate the activities of your firm. *[Used in: Part 1A, Instructions, Items 1 and 2; Schedule D; Form ADV-W, Item 1]*

36. **Private Fund:** An issuer that would be an investment company as defined in section 3 of the Investment Company Act of 1940 but for section 3(c)(1) or 3(c)(7) of that Act. *[Used in: Part 1A, Items 2, 5, 7, and 9; Schedule D; General Instructions; Part 1A, Instructions]*

37. **Proceeding:** This term includes a formal administrative or civil action initiated by a governmental agency, ***self-regulatory organization*** or ***foreign financial regulatory authority***; a ***felony*** criminal indictment or information (or equivalent formal charge); or a ***misdemeanor*** criminal information (or equivalent formal charge). This term does not include other civil litigation, investigations, or arrests or similar charges effected in the absence of a formal criminal indictment or information (or equivalent formal charge). *[Used in: Part 1A, Item 11; DRPs; Part 1B, Item 2; Part 2A, Item 9; Part 2B, Item 3]*

38. **Related Person:** Any ***advisory affiliate*** and any ***person*** that is under common ***control*** with your firm. *[Used in: Part 1A, Items 7, 8, 9; Schedule D; Form ADV-W, Item 3; Part 2A, Items 10, 11, 12, 14; Part 2A, Appendix 1, Item 6]*

39. **Self-Regulatory Organization** or **SRO:** Any national securities or commodities exchange, registered securities association, or registered clearing agency. For example, the Chicago Board of Trade ("CBOT"), FINRA and New York Stock Exchange ("NYSE") are self-regulatory organizations. *[Used in: Part 1A, Item 11; DRPs; Part 1B, Item 2; Part 2A, Items 9 and 19; Part 2B, Items 3 and 7]*

40. **Sponsor:** A sponsor of a ***wrap fee program*** sponsors, organizes, or administers the program or selects, or provides advice to ***clients*** regarding the selection of, other investment advisers in the program. *[Used in: Part 1A, Item 5; Schedule D; Part 2A, Instructions, Appendix 1 Instructions]*

41. **State Securities Authority:** The securities commissioner or commission (or any agency, office or officer performing like functions) of any state of the United States, the District of Columbia, Puerto Rico, the Virgin Islands, or any other possession of the United States. *[Used throughout Form ADV]*

42. **Supervised Person:** Any of your officers, partners, directors (or other ***persons*** occupying a similar status or performing similar functions), or ***employees***, or any other ***person*** who provides investment advice on your behalf and is subject to your supervision or ***control***. *[Used throughout Part 2]*

43. **United States person:** This term has the same meaning as in rule 203(m)-1 under the Advisers Act, which includes any natural person that is resident in the United States. *[Used in: Part 1A, Instructions; Item 5; Schedule D]*

44. **Wrap Brochure** or **Wrap Fee Program Brochure:** The written disclosure statement that ***sponsors*** of ***wrap fee programs*** must provide to each of their ***wrap fee program clients***. *[Used in: Part 2, General Instructions; Used throughout Part 2A, Appendix 1]*

45. **Wrap Fee Program:** Any advisory program under which a specified fee or fees not based directly upon transactions in a ***client's*** account is charged for investment advisory services

(which may include portfolio management or advice concerning the selection of other investment advisers) and the execution of ***client*** transactions. *[Used in: Part 1, Item 5; Schedule D; Part 2A, Instructions, Item 4, used throughout Appendix 1; Part 2B, Instructions]*

FORM ADV (Paper Version)

- **UNIFORM APPLICATION FOR INVESTMENT ADVISER REGISTRATION AND**
- **REPORT BY EXEMPT REPORTING ADVISERS**

PART 1A

WARNING: Complete this form truthfully. False statements or omissions may result in denial of your application, revocation of your registration, or criminal prosecution. You must keep this form updated by filing periodic amendments. See Form ADV General Instruction 4.

Check the box that indicates what you would like to do (check all that apply):

SEC or State Registration:

☐ Submit an initial application to register as an investment adviser with the SEC.
☐ Submit an initial application to register as an investment adviser with one or more states.
☐ Submit an *annual updating amendment* to your registration for your fiscal year ended _________.
☐ Submit an other-than-annual amendment to your registration.

SEC or State Report by *Exempt Reporting Advisers*:

☐ Submit an initial report to the SEC.
☐ Submit a report to one or more *state securities authorities*.
☐ Submit an *annual updating amendment* to your report for your fiscal year ended _________.
☐ Submit an other-than-annual amendment to your report.
☐ Submit a final report.

Item 1 Identifying Information

Responses to this Item tell us who you are, where you are doing business, and how we can contact you.

A. Your full legal name (if you are a sole proprietor, your last, first, and middle names):

____

B. Name under which you primarily conduct your advisory business, if different from Item 1.A.

____

List on Section 1.B. of Schedule D any additional names under which you conduct your advisory business.

C. If this filing is reporting a change in your legal name (Item 1.A.) or primary business name (Item 1.B.), enter the new name and specify whether the name change is of ☐ your legal name or ☐ your primary business name:

____

D. (1) If you are registered with the SEC as an investment adviser, your SEC file number: 801-___________

(2) If you report to the SEC as an *exempt reporting adviser*, your SEC file number: 802-___________

E. If you have a number ("*CRD* Number") assigned by the *FINRA's CRD* system or by the IARD system, your *CRD* number: ___________

SEC 1707 (09-11)
File 2 of 4

If your firm does not have a CRD number, skip this Item 1.E. Do not provide the CRD number of one of your officers, employees, or affiliates.

F. *Principal Office and Place of Business*

(1) Address (do not use a P.O. Box):

____
(number and street)

____
(city) (state/country) (zip+4/postal code)

If this address is a private residence, check this box: ☐

List on Section 1.F. of Schedule D any office, other than your principal office and place of business, at which you conduct investment advisory business. If you are applying for registration, or are registered, with one or more state securities authorities, you must list all of your offices in the state or states to which you are applying for registration or with whom you are registered. If you are applying for SEC registration, if you are registered only with the SEC, or if you are reporting to the SEC as an exempt reporting adviser, list the largest five offices in terms of numbers of employees.

(2) Days of week that you normally conduct business at your *principal office and place of business*:

☐ Monday - Friday ☐ Other: ____________________

Normal business hours at this location: ____________________

(3) Telephone number at this location: ____________________
(area code) (telephone number)

(4) Facsimile number at this location: ____________________
(area code) (facsimile number)

G. Mailing address, if different from your *principal office and place of business* address:

____
(number and street)

____
(city) (state/country) (zip+4/postal code)

If this address is a private residence, check this box: ☐

H. If you are a sole proprietor, state your full residence address, if different from your *principal office and place of business* address in Item 1.F.:

____
(number and street)

____
(city) (state/country) (zip+4/postal code)

I. Do you have one or more websites? Yes ☐ No ☐

If "yes," list all website addresses on Section 1.I. of Schedule D. If a website address serves as a portal through which to access other information you have published on the web, you may list the portal without listing addresses for all of the other information. Some advisers may need to list more than one portal address. Do not provide individual electronic mail (e-mail) addresses in response to this Item.

J. Provide the name and contact information of your Chief Compliance Officer: If you are an *exempt reporting adviser*, you must provide the contact information for your Chief Compliance Officer, if you have one. If not, you must complete Item 1.K. below.

(name)

(other titles, if any)

(area code) (telephone number) (area code) (facsimile number)

(number and street)

(city) (state/country) (zip+4/postal code)

(electronic mail (e-mail) address, if Chief Compliance Officer has one)

K. Additional Regulatory Contact Person: If a person other than the Chief Compliance Officer is authorized to receive information and respond to questions about this Form ADV, you may provide that information here.

(name)

(titles)

(area code) (telephone number) (area code) (facsimile number)

(number and street)

(city) (state/country) (zip+4/postal code)

(electronic mail (e-mail) address, if contact person has one)

L. Do you maintain some or all of the books and records you are required to keep under Section 204 of the Advisers Act, or similar state law, somewhere other than your *principal office and place of business*?

Yes ☐ No ☐

If "yes," complete Section 1.L. of Schedule D.

M. Are you registered with a *foreign financial regulatory authority*? Yes ☐ No ☐

Answer "no" if you are not registered with a foreign financial regulatory authority, even if you have an affiliate that is registered with a foreign financial regulatory authority. If "yes," complete Section 1.M. of Schedule D.

N. Are you a public reporting company under Sections 12 or 15(d) of the Securities Exchange Act of 1934?

Yes ☐ No ☐

If "yes," provide your CIK number (Central Index Key number that the SEC assigns to each public reporting company): ________________

O. Did you have $1 billion or more in assets on the last day of your most recent fiscal year?

Yes ☐ No ☐

P. Provide your *Legal Entity Identifier* if you have one: ________________

A *legal entity identifier* is a unique number that companies use to identify each other in the financial marketplace. In the first half of 2011, the *legal entity identifier* standard was still in development. You may not have a *legal entity identifier*.

Item 2

SEC Registration

Responses to this Item help us (and you) determine whether you are eligible to register with the SEC. Complete this Item 2.A. only if you are applying for SEC registration or submitting an *annual updating amendment* to your SEC registration.

A. To register (or remain registered) with the SEC, you must check **at least one** of the Items 2.A.(1) through 2.A.(12), below. If you are submitting an *annual updating amendment* to your SEC registration and you are no longer eligible to register with the SEC, check Item 2.A.(13). Part 1A Instruction 2 provides information to help you determine whether you may affirmatively respond to each of these items.

You (the adviser):

☐ (1) are a **large advisory firm** that either:

(a) has regulatory assets under management of $100 million (in U.S. dollars) or more, or

(b) has regulatory assets under management of $90 million (in U.S. dollars) or more at the time of filing its most recent *annual updating amendment* and is registered with the SEC;

☐ (2) are a **mid-sized advisory firm** that has regulatory assets under management of $25 million (in U.S. dollars) or more but less than $100 million (in U.S. dollars) and you are either:

(a) not required to be registered as an adviser with the *state securities authority* of the state where you maintain your *principal office and place of business*, or

(b) not subject to examination by the *state securities authority* of the state where you maintain your *principal office and place of business*;

*Click **HERE** for a list of states in which an investment adviser, if registered, would not be subject to examination by the state securities authority.*

☐ (3) have your *principal office and place of business* **in Wyoming** (which does not regulate advisers);

☐ (4) have your *principal office and place of business* **outside the United States;**

☐ (5) are **an investment adviser (or sub-adviser) to an investment company** registered under the Investment Company Act of 1940;

☐ (6) are **an investment adviser to a company which has elected to be a business development company** pursuant to section 54 of the Investment Company Act of 1940 and has not withdrawn the election, and you have at least $25 million of regulatory assets under management;

☐ (7) are a **pension consultant** with respect to assets of plans having an aggregate value of at least $200,000,000 that qualifies for the exemption in rule 203A-2(a);

☐ (8) are a **related adviser** under rule 203A-2(b) that *controls,* is *controlled* by, or is under common *control* with, an investment adviser that is registered with the SEC, and your *principal office and place of business* is the same as the registered adviser;

If you check this box, complete Section 2.A.(8) of Schedule D.

☐ (9) are a **newly formed adviser** relying on rule 203A-2(c) because you expect to be eligible for SEC registration within 120 days;

If you check this box, complete Section 2.A.(9) of Schedule D.

☐ (10) are a **multi-state adviser** that is required to register in 15 or more states and is relying on rule 203A-2(d);

If you check this box, complete Section 2.A.(10) of Schedule D.

☐ (11) are an **Internet adviser** relying on rule 203A-2(e);

☐ (12) have **received an SEC order** exempting you from the prohibition against registration with the SEC;

If you check this box, complete Section 2.A.(12) of Schedule D.

☐ (13) are **no longer eligible** to remain registered with the SEC.

SEC Reporting by *Exempt Reporting Advisers*

B. Complete this Item 2.B. only if you are reporting to the SEC as an *exempt reporting adviser.* Check all that apply. You:

☐ (1) qualify for the exemption from registration as an adviser solely to one or more venture capital funds;

Your Name____________________ *CRD* Number____________________
Date____________________ SEC 801- or 802 Number____________________

☐ (2) qualify for the exemption from registration because you act solely as an adviser to *private funds* and have assets under management in the United States of less than $150 million;

☐ (3) act solely as an adviser to *private funds* but you are no longer eligible to check box 2.B.(2) because you have assets under management in the United States of $150 million or more.

If you check box (2) or (3), complete Section 2.B. of Schedule D.

State Securities Authority Notice Filings and State Reporting by *Exempt Reporting Advisers*

C. Under state laws, SEC-registered advisers may be required to provide to *state securities authorities* a copy of the Form ADV and any amendments they file with the SEC. These are called *notice filings*. In addition, *exempt reporting advisers* may be required to provide *state securities authorities* with a copy of reports and any amendments they file with the SEC. If this is an initial application or report, check the box(es) next to the state(s) that you would like to receive notice of this and all subsequent filings or reports you submit to the SEC. If this is an amendment to direct your *notice filings* or reports to additional state(s), check the box(es) next to the state(s) that you would like to receive notice of this and all subsequent filings or reports you submit to the SEC. If this is an amendment to your registration to stop your *notice filings* or reports from going to state(s) that currently receive them, uncheck the box(es) next to those state(s).

☐ AL	☐ CT	☐ HI	☐ KY	☐ MN	☐ NH	☐ OH	☐ SC	☐ VI
☐ AK	☐ DE	☐ ID	☐ LA	☐ MS	☐ NJ	☐ OK	☐ SD	☐ VA
☐ AZ	☐ DC	☐ IL	☐ ME	☐ MO	☐ NM	☐ OR	☐ TN	☐ WA
☐ AR	☐ FL	☐ IN	☐ MD	☐ MT	☐ NY	☐ PA	☐ TX	☐ WV
☐ CA	☐ GA	☐ IA	☐ MA	☐ NE	☐ NC	☐ PR	☐ UT	☐ WI
☐ CO	☐ GU	☐ KS	☐ MI	☐ NV	☐ ND	☐ RI	☐ VT	

If you are amending your registration to stop your notice filings or reports from going to a state that currently receives them and you do not want to pay that state's notice filing or report filing fee for the coming year, your amendment must be filed before the end of the year (December 31).

Item 3 Form of Organization

A. How are you organized?

☐ Corporation ☐ Sole Proprietorship ☐ Limited Liability Partnership (LLP)
☐ Partnership ☐ Limited Liability Company (LLC) ☐ Limited Partnership (LP)
☐ Other (specify):____________________

If you are changing your response to this Item, see Part 1A Instruction 4.

B. In what month does your fiscal year end each year? ____________________

C. Under the laws of what state or country are you organized? ____________________

If you are a partnership, provide the name of the state or country under whose laws your partnership was formed. If you are a sole proprietor, provide the name of the state or country where you reside.

If you are changing your response to this Item, see Part 1A Instruction 4.

Item 4 Successions

A. Are you, at the time of this filing, succeeding to the business of a registered investment adviser?

☐ Yes ☐ No

If "yes," complete Item 4.B. and Section 4 of Schedule D.

B. Date of Succession: __________
(mm/dd/yyyy)

If you have already reported this succession on a previous Form ADV filing, do not report the succession again. Instead, check "No." See Part 1A Instruction 4.

Item 5 Information About Your Advisory Business

Responses to this Item help us understand your business, assist us in preparing for on-site examinations, and provide us with data we use when making regulatory policy. Part 1A Instruction 5.a. provides additional guidance to newly formed advisers for completing this Item 5.

Employees

If you are organized as a sole proprietorship, include yourself as an employee in your responses to Item 5.A and Items 5.B.(1), (2), (3), (4), and (5). If an employee performs more than one function, you should count that employee in each of your responses to Items 5.B.(1), (2), (3), (4) and (5).

A. Approximately how many *employees* do you have? Include full- and part-time *employees* but do not include any clerical workers.

____

B.

(1) Approximately how many of the *employees* reported in 5.A. perform investment advisory functions (including research)?

____

(2) Approximately how many of the *employees* reported in 5.A. are registered representatives of a broker-dealer?

____

(3) Approximately how many of the *employees* reported in 5.A. are registered with one or more *state securities authorities* as *investment adviser representatives*?

____

(4) Approximately how many of the *employees* reported in 5.A. are registered with one or more *state securities authorities* as *investment adviser representatives* for an investment adviser other than you?

____

(5) Approximately how many of the *employees* reported in 5.A. are licensed agents of an insurance company or agency?

____

(6) Approximately how many firms or other *persons* solicit advisory *clients* on your behalf? ________

In your response to Item 5.B.(6), do not count any of your employees and count a firm only once – do not count each of the firm's employees that solicit on your behalf.

Clients

In your responses to Items 5.C. and 5.D. do not include as "clients" the investors in a private fund you advise, unless you have a separate advisory relationship with those investors.

C. (1) To approximately how many *clients* did you provide investment advisory services during your most recently completed fiscal year?

☐0 ☐1-10 ☐11-25 ☐26-100

If more than 100, how many? ______ (round to the nearest 100)

(2) Approximately what percentage of your *clients* are non-*United States persons*? ______%

D. *For purposes of this Item 5.D., the category "individuals" includes trusts, estates, and 401(k) plans and IRAs of individuals and their family members, but does not include businesses organized as sole proprietorships.*
The category "business development companies" consists of companies that have made an election pursuant to section 54 of the Investment Company Act of 1940. Unless you provide advisory services pursuant to an investment advisory contract to an investment company registered under the Investment Company Act of 1940, check "None" in response to Item 5.D.(1)(d) and do not check any of the boxes in response to Item 5.D.(2)(d).

(1) What types of *clients* do you have? Indicate the approximate percentage that each type of *client* comprises of your total number of *clients*. If a *client* fits into more than one category, check all that apply.

	None	Up to 10%	11-25%	26-50%	51-75%	76-99%	100%
(a) Individuals (other than *high net worth individuals*)	☐	☐	☐	☐	☐	☐	☐
(b) *High net worth individuals*	☐	☐	☐	☐	☐	☐	☐
(c) Banking or thrift institutions	☐	☐	☐	☐	☐	☐	☐
(d) Investment companies	☐	☐	☐	☐	☐	☐	☐
(e) Business development companies	☐	☐	☐	☐	☐	☐	☐
(f) Pooled investment vehicles (other than investment companies)	☐	☐	☐	☐	☐	☐	☐
(g) Pension and profit sharing plans (but not the plan participants)	☐	☐	☐	☐	☐	☐	☐
(h) Charitable organizations	☐	☐	☐	☐	☐	☐	☐
(i) Corporations or other businesses not listed above	☐	☐	☐	☐	☐	☐	☐
(j) State or municipal *government entities*	☐	☐	☐	☐	☐	☐	☐
(k) Other investment advisers	☐	☐	☐	☐	☐	☐	☐
(l) Insurance companies	☐	☐	☐	☐	☐	☐	☐

(m) Other: ________ ☐ ☐ ☐ ☐ ☐ ☐ ☐

(2) Indicate the approximate amount of your regulatory assets under management (reported in Item 5.F. below) attributable to each of the following type of *client*. If a *client* fits into more than one category, check all that apply.

	None	Up to 25%	Up to 50%	Up to 75%	>75%
(a) Individuals (other than *high net worth individuals*)	☐	☐	☐	☐	☐
(b) *High net worth individuals*	☐	☐	☐	☐	☐
(c) Banking or thrift institutions	☐	☐	☐	☐	☐
(d) Investment companies	☐	☐	☐	☐	☐
(e) Business development companies	☐	☐	☐	☐	☐
(f) Pooled investment vehicles (other than investment companies)	☐	☐	☐	☐	☐
(g) Pension and profit sharing plans (but not the plan participants)	☐	☐	☐	☐	☐
(h) Charitable organizations	☐	☐	☐	☐	☐
(i) Corporations or other businesses not listed above	☐	☐	☐	☐	☐
(j) State or municipal *government entities*	☐	☐	☐	☐	☐
(k) Other investment advisers	☐	☐	☐	☐	☐
(l) Insurance companies	☐	☐	☐	☐	☐
(m) Other: ________	☐	☐	☐	☐	☐

Compensation Arrangements

E. You are compensated for your investment advisory services by (check all that apply):

- ☐ (1) A percentage of assets under your management
- ☐ (2) Hourly charges
- ☐ (3) Subscription fees (for a newsletter or periodical)
- ☐ (4) Fixed fees (other than subscription fees)
- ☐ (5) Commissions
- ☐ (6) *Performance-based fees*
- ☐ (7) Other (specify): ________

Regulatory Assets Under Management

F. (1) Do you provide continuous and regular supervisory or management services to securities portfolios? ☐ Yes ☐ No

(2) If yes, what is the amount of your regulatory assets under management and total number of accounts?

	U.S. Dollar Amount	Total Number of Accounts
Discretionary:	(a) $________.00	(d) ________

Non-Discretionary:	(b) $____________.00	(e) ____________
Total:	(c) $____________.00	(f) ____________

Part 1A Instruction 5.b. explains how to calculate your regulatory assets under management. You must follow these instructions carefully when completing this Item.

Advisory Activities

G. What type(s) of advisory services do you provide? Check all that apply.

- ☐ (1) Financial planning services
- ☐ (2) Portfolio management for individuals and/or small businesses
- ☐ (3) Portfolio management for investment companies (as well as "business development companies" that have made an election pursuant to section 54 of the Investment Company Act of 1940)
- ☐ (4) Portfolio management for pooled investment vehicles (other than investment companies)
- ☐ (5) Portfolio management for businesses (other than small businesses) or institutional *clients* (other than registered investment companies and other pooled investment vehicles)
- ☐ (6) Pension consulting services
- ☐ (7) Selection of other advisers (including *private fund* managers)
- ☐ (8) Publication of periodicals or newsletters
- ☐ (9) Security ratings or pricing services
- ☐ (10) Market timing services
- ☐ (11) Educational seminars/workshops
- ☐ (12) Other (specify): ____

Do not check Item 5.G.(3) unless you provide advisory services pursuant to an investment advisory contract to an investment company registered under the Investment Company Act of 1940, including as a subadviser. If you check Item 5.G.(3), report the 811 or 814 number of the investment company or investment companies to which you provide advice in Section 5.G. of Schedule D.

H. If you provide financial planning services, to how many *clients* did you provide these services during your last fiscal year?

☐ 0 ☐ 1-10 ☐ 11-25 ☐ 26-50 ☐ 51-100 ☐ 101-250 ☐ 251 – 500
☐ More than 500 If more than 500, how many? ______ (round to the nearest 500)

In your responses to this Item 5.H., do not include as "clients" the investors in a private fund you advise, unless you have a separate advisory relationship with those investors.

I. If you participate in a *wrap fee program*, do you (check all that apply):

- ☐ (1) *sponsor* the *wrap fee program*?
- ☐ (2) act as a portfolio manager for the *wrap fee program*?

If you are a portfolio manager for a wrap fee program, list the names of the programs and their sponsors in Section 5.I.(2) of Schedule D.

If your involvement in a wrap fee program is limited to recommending wrap fee programs to your clients, or you advise a mutual fund that is offered through a wrap fee program, do not check either Item 5.I.(1) or 5.I(2).

J. In response to Item 4.B. of Part 2A of Form ADV, do you indicate that you provide investment advice only with respect to limited types of investments? ☐ Yes ☐ No

Item 6 Other Business Activities

In this Item, we request information about your firm's other business activities.

A. You are actively engaged in business as a (check all that apply):

☐ (1) broker-dealer (registered or unregistered)
☐ (2) registered representative of a broker-dealer
☐ (3) commodity pool operator or commodity trading advisor (whether registered or exempt from registration)
☐ (4) futures commission merchant
☐ (5) real estate broker, dealer, or agent
☐ (6) insurance broker or agent
☐ (7) bank (including a separately identifiable department or division of a bank)
☐ (8) trust company
☐ (9) registered municipal advisor
☐ (10) registered security-based swap dealer
☐ (11) major security-based swap participant
☐ (12) accountant or accounting firm
☐ (13) lawyer or law firm
☐ (14) other financial product salesperson (specify): ________________

If you engage in other business using a name that is different from the names reported in Items 1.A. or 1.B, complete Section 6.A. of Schedule D.

B. (1) Are you actively engaged in any other business not listed in Item 6.A. (other than giving investment advice)? ☐ Yes ☐ No

(2) If yes, is this other business your primary business? ☐ Yes ☐ No

If "yes," describe this other business on Section 6.B.(2) of Schedule D, and if you engage in this business under a different name, provide that name.

(3) Do you sell products or provide services other than investment advice to your advisory *clients*? ☐ Yes ☐ No

If "yes," describe this other business on Section 6.B.(3) of Schedule D, and if you engage in this business under a different name, provide that name.

Item 7 Financial Industry Affiliations and *Private Fund* Reporting

In this Item, we request information about your financial industry affiliations and activities. This information identifies areas in which conflicts of interest may occur between you and your *clients*.

A. This part of Item 7 requires you to provide information about you and your *related persons*, including foreign affiliates. Your *related persons* are all of your *advisory affiliates* and any *person* that is under common *control* with you.

You have a *related person* that is a (check all that apply):

☐ (1) broker-dealer, municipal securities dealer, or government securities broker or dealer (registered or unregistered)

- ☐ (2) other investment adviser (including financial planners)
- ☐ (3) registered municipal advisor
- ☐ (4) registered security-based swap dealer
- ☐ (5) major security-based swap participant
- ☐ (6) commodity pool operator or commodity trading advisor (whether registered or exempt from registration)
- ☐ (7) futures commission merchant
- ☐ (8) banking or thrift institution
- ☐ (9) trust company
- ☐ (10) accountant or accounting firm
- ☐ (11) lawyer or law firm
- ☐ (12) insurance company or agency
- ☐ (13) pension consultant
- ☐ (14) real estate broker or dealer
- ☐ (15) sponsor or syndicator of limited partnerships (or equivalent), excluding pooled investment vehicles
- ☐ (16) sponsor, general partner, managing member (or equivalent) of pooled investment vehicles

For each related person, including foreign affiliates that may not be registered or required to be registered in the United States, complete Section 7.A. of Schedule D.

You do not need to complete Section 7.A. of Schedule D for any related person if: (1) you have no business dealings with the related person in connection with advisory services you provide to your clients; (2) you do not conduct shared operations with the related person; (3) you do not refer clients or business to the related person, and the related person does not refer prospective clients or business to you; (4) you do not share supervised persons or premises with the related person; and (5) you have no reason to believe that your relationship with the related person otherwise creates a conflict of interest with your clients.

You must complete Section 7.A. of Schedule D for each related person acting as qualified custodian in connection with advisory services you provide to your clients (other than any mutual fund transfer agent pursuant to rule 206(4)-2(b)(1)), regardless of whether you have determined the related person to be operationally independent under rule 206(4)-2 of the Advisers Act.

B. Are you an adviser to any *private fund*? ☐ Yes ☐ No

If "yes," then for each private fund that you advise, you must complete a Section 7.B.(1) of Schedule D, except in certain circumstances described in the next sentence and in Instruction 6 of the Instructions to Part 1A. If another adviser reports this information with respect to any such private fund in Section 7.B.(1) of Schedule D of its Form ADV (e.g., if you are a subadviser), do not complete Section 7.B.(1) of Schedule D with respect to that private fund. You must, instead, complete Section 7.B.(2) of Schedule D.

In either case, if you seek to preserve the anonymity of a private fund client by maintaining its identity in your books and records in numerical or alphabetical code, or similar designation, pursuant to rule 204-2(d), you may identify the private fund in Section 7.B.(1) or 7.B.(2) of Schedule D using the same code or designation in place of the fund's name.

Item 8 Participation or Interest in *Client* Transactions

In this Item, we request information about your participation and interest in your *clients'* transactions. This information identifies additional areas in which conflicts of interest may occur between you and your *clients*.

Like Item 7, Item 8 requires you to provide information about you and your *related persons*, including foreign affiliates.

Proprietary Interest in *Client* Transactions

A. Do you or any *related person*: Yes No

(1) buy securities for yourself from advisory *clients*, or sell securities you own to advisory *clients* (principal transactions)? ☐ ☐

(2) buy or sell for yourself securities (other than shares of mutual funds) that you also recommend to advisory *clients*? ☐ ☐

(3) recommend securities (or other investment products) to advisory *clients* in which you or any *related person* has some other proprietary (ownership) interest (other than those mentioned in Items 8.A.(1) or (2))? ☐ ☐

Sales Interest in *Client* Transactions

B. Do you or any *related person*: Yes No

(1) as a broker-dealer or registered representative of a broker-dealer, execute securities trades for brokerage customers in which advisory *client* securities are sold to or bought from the brokerage customer (agency cross transactions)? ☐ ☐

(2) recommend purchase of securities to advisory *clients* for which you or any *related person* serves as underwriter, general or managing partner, or purchaser representative? ☐ ☐

(3) recommend purchase or sale of securities to advisory *clients* for which you or any *related person* has any other sales interest (other than the receipt of sales commissions as a broker or registered representative of a broker-dealer)? ☐ ☐

Investment or Brokerage Discretion

C. Do you or any *related person* have *discretionary authority* to determine the: Yes No

(1) securities to be bought or sold for a *client's* account? ☐ ☐

(2) amount of securities to be bought or sold for a *client's* account? ☐ ☐

(3) broker or dealer to be used for a purchase or sale of securities for a *client's* account? ☐ ☐

(4) commission rates to be paid to a broker or dealer for a *client's* securities transactions? ☐ ☐

Yes No

D. If you answer "yes" to C.(3) above, are any of the brokers or dealers *related persons*? ☐ ☐

E. Do you or any *related person* recommend brokers or dealers to *clients*? ☐ ☐

F. If you answer "yes" to E above, are any of the brokers or dealers *related persons*? ☐ ☐

G. (1) Do you or any *related person* receive research or other products or services other than execution from a broker-dealer or a third party ("soft dollar benefits") in connection with *client* securities transactions? ☐ ☐

(2) If "yes" to G.(1) above, are all the "soft dollar benefits" you or any *related persons* receive eligible "research or brokerage services" under section 28(e) of the Securities Exchange Act of 1934? ☐ ☐

H. Do you or any *related person*, directly or indirectly, compensate any *person* for *client* referrals? ☐ ☐

I. Do you or any *related person*, directly or indirectly, receive compensation from any *person* for *client* referrals? ☐ ☐

In responding to Items 8.H and 8.I., consider all cash and non-cash compensation that you or a related person gave to (in answering Item 8.H) or received from (in answering Item 8.I) any person in exchange for client referrals, including any bonus that is based, at least in part, on the number or amount of client referrals.

Item 9 Custody

In this Item, we ask you whether you or a *related person* has *custody* of *client* (other than *clients* that are investment companies registered under the Investment Company Act of 1940) assets and about your custodial practices.

A. (1) Do you have *custody* of any advisory *clients'*: Yes No

(a) cash or bank accounts? ☐ ☐
(b) securities? ☐ ☐

If you are registering or registered with the SEC, answer "No" to Item 9.A.(1)(a) and (b) if you have custody solely because (i) you deduct your advisory fees directly from your clients' accounts, or (ii) a related person has custody of client assets in connection with advisory services you provide to clients, but you have overcome the presumption that you are not operationally independent (pursuant to Advisers Act rule 206(4)-(2)(d)(5)) from the related person.

(2) If you checked "yes" to Item 9.A.(1)(a) or (b), what is the approximate amount of *client* funds and securities and total number of *clients* for which you have *custody*:

U.S. Dollar Amount	Total Number of *Clients*
(a) $______________	(b) ______________

If you are registering or registered with the SEC and you have custody solely because you deduct your advisory fees directly from your clients' accounts, do not include the amount of those assets and the number of those clients in your response to Item 9.A.(2). If your related person has custody of client assets in connection with advisory services you provide to clients, do not include the amount of those assets and the number of those clients in your response to Item 9.A.(2). Instead, include that information in your response to Item 9.B.(2).

B. (1) In connection with advisory services you provide to *clients*, do any of your *related persons* have *custody* of any of your advisory *clients'*:

	Yes	No
(a) cash or bank accounts?	☐	☐
(b) securities?	☐	☐

You are required to answer this item regardless of how you answered Item 9.A.(1)(a) or (b).

(2) If you checked "yes" to Item 9.B.(1)(a) or (b), what is the approximate amount of *client* funds and securities and total number of *clients* for which your *related persons* have *custody*:

U.S. Dollar Amount	Total Number of *Clients*
(a) $____________	(b) ____________

C. If you or your *related persons* have *custody* of *client* funds or securities in connection with advisory services you provide to *clients*, check all the following that apply:

☐ (1) A qualified custodian(s) sends account statements at least quarterly to the investors in the pooled investment vehicle(s) you manage.

☐ (2) An *independent public accountant* audits annually the pooled investment vehicle(s) that you manage and the audited financial statements are distributed to the investors in the pools.

☐ (3) An *independent public accountant* conducts an annual surprise examination of *client* funds and securities.

☐ (4) An *independent public accountant* prepares an internal control report with respect to custodial services when you or your *related persons* are qualified custodians for *client* funds and securities.

If you checked Item 9.C.(2), C.(3) or C.(4), list in Section 9.C. of Schedule D the accountants that are engaged to perform the audit or examination or prepare an internal control report. (If you checked Item 9.C.(2), you do not have to list auditor information in Section 9.C. of Schedule D if you already provided this information with respect to the private funds you advise in Section 7.B.(1) of Schedule D).

D. Do you or your *related person(s)* act as qualified custodians for your *clients* in connection with advisory services you provide to *clients*?

	Yes	No
(1) you act as a qualified custodian	☐	☐
(2) your *related person(s)* act as qualified custodian(s)	☐	☐

If you checked "yes" to Item 9.D.(2), all related persons that act as qualified custodians (other than any mutual fund transfer agent pursuant to rule 206(4)-2(b)(1)) must be identified in Section 7.A. of Schedule D, regardless of whether you have determined the related person to be operationally independent under rule 206(4)-2 of the Advisers Act.

E. If you are filing your *annual updating amendment* and you were subject to a surprise examination by an *independent public accountant* during your last fiscal year, provide the date (MM/YYYY) the examination commenced: ____________

F. If you or your *related persons* have *custody* of *client* funds or securities, how many *persons*, including, but not limited to, you and your *related persons*, act as qualified custodians for your *clients* in connection with advisory services you provide to *clients*? __________

Item 10 Control Persons

In this Item, we ask you to identify every *person* that, directly or indirectly, *controls* you.

If you are submitting an initial application or report, you must complete Schedule A and Schedule B. Schedule A asks for information about your direct owners and executive officers. Schedule B asks for information about your indirect owners. If this is an amendment and you are updating information you reported on either Schedule A or Schedule B (or both) that you filed with your initial application or report, you must complete Schedule C.

A. Does any *person* not named in Item 1.A. or Schedules A, B, or C, directly or indirectly, *control* your management or policies? ☐ Yes ☐ No

If yes, complete Section 10.A. of Schedule D.

B. If any *person* named in Schedules A, B, or C or in Section 10.A. of Schedule D is a public reporting company under Sections 12 or 15(d) of the Securities Exchange Act of 1934, please complete Section 10.B. of Schedule D.

Item 11 Disclosure Information

In this Item, we ask for information about your disciplinary history and the disciplinary history of all your *advisory affiliates*. We use this information to determine whether to grant your application for registration, to decide whether to revoke your registration or to place limitations on your activities as an investment adviser, and to identify potential problem areas to focus on during our on-site examinations. One event may result in "yes" answers to more than one of the questions below.

Your *advisory affiliates* are: (1) all of your current *employees* (other than *employees* performing only clerical, administrative, support or similar functions); (2) all of your officers, partners, or directors (or any *person* performing similar functions); and (3) all *persons* directly or indirectly *controlling* you or *controlled* by you. If you are a "separately identifiable department or division" (SID) of a bank, see the Glossary of Terms to determine who your *advisory affiliates* are.

If you are registered or registering with the SEC or if you are an exempt reporting adviser, you may limit your disclosure of any event listed in Item 11 to ten years following the date of the event. If you are registered or registering with a state, you must respond to the questions as posed; you may, therefore, limit your disclosure to ten years following the date of an event only in responding to Items 11.A.(1), 11.A.(2), 11.B.(1), 11.B.(2), 11.D.(4), and 11.H(1)(a). For purposes of calculating this ten-year period, the date of an event is the date the final order, judgment, or decree was entered, or the date any rights of appeal from preliminary orders, judgments, or decrees lapsed.

You must complete the appropriate Disclosure Reporting Page ("DRP") for "yes" answers to the questions in this Item 11.

	Yes	No
Do any of the events below involve you or any of your *supervised persons?*	☐	☐

For "yes" answers to the following questions, complete a Criminal Action DRP:

	Yes	No
A. In the past ten years, have you or any *advisory affiliate*:		
(1) been convicted of or pled guilty or nolo contendere ("no contest") in a domestic, foreign, or military court to any *felony*?	☐	☐
(2) been *charged* with any *felony*?	☐	☐

If you are registered or registering with the SEC, or if you are reporting as an exempt reporting adviser, you may limit your response to Item 11.A.(2) to charges that are currently pending.

	Yes	No
B. In the past ten years, have you or any *advisory affiliate*:		
(1) been convicted of or pled guilty or nolo contendere ("no contest") in a domestic, foreign, or military court to a *misdemeanor* involving: investments or an *investment-related* business, or any fraud, false statements, or omissions, wrongful taking of property, bribery, perjury, forgery, counterfeiting, extortion, or a conspiracy to commit any of these offenses?	☐	☐
(2) been *charged* with a *misdemeanor* listed in Item 11.B.(1)?	☐	☐

If you are registered or registering with the SEC, or if you are reporting as an exempt reporting adviser, you may limit your response to Item 11.B.(2) to charges that are currently pending.

For "yes" answers to the following questions, complete a Regulatory Action DRP:

	Yes	No
C. Has the SEC or the Commodity Futures Trading Commission (CFTC) ever:		
(1) *found* you or any *advisory affiliate* to have made a false statement or omission?	☐	☐
(2) *found* you or any *advisory affiliate* to have been *involved* in a violation of SEC or CFTC regulations or statutes?	☐	☐
(3) *found* you or any *advisory affiliate* to have been a cause of an *investment-related* business having its authorization to do business denied, suspended, revoked, or restricted?	☐	☐
(4) entered an *order* against you or any *advisory affiliate* in connection with *investment-related* activity?	☐	☐
(5) imposed a civil money penalty on you or any *advisory affiliate*, or *ordered* you or any *advisory affiliate* to cease and desist from any activity?	☐	☐
D. Has any other federal regulatory agency, any state regulatory agency, or any *foreign financial regulatory authority*:		
(1) ever *found* you or any *advisory affiliate* to have made a false statement or omission, or been dishonest, unfair, or unethical?	☐	☐
(2) ever *found* you or any *advisory affiliate* to have been *involved* in a violation of *investment-related* regulations or statutes?	☐	☐

	Yes	No
(3) ever *found* you or any *advisory affiliate* to have been a cause of an *investment-related* business having its authorization to do business denied, suspended, revoked, or restricted?	☐	☐
(4) in the past ten years, entered an *order* against you or any *advisory affiliate* in connection with an *investment-related* activity?	☐	☐
(5) ever denied, suspended, or revoked your or any *advisory affiliate's* registration or license, or otherwise prevented you or any *advisory affiliate*, by *order*, from associating with an *investment-related* business or restricted your or any *advisory affiliate's* activity?	☐	☐
E. Has any *self-regulatory organization* or commodities exchange ever:		
(1) *found* you or any *advisory affiliate* to have made a false statement or omission?	☐	☐
(2) *found* you or any *advisory affiliate* to have been *involved* in a violation of its rules (other than a violation designated as a "*minor rule violation*" under a plan approved by the SEC)?	☐	☐
(3) *found* you or any *advisory affiliate* to have been the cause of an *investment-related* business having its authorization to do business denied, suspended, revoked, or restricted?	☐	☐
(4) disciplined you or any *advisory affiliate* by expelling or suspending you or the *advisory affiliate* from membership, barring or suspending you or the *advisory affiliate* from association with other members, or otherwise restricting your or the *advisory affiliate's* activities?	☐	☐
F. Has an authorization to act as an attorney, accountant, or federal contractor granted to you or any *advisory affiliate* ever been revoked or suspended?	☐	☐
G. Are you or any *advisory affiliate* now the subject of any regulatory *proceeding* that could result in a "yes" answer to any part of Item 11.C., 11.D., or 11.E.?	☐	☐

For "yes" answers to the following questions, complete a Civil Judicial Action DRP:

	Yes	No
H. (1) Has any domestic or foreign court:		
(a) in the past ten years, *enjoined* you or any *advisory affiliate* in connection with any *investment-related* activity?	☐	☐
(b) ever *found* that you or any *advisory affiliate* were *involved* in a violation of *investment-related* statutes or regulations?	☐	☐
(c) ever dismissed, pursuant to a settlement agreement, an *investment-related* civil action brought against you or any *advisory affiliate* by a state or *foreign financial regulatory authority*?	☐	☐

(2) Are you or any *advisory affiliate* now the subject of any civil *proceeding* that could result in a "yes" answer to any part of Item 11.H(1)? ☐ ☐

Item 12 Small Businesses

The SEC is required by the Regulatory Flexibility Act to consider the effect of its regulations on small entities. In order to do this, we need to determine whether you meet the definition of "small business" or "small organization" under rule 0-7.

Answer this Item 12 only if you are registered or registering with the SEC and you indicated in response to Item 5.F.(2)(c) that you have regulatory assets under management of less than $25 million. You are not required to answer this Item 12 if you are filing for initial registration as a state adviser, amending a current state registration, or switching from SEC to state registration.

For purposes of this Item 12 only:

- Total Assets refers to the total assets of a firm, rather than the assets managed on behalf of *clients*. In determining your or another *person's* total assets, you may use the total assets shown on a current balance sheet (but use total assets reported on a consolidated balance sheet with subsidiaries included, if that amount is larger).

- *Control* means the power to direct or cause the direction of the management or policies of a *person*, whether through ownership of securities, by contract, or otherwise. Any *person* that directly or indirectly has the right to vote 25 percent or more of the voting securities, or is entitled to 25 percent or more of the profits, of another *person* is presumed to *control* the other *person*.

	Yes	No
A. Did you have total assets of $5 million or more on the last day of your most recent fiscal year?	☐	☐

If "yes," you do not need to answer Items 12.B. and 12.C.

B. Do you:

	Yes	No
(1) *control* another investment adviser that had regulatory assets under management (calculated in response to Item 5.F.(2)(c) of Form ADV) $25 million or more on the last day of its most recent fiscal year?	☐	☐
(2) *control* another *person* (other than a natural person) that had total assets of $5 million or more on the last day of its most recent fiscal year?	☐	☐

C. Are you:

	Yes	No
(1) *controlled* by or under common *control* with another investment adviser that had regulatory assets under management (calculated in response to Item 5.F.(2)(c) of Form ADV) of $25 million or more on the last day of its most recent fiscal year?	☐	☐
(2) *controlled* by or under common *control* with another *person* (other than a natural person) that had total assets of $5 million or more on the last day of its most recent fiscal year?	☐	☐

FORM ADV Schedule A	Your Name________ Date________	SEC File No.________ *CRD* No.________

Direct Owners and Executive Officers

1. Complete Schedule A only if you are submitting an initial application or report. Schedule A asks for information about your direct owners and executive officers. Use Schedule C to amend this information.

2. Direct Owners and Executive Officers. List below the names of:

   (a) each Chief Executive Officer, Chief Financial Officer, Chief Operations Officer, Chief Legal Officer, Chief Compliance Officer (Chief Compliance Officer is required if you are registered or applying for registration and cannot be more than one individual), director and any other individuals with similar status or functions;

   (b) if you are organized as a corporation, each shareholder that is a direct owner of 5% or more of a class of your voting securities, unless you are a public reporting company (a company subject to Section 12 or 15(d) of the Exchange Act);

   Direct owners include any *person* that owns, beneficially owns, has the right to vote, or has the power to sell or direct the sale of, 5% or more of a class of your voting securities. For purposes of this Schedule, a *person* beneficially owns any securities: (i) owned by his/her child, stepchild, grandchild, parent, stepparent, grandparent, spouse, sibling, mother-in-law, father-in-law, son-in-law, daughter-in-law, brother-in-law, or sister-in-law, sharing the same residence; or (ii) that he/she has the right to acquire, within 60 days, through the exercise of any option, warrant, or right to purchase the security.

   (c) if you are organized as a partnership, <u>all</u> general partners and those limited and special partners that have the right to receive upon dissolution, or have contributed, 5% or more of your capital;

   (d) in the case of a trust that directly owns 5% or more of a class of your voting securities, or that has the right to receive upon dissolution, or has contributed, 5% or more of your capital, the trust and each trustee; and

   (e) if you are organized as a limited liability company ("LLC"), (i) those members that have the right to receive upon dissolution, or have contributed, 5% or more of your capital, and (ii) if managed by elected managers, all elected managers.

3. Do you have any indirect owners to be reported on Schedule B? ☐ Yes ☐ No

4. In the DE/FE/I column below, enter "DE" if the owner is a domestic entity, "FE" if the owner is an entity incorporated or domiciled in a foreign country, or "I" if the owner or executive officer is an individual.

5. Complete the Title or Status column by entering board/management titles; status as partner, trustee, sole proprietor, elected manager, shareholder, or member; and for shareholders or members, the class of securities owned (if more than one is issued).

6. Ownership codes are: NA - less than 5% | A - 5% but less than 10% | B - 10% but less than 25% | C - 25% but less than 50% | D - 50% but less than 75% | E - 75% or more

7. (a) In the *Control Person* column, enter "Yes" if the *person* has *control* as defined in the Glossary of Terms to Form ADV, and enter "No" if the *person* does not have *control.* Note that under this definition, most executive officers and all 25% owners, general partners, elected managers, and trustees are *control persons*.
   (b) In the PR column, enter "PR" if the owner is a public reporting company under Sections 12 or 15(d) of the Exchange Act.
   (c) Complete each column.

FULL LEGAL NAME (Individuals: Last Name, First Name, Middle Name)	DE/FE/I	Title or Status	Date Title or Status Acquired MM	YYYY	Ownership Code	*Control Person*	PR	*CRD* No. If None: S.S. No. and Date of Birth, IRS Tax No. or Employer ID No.

FORM ADV Schedule B	Your Name____________ Date____________	SEC File No.____________ *CRD* No.____________

Indirect Owners

1. Complete Schedule B only if you are submitting an initial application or report. Schedule B asks for information about your indirect owners; you must first complete Schedule A, which asks for information about your direct owners. Use Schedule C to amend this information.

2. Indirect Owners. With respect to each owner listed on Schedule A (except individual owners), list below:

   (a) in the case of an owner that is a corporation, each of its shareholders that beneficially owns, has the right to vote, or has the power to sell or direct the sale of, 25% or more of a class of a voting security of that corporation;

   For purposes of this Schedule, a *person* beneficially owns any securities: (i) owned by his/her child, stepchild, grandchild, parent, stepparent, grandparent, spouse, sibling, mother-in-law, father-in-law, son-in-law, daughter-in-law, brother-in-law, or sister-in-law, sharing the same residence; or (ii) that he/she has the right to acquire, within 60 days, through the exercise of any option, warrant, or right to purchase the security.

   (b) in the case of an owner that is a partnership, all general partners and those limited and special partners that have the right to receive upon dissolution, or have contributed, 25% or more of the partnership's capital;

   (c) in the case of an owner that is a trust, the trust and each trustee; and

   (d) in the case of an owner that is a limited liability company ("LLC"), (i) those members that have the right to receive upon dissolution, or have contributed, 25% or more of the LLC's capital, and (ii) if managed by elected managers, all elected managers.

3. Continue up the chain of ownership listing all 25% owners at each level. Once a public reporting company (a company subject to Sections 12 or 15(d) of the Exchange Act) is reached, no further ownership information need be given.

4. In the DE/FE/I column below, enter "DE" if the owner is a domestic entity, "FE" if the owner is an entity incorporated or domiciled in a foreign country, or "I" if the owner is an individual.

5. Complete the Status column by entering the owner's status as partner, trustee, elected manager, shareholder, or member; and for shareholders or members, the class of securities owned (if more than one is issued).

6. Ownership codes are: C - 25% but less than 50% D - 50% but less than 75% E - 75% or more F - Other (general partner, trustee, or elected manager)

7. (a) In the *Control Person* column, enter "Yes" if the *person* has *control* as defined in the Glossary of Terms to Form ADV, and enter "No" if the *person* does not have *control*. Note that under this definition, most executive officers and all 25% owners, general partners, elected managers, and trustees are *control persons*.
   (b) In the PR column, enter "PR" if the owner is a public reporting company under Sections 12 or 15(d) of the Exchange Act.
   (c) Complete each column.

FULL LEGAL NAME (Individuals: Last Name, First Name, Middle Name)	DE/FE/I	Entity in Which Interest is Owned	Status	Date Status Acquired MM	YYYY	Ownership Code	Control Person	PR	CRD No. If None: S.S. No. and Date of Birth, IRS Tax No. or Employer ID No.

FORM ADV Schedule C	Your Name____________ Date____________	SEC File No.____________ *CRD* No.____________

Amendments to Schedules A and B

1. Use Schedule C only to amend information requested on either Schedule A or Schedule B. Refer to Schedule A and Schedule B for specific instructions for completing this Schedule C. Complete each column.

2. In the Type of Amendment column, indicate "A" (addition), "D" (deletion), or "C" (change in information about the same *person*).

3. Ownership codes are: NA - less than 5% | A - 5% but less than 10% | B - 10% but less than 25% | C - 25% but less than 50% | D - 50% but less than 75% | E - 75% or more | G - Other (general partner, trustee, or elected member)

4. List below all changes to Schedule A (Direct Owners and Executive Officers):

FULL LEGAL NAME (Individuals: Last Name, First Name, Middle Name)	DE/FE/I	Type of Amendment	Title or Status	Date Title or Status Acquired MM/YYYY	Ownership Code	Control Person	PR	CRD No. If None: S.S. No. and Date of Birth, IRS Tax No. or Employer ID No.

5. List below all changes to Schedule B (Indirect Owners):

FULL LEGAL NAME (Individuals: Last Name, First Name, Middle Name)	DE/FE/I	Type of Amendment	Title or Status	Date Title or Status Acquired MM/YYYY	Ownership Code	Control Person	PR	CRD No. If None: S.S. No. and Date of Birth, IRS Tax No. or Employer ID No.

FORM ADV Schedule D Page 1 of 13	Your Name____________________ Date____________________	*CRD* Number____________________ SEC 801- or 802 Number____________________

Certain items in Part 1A of Form ADV require additional information on Schedule D. Use this Schedule D to report details for items listed below. Report only new information or changes/updates to previously submitted information. Do not repeat previously submitted information.

This is an ☐ INITIAL or ☐ AMENDED Schedule D

SECTION 1.B. Other Business Names

List your other business names and the jurisdictions in which you use them. You must complete a separate Schedule D Section 1.B. for each business name.

Check only one box: ☐ Add ☐ Delete ☐ Amend

Name ____ Jurisdictions __________________________

SECTION 1.F. Other Offices

Complete the following information for each office, other than your *principal office and place of business*, at which you conduct investment advisory business. You must complete a separate Schedule D Section 1.F. for each location. If you are applying for SEC registration, if you are registered only with the SEC, or if you are an *exempt reporting adviser*, list only the largest five offices (in terms of numbers of *employees*).

Check only one box: ☐ Add ☐ Delete

____
(number and street)

____
(city) (state/country) (zip+4/postal code)

If this address is a private residence, check this box: ☐

__________________________ __________________________
(area code) (telephone number) (area code) (facsimile number)

SECTION 1.I. Website Addresses

List your website addresses. You must complete a separate Schedule D Section 1.I. for each website address.

Check only one box: ☐ Add ☐ Delete

Website Address: ____________________________________

SECTION 1.L. Location of Books and Records

Complete the following information for each location at which you keep your books and records, other than your *principal office and place of business*. You must complete a separate Schedule D Section 1.L. for each location.

Check only one box: ☐ Add ☐ Delete ☐ Amend

Name of entity where books and records are kept: ____

____
(number and street)

____
(city) (state/country) (zip+4/postal code)

If this address is a private residence, check this box: ☐

__________________________ __________________________
(area code) (telephone number) (area code) (facsimile number)

This is (check one):
☐ one of your branch offices or affiliates.
☐ a third-party unaffiliated recordkeeper.
☐ other.

Briefly describe the books and records kept at this location. ____

____

Your Name____________________ Date____________________ *CRD* Number____________________ SEC 801- or 802 Number____________________

Certain items in Part 1A of Form ADV require additional information on Schedule D. Use this Schedule D to report details for items listed below. Report only new information or changes/updates to previously submitted information. Do not repeat previously submitted information.

This is an ☐ INITIAL or ☐ AMENDED Schedule D

SECTION 1.M. Registration with *Foreign Financial Regulatory Authorities*

List the name and country, in English, of each *foreign financial regulatory authority* with which you are registered. You must complete a separate Schedule D Section 1.M. for each *foreign financial regulatory authority* with whom you are registered.

Check only one box: ☐ Add ☐ Delete

Name of *Foreign Financial Regulatory Authority* ____________________
Name of Country ____________________

SECTION 2.A.(8) Related Adviser

If you are relying on the exemption in rule 203A-2(b) from the prohibition on registration because you *control,* are *controlled* by, or are under common *control* with an investment adviser that is registered with the SEC and your *principal office and place of business* is the same as that of the registered adviser, provide the following information:

Name of Registered Investment Adviser ____________________
CRD Number of Registered Investment Adviser ____________________
SEC Number of Registered Investment Adviser 801-____________________

SECTION 2.A.(9) Newly Formed Adviser

If you are relying on rule 203A-2(c), the newly formed adviser exemption from the prohibition on registration, you are required to make certain representations about your eligibility for SEC registration. By checking the appropriate boxes, you will be deemed to have made the required representations. You must make both of these representations:

☐ I am not registered or required to be registered with the SEC or a *state securities authority* and I have a reasonable expectation that I will be eligible to register with the SEC within 120 days after the date my registration with the SEC becomes effective.

☐ I undertake to withdraw from SEC registration if, on the 120th day after my registration with the SEC becomes effective, I would be prohibited by Section 203A(a) of the Advisers Act from registering with the SEC.

SECTION 2.A.(10) Multi-State Adviser

If you are relying on rule 203A-2(d), the multi-state adviser exemption from the prohibition on registration, you are required to make certain representations about your eligibility for SEC registration. By checking the appropriate boxes, you will be deemed to have made the required representations.

If you are applying for registration as an investment adviser with the SEC, you must make both of these representations:

☐ I have reviewed the applicable state and federal laws and have concluded that I am required by the laws of 15 or more states to register as an investment adviser with the *state securities authorities* in those states.

☐ I undertake to withdraw from SEC registration if I file an amendment to this registration indicating that I would be required by the laws of fewer than 15 states to register as an investment adviser with the *state securities authorities* of those states.

If you are submitting your *annual updating amendment*, you must make this representation:

☐ Within 90 days prior to the date of filing this amendment, I have reviewed the applicable state and federal laws and have concluded that I am required by the laws of at least 15 states to register as an investment adviser with the *state securities authorities* in those states.

FORM ADV Schedule D Page 3 of 13	Your Name____________ Date____________	*CRD* Number____________ SEC 801- or 802 Number____________

Certain items in Part 1A of Form ADV require additional information on Schedule D. Use this Schedule D to report details for items listed below. Report only new information or changes/updates to previously submitted information. Do not repeat previously submitted information.

This is an ☐ INITIAL or ☐ AMENDED Schedule D

SECTION 2.A.(12) SEC Exemptive *Order*

If you are relying upon an SEC *order* exempting you from the prohibition on registration, provide the following information:

Application Number: 803-__________ Date of *order*: __________
(mm/dd/yyyy)

SECTION 2.B. *Private Fund* Assets

If you check Item 2.B.(2) or (3), what is the amount of the *private fund* assets that you manage? __________.

NOTE: "*Private fund* assets" has the same meaning here as it has under rule 203(m)-1. If you are an investment adviser with its *principal office and place of business* outside of the United States only include *private fund* assets that you manage at a place of business in the United States.

SECTION 4 Successions

Complete the following information if you are succeeding to the business of a currently registered investment adviser. If you acquired more than one firm in the succession you are reporting on this Form ADV, you must complete a separate Schedule D Section 4 for each acquired firm. See Part 1A Instruction 4.

Name of Acquired Firm ____________________

Acquired Firm's SEC File No. (if any) 801-__________ Acquired Firm's *CRD* Number (if any) __________

SECTION 5.G.(3) Advisers to Registered Investment Companies and Business Development Companies

If you check Item 5.G (3), what is the SEC file number (811 or 814 number) of each of the registered investment companies and business development companies to which you act as an adviser pursuant to an advisory contract? You must complete a separate Schedule D Section 5.G.(3) for each registered investment company and business development company to which you act as an adviser.

Check only one box: ☐ Add ☐ Delete

SEC File Number 811- or 814-__________

SECTION 5.I.(2) *Wrap Fee Programs*

If you are a portfolio manager for one or more *wrap fee programs*, list the name of each program and its *sponsor*. You must complete a separate Schedule D Section 5.I.(2) for each *wrap fee program* for which you are a portfolio manager.

Check only one box: ☐ Add ☐ Delete ☐ Amend

Name of *Wrap Fee Program* ____________________

Name of *Sponsor* ____________________

Your Name____________________ *CRD* Number____________________
Date____________________ SEC 801- or 802 Number____________________

Certain items in Part 1A of Form ADV require additional information on Schedule D. Use this Schedule D to report details for items listed below. Report only new information or changes/updates to previously submitted information. Do not repeat previously submitted information.

This is an ☐ INITIAL or ☐ AMENDED Schedule D

SECTION 6.A. Names of Your Other Businesses

If you are actively engaged in other business using a different name, provide that name and the other line(s) of business.

☐ Add ☐ Delete ☐ Amend

Other Business Name: ____

Other line(s) of business in which you engage using this name: (check all that apply)

☐ (1) broker-dealer (registered or unregistered)
☐ (2) registered representative of a broker-dealer
☐ (3) commodity pool operator or commodity trading advisor (whether registered or exempt from registration)
☐ (4) futures commission merchant
☐ (5) real estate broker, dealer, or agent
☐ (6) insurance broker or agent
☐ (7) bank (including a separately identifiable department or division of a bank)
☐ (8) trust company
☐ (9) registered municipal advisor
☐ (10) registered security-based swap dealer
☐ (11) major security-based swap participant
☐ (12) accountant or accounting firm
☐ (13) lawyer or law firm
☐ (14) other financial product salesperson (specify): ____________________________

SECTION 6.B.(2) Description of Primary Business

Describe your primary business (not your investment advisory business):

If you engage in that business under a different name, provide that name:

SECTION 6.B.(3) Description of Other Products and Services

Describe other products or services you sell to your client. You may omit products and services that you listed in Section 6.B.2. above.

If you engage in that business under a different name, provide that name:

SECTION 7.A. Financial Industry Affiliations

Complete a separate Schedule D Section 7.A. for each *related person* listed in Item 7.A.

Check only one box: ☐ Add ☐ Delete ☐ Amend

FORM ADV Schedule D Page 5 of 13	Your Name____________________ Date____________________	*CRD* Number____________________ SEC 801- or 802 Number____________________

Certain items in Part 1A of Form ADV require additional information on Schedule D. Use this Schedule D to report details for items listed below. Report only new information or changes/updates to previously submitted information. Do not repeat previously submitted information.

This is an ☐ INITIAL or ☐ AMENDED Schedule D

1. Legal Name of *Related Person*: ____

2. Primary Business Name of *Related Person*: ____

3. *Related Person*'s SEC File Number (if any) (*e.g.*, 801-, 8-, 866-, 802-) ________________

4. *Related Person's CRD* Number (if any): ____________

5. *Related Person* is: (check all that apply)

   ☐ (a) broker-dealer, municipal securities dealer, or government securities broker or dealer
   ☐ (b) other investment adviser (including financial planners)
   ☐ (c) registered municipal advisor
   ☐ (d) registered security-based swap dealer
   ☐ (e) major security-based swap participant
   ☐ (f) commodity pool operator or commodity trading advisor (whether registered or exempt from registration)
   ☐ (g) futures commission merchant
   ☐ (h) banking or thrift institution
   ☐ (i) trust company
   ☐ (j) accountant or accounting firm
   ☐ (k) lawyer or law firm
   ☐ (l) insurance company or agency
   ☐ (m) pension consultant
   ☐ (n) real estate broker or dealer
   ☐ (o) sponsor or syndicator of limited partnerships (or equivalent), excluding pooled investment vehicles
   ☐ (p) sponsor, general partner, managing member (or equivalent) of pooled investment vehicles

6. Do you *control* or are you *controlled* by the *related person*? ☐ Yes ☐ No

7. Are you and the *related person* under common *control*? ☐ Yes ☐ No

8. (a) Does the *related person* act as a qualified custodian for your *clients* in connection with advisory services you provide to *clients*? ☐ Yes ☐ No

   (b) If you are registering or registered with the SEC and you have answered "yes" to question 8.(a) above, have you overcome the presumption that you are not operationally independent (pursuant to rule 206(4)-(2)(d)(5)) from the *related person* and thus are not required to obtain a surprise examination for your *clients'* funds or securities that are maintained at the *related person*?

   ☐ Yes ☐ No

   (c) If you have answered "yes" to question 8.(a) above, provide the location of the *related person*'s office responsible for *custody* of your *clients'* assets:

   ____
   (number and street)

   ____
   (city) (state/country) (zip+4/postal code)

9. (a) If the *related person* is an investment adviser, is it exempt from registration? ☐ Yes ☐ No

   (b) If the answer is yes, under what exemption? ______

10. (a) Is the *related person* registered with a *foreign financial regulatory authority?* ☐ Yes ☐ No

    (b) If the answer is yes, list the name and country, in English, of each *foreign financial regulatory authority* with which the *related person* is registered. ______________________________

11. Do you and the *related person* share any *supervised persons*? ☐ Yes ☐ No

FORM ADV Schedule D Page 6 of 13	Your Name____________________ Date____________________	*CRD* Number____________________ SEC 801- or 802 Number____________________

Certain items in Part 1A of Form ADV require additional information on Schedule D. Use this Schedule D to report details for items listed below. Report only new information or changes/updates to previously submitted information. Do not repeat previously submitted information.

This is an ☐ INITIAL or ☐ AMENDED Schedule D

12. Do you and the *related person* share the same physical location? ☐ Yes ☐ No

---

SECTION 7.B.(1) *Private Fund* Reporting

Check only one box: ☐ Add ☐ Delete ☐ Amend

A. PRIVATE FUND

Information About the *Private Fund*

1. (a) Name of the *private fund*: __________________

   (b) *Private fund* identification number: __________________

2. Under the laws of what state or country is the *private fund* organized: _______________________

3. Name(s) of General Partner, Manager, Trustee, or Directors (or persons serving in a similar capacity):

   Check only one box: ☐ Add ☐ Delete ☐ Amend

   ____

4. The *private fund* (check all that apply; you must check at least one):

   ☐ (1) qualifies for the exclusion from the definition of investment company under section 3(c)(1) of the Investment Company Act of 1940

   ☐ (2) qualifies for the exclusion from the definition of investment company under section 3(c)(7) of the Investment Company Act of 1940

5. List the name and country, in English, of each *foreign financial regulatory authority* with which the *private fund* is registered.

   Check only one box: ☐ Add ☐ Delete ☐ Amend

   English Name of *Foreign Financial Regulatory Authority* ______________ Name of Country ______________

6. (a) Is this a "master fund" in a master-feeder arrangement? ☐ Yes ☐ No

   (b) If yes, what is the name and *private fund* identification number (if any) of the feeder funds investing in this *private fund*?

   Check only one box: ☐ Add ☐ Delete ☐ Amend

   ________ ________

   (c) Is this a "feeder fund" in a master-feeder arrangement? ☐ Yes ☐ No

   (d) If yes, what is the name and *private fund* identification number (if any) of the master fund in which this *private fund* invests?

   Check only one box: ☐ Add ☐ Delete ☐ Amend

   ________ ________

   NOTE: You must complete question 6 for each master-feeder arrangement regardless of whether you are filing a single Schedule D, Section 7.B.(1) for the master-feeder arrangement or reporting on the funds separately.

FORM ADV Schedule D Page 7 of 13	Your Name____________________ Date____________________	*CRD* Number____________________ SEC 801- or 802 Number____________________

Certain items in Part 1A of Form ADV require additional information on Schedule D. Use this Schedule D to report details for items listed below. Report only new information or changes/updates to previously submitted information. Do not repeat previously submitted information.

This is an ☐ INITIAL or ☐ AMENDED Schedule D

7. If you are filing a single Schedule D, Section 7.B.(1) for a master-feeder arrangement according to the instructions to this Section 7.B.(1), for each of the feeder funds answer the following questions:

   Check only one box: ☐ Add ☐ Delete ☐ Amend

   (a) Name of the *private fund*: ___________

   (b) *Private fund* identification number: _______________

   (c) Under the laws of what state or country is the *private fund* organized: ___________________

   (d) Name(s) of General Partner, Manager, Trustee, or Directors (or persons serving in a similar capacity):

   Check only one box: ☐ Add ☐ Delete ☐ Amend

   ____

   (e) The *private fund* (check all that apply; you must check at least one):

   ☐ (1) qualifies for the exclusion from the definition of investment company under section 3(c)(1) of the Investment Company Act of 1940

   ☐ (2) qualifies for the exclusion from the definition of investment company under section 3(c)(7) of the Investment Company Act of 1940

   (f) List the name and country, in English, of each *foreign financial regulatory authority* with which the *private fund* is registered.

   Check only one box: ☐ Add ☐ Delete ☐ Amend

   English Name of *Foreign Financial Regulatory Authority* ______________ Name of Country ______________

   NOTE: For purposes of questions 6 and 7, in a master-feeder arrangement, one or more funds ("feeder funds") invest all or substantially all of their assets in a single fund ("master fund"). A fund would also be a "feeder fund" investing in a "master fund" for purposes of this question if it issued multiple classes (or series) of shares or interests, and each class (or series) invests substantially all of its assets in a single master fund.

8. (a) Is this *private fund* a "fund of funds"? ☐ Yes ☐ No

   (b) If yes, does the *private fund* invest in funds managed by you or by a *related person?* ☐ Yes ☐ No

   NOTE: For purposes of this question only, answer "yes" if the fund invests 10 percent or more of its total assets in other pooled investment vehicles, whether or not they are also *private funds*, or registered investment companies.

9. During your last fiscal year, did the *private fund* invest in securities issued by investment companies registered under the Investment Company Act of 1940 (other than "money market funds," to the extent provided in Instruction 6.e.)? ☐ Yes ☐ No

10. What type of fund is the *private fund*?

    ☐ hedge fund ☐ liquidity fund ☐ private equity fund ☐ real estate fund ☐ securitized asset fund ☐ venture capital fund

    ☐Other *private fund*: ____________

    NOTE: For funds of funds, refer to the funds in which the *private fund* invests. For definitions of these fund types, please see Instruction 6 of the Instructions to Part 1A.

11. Current gross asset value of the *private fund*: $_____

Certain items in Part 1A of Form ADV require additional information on Schedule D. Use this Schedule D to report details for items listed below. Report only new information or changes/updates to previously submitted information. Do not repeat previously submitted information.

This is an ☐ INITIAL or ☐ AMENDED Schedule D

Ownership

12. Minimum investment commitment required of an investor in the *private fund*: $____________

    NOTE: Report the amount routinely required of investors who are not your *related persons* (even if different from the amount set forth in the organizational documents of the fund).

13. Approximate number of the *private fund*'s beneficial owners: ____

14. What is the approximate percentage of the *private fund* beneficially owned by you and your *related persons*:

    _____%

15. What is the approximate percentage of the *private fund* beneficially owned (in the aggregate) by funds of funds:

    _____%

16. What is the approximate percentage of the *private fund* beneficially owned by *non-United States persons*:

    _____%

Your Advisory Services

17. (a) Are you a subadviser to this *private fund*? ☐ Yes ☐ No

    (b) If the answer to question 17(a) is "yes," provide the name and SEC file number, if any, of the adviser of the *private fund*. If the answer to question 17(a) is "no," leave this question blank. ____________

18. (a) Do any other investment advisers advise the *private fund*? ☐ Yes ☐ No

    (b) If the answer to question 18(a) is "yes," provide the name and SEC file number, if any, of the other advisers to the *private fund*. If the answer to question 18(a) is "no," leave this question blank.

    Check only one box: ☐ Add ☐ Delete ☐ Amend

    ____________ ____________

19. Are your *clients* solicited to invest in the *private fund*? ☐ Yes ☐ No

20. Approximately what percentage of your *clients* has invested in the *private fund*? _____%

Private Offering

21. Does the *private fund* rely on an exemption from registration of its securities under Regulation D of the Securities Act of 1933? ☐ Yes ☐ No

22. If yes, provide the *private fund*'s Form D file number (if any):

    Check only one box: ☐ Add ☐ Delete ☐ Amend

    021-____________

FORM ADV Schedule D Page 9 of 13	Your Name____________________ Date____________________	*CRD* Number____________________ SEC 801- or 802 Number____________________

Certain items in Part 1A of Form ADV require additional information on Schedule D. Use this Schedule D to report details for items listed below. Report only new information or changes/updates to previously submitted information. Do not repeat previously submitted information.

This is an ☐ INITIAL or ☐ AMENDED Schedule D

B. SERVICE PROVIDERS

☐ Check this box if you are filing this Form ADV through the IARD system and want the IARD system to create a new Schedule D, Section 7.B.(1) with the same service provider information you have given here in Questions 23 - 28 for a new *private fund* for which you are required to complete Section 7.B.(1) If you check the box, the system will pre-fill those fields for you, but you will be able to manually edit the information after it is pre-filled and before you submit your filing.

Auditors

23. (a) (1) Are the *private fund*'s financial statements subject to an annual audit? ☐ Yes ☐ No

(2) Are the financial statements prepared in accordance with U.S. GAAP? ☐ Yes ☐ No

If the answer to 23(a)(1) is "yes," respond to questions (b) through (f) below. If the *private fund* uses more than one auditing firm, you must complete questions (b) through (f) separately for each auditing firm.

Check only one box: ☐ Add ☐ Delete ☐ Amend

(b) Name of the auditing firm: ____

(c) The location of the auditing firm's office responsible for the *private fund's* audit (city, state and country): _______________

(d) Is the auditing firm an *independent public accountant*? ☐ Yes ☐ No

(e) Is the auditing firm registered with the Public Company Accounting Oversight Board? ☐ Yes ☐ No

(f) If "yes" to (e) above, is the auditing firm subject to regular inspection by the Public Company Accounting Oversight Board in accordance with its rules? ☐ Yes ☐ No

(g) Are the *private fund*'s audited financial statements distributed to the *private fund*'s investors? ☐ Yes ☐ No

(h) Does the report prepared by the auditing firm contain an unqualified opinion? ☐ Yes ☐ No ☐ Report Not Yet Received

If you check "Report Not Yet Received," you must promptly file an amendment to your Form ADV to update your response when the report is available.

Prime Broker

24. (a) Does the *private fund* use one or more prime brokers? ☐ Yes ☐ No

If the answer to 24(a) is "yes," respond to questions (b) through (e) below for each prime broker the *private fund* uses. If the *private fund* uses more than one prime broker, you must complete questions (b) through (e) separately for each prime broker.

Check only one box: ☐ Add ☐ Delete ☐ Amend

(b) Name of the prime broker: __________

(c) If the prime broker is registered with the SEC, its registration number: 8-____________

(d) Location of prime broker's office used principally by the *private fund* (city, state and country):

____

(e) Does this prime broker act as custodian for some or all of the *private fund*'s assets? ☐ Yes ☐ No

Custodian

25. (a) Does the *private fund* use any custodians (including the prime brokers listed above) to hold some or all of its assets? ☐ Yes ☐ No

If the answer to 25(a) is "yes," respond to questions (b) through (f) below for each custodian the *private fund* uses. If the *private fund* uses more than one custodian, you must complete questions (b) through (f) separately for each custodian.

Certain items in Part 1A of Form ADV require additional information on Schedule D. Use this Schedule D to report details for items listed below. Report only new information or changes/updates to previously submitted information. Do not repeat previously submitted information.

This is an ☐ INITIAL or ☐ AMENDED Schedule D

Check only one box: ☐ Add ☐ Delete ☐ Amend

(b) Legal name of custodian: __________

(c) Primary business name of custodian: __________

(d) The location of the custodian's office responsible for *custody* of the *private fund*'s assets (city, state and country): __________

(e) Is the custodian a *related person* of your firm? ☐ Yes ☐ No

(f) If the custodian is a broker-dealer, provide its SEC registration number (if any) 8-__________

Administrator

26. (a) Does the *private fund* use an administrator other than your firm? ☐ Yes ☐ No

If the answer to 26(a) is "yes," respond to questions (b) through (f) below. If the *private fund* uses more than one administrator, you must complete questions (b) through (f) separately for each administrator.

Check only one box: ☐ Add ☐ Delete ☐ Amend

(b) Name of administrator: __________

(c) Location of administrator (city, state and country): __________

(d) Is the administrator a *related person* of your firm? ☐ Yes ☐ No

(e) Does the administrator prepare and send investor account statements to the *private fund*'s investors?

☐ Yes (provided to all investors) ☐ Some (provided to some but not all investors) ☐ No (provided to no investors)

(f) If the answer to 26(e) is "no" or "some," who sends the investor account statements to the (rest of the) *private fund*'s investors? If investor account statements are not sent to the (rest of the) private fund's investors, respond "not applicable."

__________.

27. During your last fiscal year, what percentage of the *private fund*'s assets (by value) was valued by a *person*, such as an administrator, that is not your *related person*?

__________%

Include only those assets where (i) such person carried out the valuation procedure established for that asset, if any, including obtaining any relevant quotes, and (ii) the valuation used for purposes of investor subscriptions, redemptions or distributions, and fee calculations (including allocations) was the valuation determined by such person.

Marketers

28. (a) Does the *private fund* use the services of someone other than you or your *employees* for marketing purposes? ☐ Yes ☐ No

You must answer "yes" whether the person acts as a placement agent, consultant, finder, introducer, municipal advisor or other solicitor, or similar person. If the answer to 28(a) is "yes", respond to questions (b) through (g) below for each such marketer the *private fund* uses. If the *private fund* uses more than one marketer, you must complete questions (b) through (g) separately for each marketer.

Check only one box: ☐ Add ☐ Delete ☐ Amend

Certain items in Part 1A of Form ADV require additional information on Schedule D. Use this Schedule D to report details for items listed below. Report only new information or changes/updates to previously submitted information. Do not repeat previously submitted information.

This is an ☐ INITIAL or ☐ AMENDED Schedule D

(b) Is the marketer a *related person* of your firm? ☐ Yes ☐ No

(c) Name of the marketer: ______________________________

(d) If the marketer is registered with the SEC, its file number (*e.g.*, 801-, 8-, or 866-): ____________ and *CRD* Number (if any) ____________

(e) Location of the marketer's office used principally by the *private fund* (city, state and country): ______________________________

(f) Does the marketer market the *private fund* through one or more websites? ☐ Yes ☐ No

(g) If the answer to 28(f) is "yes," list the website address(es): __________

SECTION 7.B.(2) *Private Fund* Reporting

(1) Name of the *private fund* ______________________

(2) *Private fund* identification number ____________

(3) Name and SEC File number of adviser that provides information about this *private fund* in Section 7.B.(1) of Schedule D of its Form ADV filing ________________________, 801- ____________ or 802-____________

(4) Are your *clients* solicited to invest in this *private fund*? ☐ Yes ☐ No

In answering this question, disregard feeder funds' investment in a master fund. For purposes of this question, in a master-feeder arrangement, one or more funds ("feeder funds") invest all or substantially all of their assets in a single fund ("master fund"). A fund would also be a "feeder fund" investing in a "master fund" for purposes of this question if it issued multiple classes (or series) of shares or interests, and each class (or series) invests substantially all of its assets in a single master fund.

SECTION 9.C. *Independent Public Accountant*

You must complete the following information for each *independent public accountant* engaged to perform a surprise examination, perform an audit of a pooled investment vehicle that you manage, or prepare an internal control report. You must complete a separate Schedule D Section 9.C. for each *independent public accountant*.

Check only one box: ☐ Add ☐ Delete ☐ Amend

(1) Name of the *independent public accountant*: ______________________________

(2) The location of the *independent public accountant*'s office responsible for the services provided:

____

(number and street)

____

(city) (state/country) (zip+4/postal code)

(3) Is the *independent public accountant* registered with the Public Company Accounting Oversight Board? ☐ Yes ☐ No

(4) If yes to (3) above, is the *independent public accountant* subject to regular inspection by the Public Company Accounting Oversight Board in accordance with its rules? ☐ Yes ☐ No

(5) The *independent public accountant* is engaged to:

Your Name________________ *CRD* Number________________
Date________________ SEC 801- or 802 Number________________

Certain items in Part 1A of Form ADV require additional information on Schedule D. Use this Schedule D to report details for items listed below. Report only new information or changes/updates to previously submitted information. Do not repeat previously submitted information.

This is an ☐ INITIAL or ☐ AMENDED Schedule D

A. ☐ audit a pooled investment vehicle
B. ☐ perform a surprise examination of *clients'* assets
C. ☐ prepare an internal control report

(6) Does any report prepared by the *independent public accountant* that audited the pooled investment vehicle or that examined internal controls contain an unqualified opinion? ☐ Yes ☐ No ☐ Report Not Yet Received

If you check "Report Not Yet Received," you must promptly file an amendment to your Form ADV to update your response when the accountant's report is available.

SECTION 10.A. *Control Persons*

You must complete a separate Schedule D Section 10.A. for each *control person* not named in Item 1.A. or Schedules A, B, or C that directly or indirectly *controls* your management or policies.

Check only one box: ☐ Add ☐ Delete ☐ Amend

(1) Firm or Organization Name

____

(2) *CRD* Number (if any) ____________ Effective Date __________ (mm/dd/yyyy) Termination Date __________ (mm/dd/yyyy)

(3) Business Address:

____
(number and street)

____
(city) (state/country) (zip+4/postal code)

If this address is a private residence, check this box: ☐

(4) Individual Name (if applicable) (Last, First, Middle)

____

(5) *CRD* Number (if any) ____________ Effective Date __________ (mm/dd/yyyy) Termination Date __________ (mm/dd/yyyy)

(6) Business Address:

____
(number and street)

____
(city) (state/country) (zip+4/postal code)

If this address is a private residence, check this box: ☐

(7) Briefly describe the nature of the *control*:

____

SECTION 10.B. *Control Person* Public Reporting Companies

If any person named in Schedules A, B, or C, or in Section 10 A. of Schedule D is a public reporting company under Sections 12 or 15(d) of the Securities Exchange Act of 1934 , please provide the following information (you must complete a separate Schedule D Section 10.B. for each public reporting company):

FORM ADV Schedule D Page 13 of 13	Your Name__________________ Date__________________	*CRD* Number__________________ SEC 801- or 802 Number__________________

Certain items in Part 1A of Form ADV require additional information on Schedule D. Use this Schedule D to report details for items listed below. Report only new information or changes/updates to previously submitted information. Do not repeat previously submitted information.

This is an ☐ INITIAL or ☐ AMENDED Schedule D

(1) Full legal name of the public reporting company: __________________________________

(2) The public reporting company's CIK number (Central Index Key number that the SEC assigns to each reporting company): ____________________

Miscellaneous

You may use the space below to explain a response to an Item or to provide any other information.

CRIMINAL DISCLOSURE REPORTING PAGE (ADV)

GENERAL INSTRUCTIONS
This Disclosure Reporting Page (DRP ADV) is an ☐ INITIAL ***OR*** ☐ AMENDED response used to report details for affirmative responses to Items 11.A. or 11.B. of Form ADV.
Check item(s) being responded to: ☐ 11.A(1) ☐ 11.A(2) ☐11.B(1) ☐11.B(2)
Use a separate DRP for each event or *proceeding*. The same event or *proceeding* may be reported for more than one *person* or entity using one DRP. File with a completed Execution Page.
Multiple counts of the same charge arising out of the same event(s) should be reported on the same DRP. Unrelated criminal actions, including separate cases arising out of the same event, must be reported on separate DRPs. Use this DRP to report all charges arising out of the same event. One event may result in more than one affirmative answer to the items listed above.

PART I

A. The *person(s)* or entity(ies) for whom this DRP is being filed is (are):
☐ You (the advisory firm)
☐ You and one or more of your *advisory affiliates*
☐ One or more of your *advisory affiliates*

If this DRP is being filed for an *advisory affiliate*, give the full name of the *advisory affiliate* below (for individuals, Last name, First name, Middle name).

If the *advisory affiliate* has a *CRD* number, provide that number. If not, indicate "non-registered" by checking the appropriate box.

Your Name	Your *CRD* Number

ADV DRP - *ADVISORY AFFILIATE*

CRD Number	This *advisory affiliate* is	☐a firm ☐an individual
	Registered:	☐Yes ☐No

Name (For individuals, Last, First, Middle)

☐ This DRP should be removed from the ADV record because the *advisory affiliate(s)* is no longer associated with the adviser.

☐ This DRP should be removed from the ADV record because: (1) the event or *proceeding* occurred more than ten years ago or (2) the adviser is registered or applying for registration with the SEC and the event was resolved in the adviser's or *advisory affiliate's* favor.

☐ This DRP should be removed from the ADV record because it was filed in error, such as due to a clerical or data-entry mistake. Explain the circumstances:

____

____

____

B. If the *advisory affiliate* is registered through the IARD system or *CRD* system, has the *advisory affiliate* submitted a DRP (with Form ADV, BD or U-4) to the IARD or *CRD* for the event? If the answer is "Yes," no other information on this DRP must be provided.
☐ Yes ☐ No

NOTE: The completion of this form does not relieve the *advisory affiliate* of its obligation to update its IARD or *CRD* records.

(continued)

CRIMINAL DISCLOSURE REPORTING PAGE (ADV)
(continuation)

PART II

1. If charge(s) were brought against an organization over which you or an *advisory affiliate* exercise(d) *control*: Enter organization name, whether or not the organization was an *investment-related* business and your or the *advisory affiliate's* position, title, or relationship.

2. Formal Charge(s) were brought in: (include name of Federal, Military, State or Foreign Court, Location of Court - City or County <u>and</u> State or Country, Docket/Case number).

3. Event Disclosure Detail (Use this for both organizational and individual charges.)

   A. Date First *Charged* (MM/DD/YYYY): ☐ Exact ☐ Explanation

   If not exact, provide explanation: ______

   B. Event Disclosure Detail (include Charge(s)/Charge Description(s), and for each charge provide: (1) number of counts, (2) *felony* or *misdemeanor*, (3) plea for each charge, and (4) product type if charge is *investment-related*).

   C. Did any of the Charge(s) within the Event involve a *felony*? ☐ Yes ☐ No

   D. Current status of the Event? ☐ Pending ☐ On Appeal ☐ Final

   E. Event Status Date (complete unless status is Pending) (MM/DD/YYYY):

   ☐ Exact ☐ Explanation

   If not exact, provide explanation: ______

4. Disposition Disclosure Detail: Include for each charge (a) Disposition Type (e.g., convicted, acquitted, dismissed, pretrial, etc.), (b) Date, (c) Sentence/Penalty, (d) Duration (if sentence-suspension, probation, etc.), (e) Start Date of Penalty, (f) Penalty/Fine Amount, and (g) Date Paid.

(continued)

CRIMINAL DISCLOSURE REPORTING PAGE (ADV)
(continuation)

5. Provide a brief summary of circumstances leading to the charge(s) as well as the disposition. Include the relevant dates when the conduct which was the subject of the charge(s) occurred. (Your response must fit within the space provided.)

REGULATORY ACTION DISCLOSURE REPORTING PAGE (ADV)

GENERAL INSTRUCTIONS

This Disclosure Reporting Page (DRP ADV) is an ☐ INITIAL ***OR*** ☐ AMENDED response used to report details for affirmative responses to Items 11.C., 11.D., 11.E., 11.F. or 11.G. of Form ADV.

Check item(s) being responded to:

☐ 11.C(1)	☐ 11.C(2)	☐ 11.C(3)	☐ 11.C(4)	☐ 11.C(5)
☐ 11.D(1)	☐ 11.D(2)	☐ 11.D(3)	☐ 11.D(4)	☐ 11.D(5)
☐ 11.E(1)	☐ 11.E(2)	☐ 11.E(3)	☐ 11.E(4)	
☐ 11.F.	☐ 11.G.			

Use a separate DRP for each event or *proceeding*. The same event or *proceeding* may be reported for more than one *person* or entity using one DRP. File with a completed Execution Page.

One event may result in more than one affirmative answer to Items 11.C., 11.D., 11.E., 11.F. or 11.G. Use only one DRP to report details related to the same event. If an event gives rise to actions by more than one regulator, provide details for each action on a separate DRP.

PART I

A. The *person(s)* or entity(ies) for whom this DRP is being filed is (are):
☐ You (the advisory firm)
☐ You and one or more of your *advisory affiliates*
☐ One or more of your *advisory affiliates*

If this DRP is being filed for an *advisory affiliate*, give the full name of the *advisory affiliate* below (for individuals, Last name, First name, Middle name).

If the *advisory affiliate* has a *CRD* number, provide that number. If not, indicate "non-registered" by checking the appropriate box.

Your Name	Your *CRD* Number

ADV DRP - *ADVISORY AFFILIATE*

CRD Number	This *advisory affiliate* is ☐ a firm ☐ an individual Registered: ☐ Yes ☐ No

Name (For individuals, Last, First, Middle)

☐ This DRP should be removed from the ADV record because the *advisory affiliate(s)* is no longer associated with the adviser.

☐ This DRP should be removed from the ADV record because: (1) the event or *proceeding* occurred more than ten years ago or (2) the adviser is registered or applying for registration with the SEC and the event was resolved in the adviser's or *advisory affiliate's* favor.

If you are registered or registering with a *state securities authority*, you may remove a DRP for an event you reported only in response to Item 11.D(4), and only if that event occurred more than ten years ago. If you are registered or registering with the SEC, you may remove a DRP for any event listed in Item 11 that occurred more than ten years ago.

☐ This DRP should be removed from the ADV record because it was filed in error, such as due to a clerical or data-entry mistake. Explain the circumstances:

____

____

B. If the *advisory affiliate* is registered through the IARD system or *CRD* system, has the *advisory affiliate* submitted a DRP (with Form ADV, BD or U-4) to the IARD or *CRD* for the event? If the answer is "Yes," no other information on this DRP must be provided.
☐ Yes ☐ No

NOTE: The completion of this form does not relieve the *advisory affiliate* of its obligation to update its IARD or *CRD* records.

(continued)

SEC 1707 (09-11)
File 2 of 4

REGULATORY ACTION DISCLOSURE REPORTING PAGE (ADV)
(continuation)

PART II

1. Regulatory Action initiated by:
☐ SEC ☐ Other Federal ☐ State ☐ *SRO* ☐ Foreign

(Full name of regulator, *foreign financial regulatory authority*, federal, state or *SRO*)

____

2. Principal Sanction (check appropriate item):

☐ Civil and Administrative Penalty(ies)/Fine(s)
☐ Bar
☐ Cease and Desist
☐ Censure
☐ Denial
☐ Disgorgement
☐ Expulsion
☐ Injunction
☐ Prohibition
☐ Reprimand
☐ Restitution
☐ Revocation
☐ Suspension
☐ Undertaking
☐ Other ____________

Other Sanctions:

____
____
____

3. Date Initiated (MM/DD/YYYY): ☐ Exact ☐ Explanation

If not exact, provide explanation: ____

4. Docket/Case Number:

5. *Advisory Affiliate* Employing Firm when activity occurred which led to the regulatory action (if applicable):

6. Principal Product Type (check appropriate item):

☐Annuity(ies) - Fixed
☐Annuity(ies) - Variable
☐CD(s)
☐Commodity Option(s)
☐Debt - Asset Backed
☐Debt - Corporate
☐Debt - Government
☐Debt - Municipal
☐Derivative(s)
☐Direct Investment(s) - DPP & LP Interest(s)
☐Equity - OTC
☐Equity Listed (Common & Preferred Stock)
☐Futures - Commodity
☐Futures - Financial
☐Index Option(s)
☐Insurance
☐Investment Contract(s)
☐Money Market Fund(s)
☐Mutual Fund(s)
☐No Product
☐Options
☐Penny Stock(s)
☐Unit Investment Trust(s)
☐Other ____________

Other Product Types:

____
____

(continued)

REGULATORY ACTION DISCLOSURE REPORTING PAGE (ADV)
(continuation)

7. Describe the allegations related to this regulatory action (your response must fit within the space provided):

8. Current status? ☐ Pending ☐ On Appeal ☐ Final

9. If on appeal, regulatory action appealed to (SEC, *SRO*, Federal or State Court) and Date Appeal Filed:

If Final or On Appeal, complete all items below. For Pending Actions, complete Item 13 only.

10. How was matter resolved (check appropriate item):

☐Acceptance, Waiver & Consent (AWC)
☐Consent
☐Decision
☐Decision & *Order* of Offer of Settlement
☐Dismissed
☐*Order*
☐Settled
☐Stipulation and Consent
☐Vacated
☐Withdrawn
☐Other ____________

11. Resolution Date (MM/DD/YYYY): ☐ Exact ☐ Explanation

If not exact, provide explanation: ____________________

12. Resolution Detail:

A. Were any of the following Sanctions *Ordered* (check all appropriate items)?

☐ Monetary/Fine ☐ Revocation/Expulsion/Denial ☐ Disgorgement/Restitution

Amount: $ ☐Censure ☐ Cease and Desist/Injunction ☐ Bar ☐ Suspension

B. Other Sanctions *Ordered*:

Sanction detail: if suspended, *enjoined* or barred, provide duration including start date and capacities affected (General Securities Principal, Financial Operations Principal, etc.). If requalification by exam/retraining was a condition of the sanction, provide length of time given to requalify/retrain, type of exam required and whether condition has been satisfied. If disposition resulted in a fine, penalty, restitution, disgorgement or monetary compensation, provide total amount, portion levied against you or an *advisory affiliate*, date paid and if any portion of penalty was waived:

(continued)

REGULATORY ACTION DISCLOSURE REPORTING PAGE (ADV)

(continuation)

13. Provide a brief summary of details related to the action status and (or) disposition and include relevant terms, conditions and dates (your response must fit within the space provided).

CIVIL JUDICIAL ACTION DISCLOSURE REPORTING PAGE (ADV)

GENERAL INSTRUCTIONS

This Disclosure Reporting Page (DRP ADV) is an ☐ INITIAL ***OR*** ☐ AMENDED response used to report details for affirmative responses to Item 11.H. of Part 1A and Item 2.F. of Part 1B of Form ADV.

Check Part 1A item(s) being responded to: ☐ 11.H(1)(a) ☐ 11.H(1)(b) ☐ 11.H(1)(c) ☐ 11.H(2)
Check Part 1B item(s) being responded to: ☐ 2.F(1) ☐ 2.F(2) ☐ 2.F(3) ☐ 2.F(4) ☐ 2.F(5)

Use a separate DRP for each event or *proceeding*. The same event or *proceeding* may be reported for more than one *person* or entity using one DRP. File with a completed Execution Page.

One event may result in more than one affirmative answer to Item 11.H. of Part 1A or Item 2.F. of Part 1B. Use only one DRP to report details related to the same event. Unrelated civil judicial actions must be reported on separate DRPs.

PART I

A. The *person(s)* or entity(ies) for whom this DRP is being filed is (are):
☐ You (the advisory firm)
☐ You and one or more of your *advisory affiliates*
☐ One or more of your *advisory affiliates*

If this DRP is being filed for an *advisory affiliate*, give the full name of the *advisory affiliate* below (for individuals, Last name, First name, Middle name).

If the *advisory affiliate* has a *CRD* number, provide that number. If not, indicate "non-registered" by checking the appropriate box.

Your Name	Your *CRD* Number

ADV DRP - *ADVISORY AFFILIATE*

CRD Number	This *advisory affiliate* is Registered:	☐ a firm ☐ Yes	☐ an individual ☐ No

Name (For individuals, Last, First, Middle)

☐ This DRP should be removed from the ADV record because the *advisory affiliate(s)* is no longer associated with the adviser.

☐ This DRP should be removed from the ADV record because: (1) the event or *proceeding* occurred more than ten years ago or (2) the adviser is registered or applying for registration with the SEC and the event was resolved in the adviser's or advisory affiliate's favor.

If you are registered or registering with a *state securities authority*, you may remove a DRP for an event you reported only in response to Item 11.H.(1)(a), and only if that event occurred more than ten years ago. If you are registered or registering with the SEC, you may remove a DRP for any event listed in Item 11 that occurred more than ten years ago.

☐ This DRP should be removed from the ADV record because it was filed in error, such as due to a clerical or data-entry mistake. Explain the circumstances:

B. If the *advisory affiliate* is registered through the IARD system or *CRD* system, has the *advisory affiliate* submitted a DRP (with Form ADV, BD or U-4) to the IARD or *CRD* for the event? If the answer is "Yes," no other information on this DRP must be provided.
☐ Yes ☐ No

NOTE: The completion of this form does not relieve the *advisory affiliate* of its obligation to update its IARD or *CRD* records.

(continued)

SEC 1707 (09-11)
File 2 of 4

CIVIL JUDICIAL ACTION DISCLOSURE REPORTING PAGE (ADV)
(continuation)

PART II

1. Court Action initiated by: (Name of regulator, *foreign financial regulatory authority, SRO*, commodities exchange, agency, firm, private plaintiff, etc.)

2. Principal Relief Sought (check appropriate item):

☐Cease and Desist ☐Disgorgement ☐Money Damages (Private/Civil Complaint) ☐Restraining Order
☐Civil Penalty(ies)/Fine(s) ☐Injunction ☐Restitution ☐Other ________

Other Relief Sought:

3. Filing Date of Court Action (MM/DD/YYYY): ☐ Exact ☐ Explanation

If not exact, provide explanation: ____

4. Principal Product Type (check appropriate item):

☐Annuity(ies) - Fixed
☐Annuity(ies) - Variable
☐CD(s)
☐Commodity Option(s)
☐Debt - Asset Backed
☐Debt - Corporate
☐Debt - Government
☐Debt - Municipal
☐Derivative(s)
☐Direct Investment(s) - DPP & LP Interest(s)
☐Equity - OTC
☐Equity Listed (Common & Preferred Stock)
☐Futures - Commodity
☐Futures - Financial
☐Index Option(s)
☐Insurance
☐Investment Contract(s)
☐Money Market Fund(s)
☐Mutual Fund(s)
☐No Product
☐Options
☐Penny Stock(s)
☐Unit Investment Trust(s)
☐Other ____________

Other Product Types:

5. Formal Action was brought in (include name of Federal, State or Foreign Court, Location of Court - City or County and State or Country, Docket/Case Number):

6. *Advisory Affiliate* Employing Firm when activity occurred which led to the civil judicial action (if applicable):

(continued)

CIVIL JUDICIAL ACTION DISCLOSURE REPORTING PAGE (ADV)
(continuation)

7. Describe the allegations related to this civil action (your response must fit within the space provided):

8. Current status? ☐ Pending ☐ On Appeal ☐ Final

9. If on appeal, action appealed to (provide name of court) and Date Appeal Filed (MM/DD/YYYY):

10. If pending, date notice/process was served (MM/DD/YYYY): ☐ Exact ☐ Explanation

If not exact, provide explanation: ____________________

If Final or On Appeal, complete all items below. For Pending Actions, complete Item 14 only.

11. How was matter resolved (check appropriate item):

☐ Consent ☐ Judgment Rendered ☐ Settled
☐ Dismissed ☐ Opinion ☐ Withdrawn ☐ Other ____________

12. Resolution Date (MM/DD/YYYY): ☐ Exact ☐ Explanation

If not exact, provide explanation: ____________________

13. Resolution Detail:

A. Were any of the following Sanctions Ordered or Relief Granted (check appropriate items)?

☐ Monetary/Fine ☐ Revocation/Expulsion/Denial ☐ Disgorgement/Restitution

Amount: $ ☐ Censure ☐ Cease and Desist/Injunction ☐Bar ☐Suspension

B. Other Sanctions:

(continued)

CIVIL JUDICIAL ACTION DISCLOSURE REPORTING PAGE (ADV)
(continuation)

C. Sanction detail: if suspended, *enjoined* or barred, provide duration including start date and capacities affected (General Securities Principal, Financial Operations Principal, etc.). If requalification by exam/retraining was a condition of the sanction, provide length of time given to requalify/retrain, type of exam required and whether condition has been satisfied. If disposition resulted in a fine, penalty, restitution, disgorgement or monetary compensation, provide total amount, portion levied against you or an *advisory affiliate*, date paid and if any portion of penalty was waived:

14. Provide a brief summary of circumstances related to the action(s), allegation(s), disposition(s) and/or finding(s) disclosed above (your response must fit within the space provided).

FORM ADV Part 1B Page 1 of 4	Your Name ________________ CRD Number ________ Date ________________ SEC 801 or 802 Number ________

FORM ADV (Paper Version)

UNIFORM APPLICATION FOR INVESTMENT ADVISER REGISTRATION

PART 1B

You must complete this Part 1B only if you are applying for registration, or are registered, as an investment adviser with any of the *state securities authorities*.

ITEM 1 STATE REGISTRATION

Complete this Item 1 if you are submitting an initial application for state registration or requesting additional state registration(s). Check the boxes next to the states to which you are submitting this application. If you are already registered with at least one state and are applying for registration with an additional state or states, check the boxes next to the states in which you are applying for registration. Do not check the boxes next to the states in which you are currently registered or where you have an application for registration pending.

❑ AL	❑ CT	❑ HI	❑ KY	❑ MN	❑ NH	❑ OH	❑ SC	❑ VA
❑ AK	❑ DE	❑ ID	❑ LA	❑ MS	❑ NJ	❑ OK	❑ SD	❑ VI
❑ AZ	❑ DC	❑ IL	❑ ME	❑ MO	❑ NM	❑ OR	❑ TN	❑ WA
❑ AR	❑ FL	❑ IN	❑ MD	❑ MT	❑ NY	❑ PA	❑ TX	❑ WV
❑ CA	❑ GA	❑ IA	❑ MA	❑ NE	❑ NC	❑ PR	❑ UT	❑ WI
❑ CO	❑ GU	❑ KS	❑ MI	❑ NV	❑ ND	❑ RI	❑ VT	

ITEM 2 ADDITIONAL INFORMATION

Complete this item 2A. only if the *person* responsible for supervision and compliance does not appear in Item 1J. or 1K. of Form ADV Part 1A:

A. *Person* responsible for supervision and compliance:

____
(Name)

____
(Title)

(Area Code) (Telephone Number) (Area Code) (Facsimile Number)

____
(Number and Street)

____
(City) (State/Country) (Zip+4/postal code)

____
Electronic mail (e-mail) address, if the person has one

If this address is a private residence, check this box: ❑

B. Bond/Capital Information, if required by your *home state*.

(1) Name of Issuing Insurance Company: ______________________

(2) Amount of Bond: $ ______________ .00

(3) Bond Policy Number: ______________________

(4) If required by your *home state*, are you in compliance with your *home state's* minimum capital requirements? ❑ Yes ❑ No

Revised 10/2012

For "yes" answers to the following question, complete a Bond DRP: Yes No

C. Has a bonding company ever denied, paid out on, or revoked a bond for you, any *advisory affiliate*, or any management person? ❑ ❑

For "yes" answers to the following question, complete a Judgment/Lien DRP:

D. Are there any unsatisfied judgments or liens against you, any *advisory affiliate*, or any *management person*? ❑ ❑

For "yes" answers to the following questions, complete an Arbitration DRP:

E. Are you, any *advisory affiliate*, or any *management person* currently the subject of, or have you, any *advisory affiliate*, or any management person been the subject of, an arbitration claim alleging damages in excess of $2,500, involving any of the following:

(1) any investment or an *investment-related* business or activity? ❑ ❑

(2) fraud, false statement, or omission? ❑ ❑

(3) theft, embezzlement, or other wrongful taking of property? ❑ ❑

(4) bribery, forgery, counterfeiting, or extortion? ❑ ❑

(5) dishonest, unfair, or unethical practices? ❑ ❑

For "yes" answers to the following questions, complete a Civil Judicial Action DRP:

F. Are you, any *advisory affiliate*, or any *management person* currently subject to, or have you, any *advisory affiliate*, or any *management person* been *found* liable in, a civil, *self-regulatory organization*, or administrative *proceeding* involving any of the following:

(1) an investment or *investment-related* business or activity? ❑ ❑

(2) fraud, false statement, or omission? ❑ ❑

(3) theft, embezzlement, or other wrongful taking of property? ❑ ❑

(4) bribery, forgery, counterfeiting, or extortion? ❑ ❑

(5) dishonest, unfair, or unethical practices? ❑ ❑

G. Other Business Activities

(1) Are you, any *advisory affiliate*, or any *management person* actively engaged in business as a(n) (check all that apply):

❑ Tax Preparer

❑ Issuer of Securities

❑ Sponsor or syndicator of limited partnerships (or equivalent), excluding pooled investment vehicles

❑ Sponsor, general partner, managing member (or equivalent) of pooled investment vehicles

❑ Real estate adviser

(2) If you, any *advisory affiliate*, or any management person are actively engaged in any business other than those listed in Item 6.A. of Part 1 A or Item 2.G(1) of Part 1B, describe the business and the approximate amount of time spent on that business: ______

H. If you provide financial planning services, the investments made based on those services at the end of your last fiscal year totaled:

	Securities Investments	Non-Securities Investments
Under $100,000	❑	❑
$100,001 to $500,000	❑	❑
$500,001 to $1,000,000	❑	❑
$1,000,001 to $2,500,000	❑	❑
$2,500,001 to $5,000,000	❑	❑
More than $5,000,000	❑	❑

If securities investments are over $5,000,000, how much? $______ (round to the nearest $1,000,000)
If non-securities investments are over $5,000,000, how much? $______ (round to the nearest $1,000,000)

I. *Custody*

	Yes	No
(1) Advisory Fees Do you withdraw advisory fees directly from your *clients'* accounts? If you answered "yes", respond to the following:	❑	❑
(a) Do you send a copy of your invoice to the custodian or trustee at the same time that you send a copy to the *client*?	❑	❑
(b) Does the custodian send quarterly statements to your *clients* showing all disbursements for the custodian account, including the amount of the advisory fees?	❑	❑
(c) Do your *clients* provide written authorization permitting you to be paid directly for their accounts held by the custodian or trustee?	❑	❑

(2) Pooled Investment Vehicles and Trusts	Yes	No
(a)(i) Do you or a *related person* act as general partner, managing member, or person serving in a similar capacity, for any pooled investment vehicle for which you are the adviser to the pooled investment vehicle, or for which you are the adviser to one or more of the investors in the pooled investment vehicle?	❑	❑

If you answered "yes", respond to the following:

(a)(ii) As the general partner, managing member, or person serving in a similar capacity, have you or a *related person* engaged any of the following to provide authority permitting each direct payment or any transfer of funds or securities from the account of the pooled investment vehicle?

	Yes	No
Attorney	❑	❑
Independent certified public accountant	❑	❑
Other independent party	❑	❑

Describe the independent party: ______

For purposes of this Item 2I.2(a), "Independent party" means a person that: (A) is engaged by the investment adviser to act as a gatekeeper for the payment of fees, expenses and capital withdrawals from the pooled investment; (B) does not control and is not controlled by and is not under common control with the investment adviser; (C) does not have, and has not had within the past two years, a material business relationship with the investment adviser; and (D) shall not negotiate or agree to have material business relations or commonly controlled relations with an investment adviser for a period of two years after serving as the person engaged in an independent party agreement.

(b) Do you or a *related person* act as investment adviser and a trustee for any trust, or act as a trustee for any trust in which your advisory clients are beneficiaries of the trust? Yes ❑ No ❑

(3) Do you require prepayment of fees of more than $500 per *client* and for six months or more in advance. Yes ❑ No ❑

J. If you are organized as a sole proprietorship, please answer the following: (Yes / No)

(1) (a) Have you passed, on or after January 1, 2000, the Series 65 examination? ❑ ❑

(b) Have you passed, on or after January 1, 2000, the Series 66 examination and also passed, at any time, the Series 7 examination? ❑ ❑

(2) (a) Do you have any investment advisory professional designations? ❑ ❑

If "no," you do not need to answer Item 2J(2)(b).

(b) I have earned and I am in good standing with the organization that issued the following credential:

- ❑ 1. Certified Financial Planner ("CFP")
- ❑ 2. Chartered Financial Analyst ("CFA")
- ❑ 3. Chartered Financial Consultant ("ChFC")
- ❑ 4. Chartered Investment Counselor ("CIC")
- ❑ 5. Personal Financial Specialist ("PFS")
- ❑ 6. None of the above

(3) Your social security number: ____________________

K. If you are organized other than as a sole proprietorship, please provide the following:

(1) Indicate the date you obtained your legal status. Date of formation: ____________________ (MM/DD/YYYY)

(2) Indicate your IRS Employer Identification Number: ____________________

BOND DISCLOSURE REPORTING PAGE (ADV)

GENERAL INSTRUCTIONS
This Disclosure Reporting Page (DRP ADV) is an ❑ INITIAL OR ❑ AMENDED response used to report details for affirmative responses to Item 2.C. of Part 1B of Form ADV. Use a separate DRP for each event or *proceeding*. The same event or *proceeding* may be reported for more than one person or entity using one DRP. File with a completed Execution Page.

Part I

A. The *person(s)* or entity(ies) for whom this DRP is being filed is (are):

❑ You (the advisory firm)

❑ You and one or more of your *advisory affiliates* or *management persons*

❑ One or more of your *advisory affiliates* or *management persons*

If this DRP is being filed for an *advisory affiliate* or *management person*, give the full name of the *advisory affiliate* or *management person* below (for individuals, Last name, First name, Middle name).

If the *advisory affiliate* or *management person* has a *CRD* number, provide that number. If not, indicate "non-registered" by checking the appropriate checkbox.

Your Name	Your *CRD* Number

ADV DRP - *ADVISORY AFFILIATE* or *MANAGEMENT PERSON*

CRD Number	This *advisory affiliate* or *management person* is: ❑ a firm ❑ an individual Registered: ❑ Yes ❑ No

Name (For individuals, Last, First, Middle)

❑ This DRP should be removed from the ADV record because the *advisory affiliate(s)* or *management person(s)* is no longer associated with the adviser.

❑ This DRP should be removed from the ADV record because it was filed in error, such as due to a clerical or data-entry mistake. Explain the circumstances: ______________________________

____

NOTE: The completion of this form does not relieve the *advisory affiliate* or *management person* of its obligation to update its IARD or *CRD* records.

Part II

1. Firm Name: (Policy Holder)

2. Bonding Company Name:

(continued)

BOND DISCLOSURE REPORTING PAGE (ADV)

(continuation)

3. Disposition Type: (check appropriate item)

❑ Denied ❑ Payout ❑ Revoked

4. Disposition Date (MM/DD/YYYY): ______________________ ❑ Exact ❑ Explanation

If not exact, provide explanation: ______________________

5. If disposition resulted in Payout, list Payout Amount and Date Paid: ______________________

6. Summarize the details of circumstances leading to the necessity of bonding company action: (your response must fit within the space provided): ______________________

JUDGMENT/LIEN DISCLOSURE REPORTING PAGE (ADV)

GENERAL INSTRUCTIONS
This Disclosure Reporting Page (DRP ADV) is an ❑ INITIAL OR ❑ AMENDED response used to report details for affirmative responses to Item 2.D. of Part 1B of Form ADV. Use a separate DRP for each event or *proceeding*. The same event or *proceeding* may be reported for more than one *person* or entity using one DRP. File with a completed Execution Page.

Part I

A. The *person(s)* or entity(ies) for whom this DRP is being filed is (are):

- ❑ You (the advisory firm)
- ❑ You and one or more of your *advisory affiliates* or management persons
- ❑ One or more of your *advisory affiliates* or *management persons*

If this DRP is being filed for an *advisory affiliate* or a *management person*, give the full name of the *advisory affiliate* or *management person* below (for individuals, Last name, First name, Middle name).

If the *advisory affiliate* or *management person* has a *CRD* number, provide that number. If not, indicate "non-registered" by checking the appropriate checkbox.

Your Name	Your *CRD* Number

ADV DRP - *ADVISORY AFFILIATE* or *MANAGEMENT PERSON*

CRD Number	This *advisory affiliate* or *management person* is: ❑ a firm ❑ an individual Registered: ❑ Yes ❑ No
Name (For individuals, Last, First, Middle)	

❑ This DRP should be removed from the ADV record because the *advisory affiliate(s)* or *management person(s)* is no longer associated with the adviser.

❑ This DRP should be removed from the ADV record because it was filed in error, such as due to a clerical or data-entry mistake. Explain the circumstances:

____

____

NOTE: The completion of this form does not relieve the *advisory affiliate* or *management person* of its obligation to update its IARD or *CRD* records.

(continued)

JUDGMENT/LIEN REPORTING PAGE (ADV)

(continuation)

Part II

1. Judgment/Lien Amount: ______

2. Judgment/Lien Holder: ______

3. Judgment/Lien Type: (check appropriate item)

❑ Civil ❑ Default ❑ Tax

4. Date Filed (MM/DD/YYYY): ______ ❑ Exact ❑ Explanation

If not exact, provide explanation: ______

5. Is Judgment/Lien outstanding? ❑ Yes ❑ No

If no, provide status date (MM/DD/YYYY): ______ ❑ Exact ❑ Explanation

If not exact, provide explanation: ______

If no, how was matter resolved? (check appropriate item)

❑ Discharged ❑ Released ❑ Removed ❑ Satisfied

6. Court (Name of Federal, State or Foreign Court), Location of Court (City or County <u>and</u> State or Country) and Docket/ Case Number: ______

7. Provide a brief summary of events leading to the action and any payment schedule details including current status (if applicable) (your response must fit within the space provided): ______

ARBITRATION DISCLOSURE REPORTING PAGE (ADV)

GENERAL INSTRUCTIONS

This Disclosure Reporting Page (DRP ADV) is an ❑ INITIAL OR ❑ AMENDED response used to report details for affirmative responses to Item 2.E. of Part 1B of Form ADV.

Check Part 1B item(s) being responded to: ❑ 2.E(1) ❑ 2.E(2) ❑ 2.E(3) ❑ 2.E(4) ❑ 2.E(5)

Use a separate DRP for each event or *proceeding*. The same event or *proceeding* may be reported for more than one *person* or entity using one DRP. File with a completed Execution Page.

One event may result in more than one affirmative answer to Item 2.E. Use only one DRP to report details related to the same event. Unrelated arbitration actions must be reported on separate DRPs.

PART I

A. The *person(s)* or entity(ies) for whom this DRP is being filed is (are):

❑ You (the advisory firm)

❑ You and one or more of your *advisory affiliates* or *management persons*

❑ One or more of your *advisory affiliates* or *management persons*

If this DRP is being filed for an *advisory affiliate* or a *management person*, give the full name of the *advisory affiliate* or *management person* below (for individuals, Last name, First name, Middle name).

If the *advisory affiliate* or *management person* has a *CRD* number, provide that number. If not, indicate "non-registered" by checking the appropriate checkbox.

Your Name	Your *CRD* Number

ADV DRP - *ADVISORY AFFILIATE* or *MANAGEMENT PERSON*

CRD Number	This *advisory affiliate* or *management person* is: ❑ a firm ❑ an individual Registered: ❑ Yes ❑ No

Name (For individuals, Last, First, Middle)

❑ This DRP should be removed from the ADV record because the *advisory affiliate(s)* or *management person(s)* is no longer associated with the adviser.

❑ This DRP should be removed from the ADV record because it was filed in error, such as due to a clerical or data-entry mistake. Explain the circumstances: ______________________________

____

NOTE: The completion of this form does not relieve the advisory affiliate or management person of its obligation to update its IARD or *CRD* records.

PART II

1. Arbitration/Reparation Claim initiated by: (Name of private plaintiff, firm, etc.) ______________________________

____

2. Principal Relief Sought (check appropriate item):

❑ Restraining *Order* ❑ Disgorgement ❑ Money Damages (Private/Civil Claim) ❑ Other ________

❑ Civil Penalty(ies)/Fine(s) ❑ Injunction ❑ Restitution

(continued)

ARBITRATION DISCLOSURE REPORTING PAGE (ADV)

(continuation)

Other Relief Sought: ______________________________

____

____

____

3. Initiation Date of Arbitration/Reparation Claim (MM/DD/YYYY): [ ]

❑ Exact ❑ Explanation

If not exact, provide explanation: ______________________________

4. Principal Product Type (check appropriate item):

❑ Annuity(ies) - Fixed	❑ Derivative(s)	❑ Investment Contract(s)
❑ Annuity(ies) - Variable	❑ Direct Investment(s) - DPP & LP Interest(s)	❑ Money Market Fund(s)
❑ CD(s)	❑ Equity - OTC	❑ Mutual Fund(s)
❑ Commodity Option(s)	❑ Equity Listed (Common & Preferred Stock)	❑ No Product
❑ Debt - Asset Backed	❑ Futures - Commodity	❑ Options
❑ Debt - Corporate	❑ Futures - Financial	❑ Penny Stock(s)
❑ Debt - Government	❑ Index Option(s)	❑ Unit Investment Trust(s)
❑ Debt - Municipal	❑ Insurance	❑ Other ______________

Other Product Types: ______________________________

____

5. Arbitration/Reparation Claim was filed with (FINRA, AAA, NYSE, CBOE, CFTC, etc.) and Docket/Case Number:

____

____

6. *Advisory Affiliate's* or *Management Person's* Employing Firm when activity occurred which led to the arbitration/reparation (if applicable): ______________________________

____

7. Describe the allegations related to this arbitration/reparation (your response must fit within the space provided):

____

____

____

____

____

8. Current status? ❑ Pending ❑ On Appeal ❑ Final

9. If on appeal, action appealed to (provide name of court) and Date Appeal Filed (MM/DD/YYYY):

____

____

____

____

____

(continued)

ARBITRATION DISCLOSURE REPORTING PAGE (ADV)

(continuation)

10. If pending, date notice/process was served (MM/DD/YYYY): ☐ Exact ☐ Explanation

If not exact, provide explanation: ______

If Final or On Appeal, complete all items below. For Pending Actions, complete Item 14 only.

11. How was matter resolved (check appropriate item):

☐ Consent ☐ Judgment Rendered ☐ Settled
☐ Dismissed ☐ Opinion ☐ Withdrawn ☐ Other ______

12. Resolution Date (MM/DD/YYYY): ☐ Exact ☐ Explanation

If not exact, provide explanation: ______

13. Resolution Detail:

A. Were any of the following Sanctions *Ordered* or Relief Granted (check appropriate items)?

☐ Monetary Award Amount: $

☐ Settlement Amount: $

☐ Disgorgement/Restitution Amount: $

☐ Injunction

B. Other Sanctions: ______

C. Sanction detail: If disposition resulted in a penalty, restitution, disgorgement or monetary compensation, provide total amount, portion levied against you, an *advisory affiliate* or *management person*, date paid and if any portion of penalty was waived: ______

14. Provide a brief summary of circumstances related to the action(s), allegation(s), disposition(s) and/or finding(s) disclosed above (your response must fit within the space provided). ______

OMB APPROVAL	
OMB Number:	3235-0049
Expires:	November 30,2014
Estimated average burden hours per response.	10.50

FORM ADV (Paper Version)
UNIFORM APPLICATION FOR INVESTMENT ADVISER REGISTRATION

PART 2: Uniform Requirements for the Investment Adviser *Brochure* and *Brochure Supplements*

General Instructions for Part 2 of Form ADV

Under SEC and similar state rules you are required to deliver to *clients* and prospective *clients* a *brochure* disclosing information about your firm. You also may be required to deliver a *brochure supplement* disclosing information about one or more of your *supervised persons*. Part 2 of Form ADV sets out the minimum required disclosure that your *brochure* (Part 2A for a firm *brochure*, or Appendix 1 for a *wrap fee program brochure*) and *brochure supplements* (Part 2B) must contain.

Read all the instructions, including General Instructions for Form ADV, General Instructions for Part 2 of Form ADV, Instructions for Part 2A of Form ADV, Instructions for Part 2B of Form ADV, and (if you are preparing or updating a *wrap fee program brochure*) Instructions for Part 2A Appendix 1 of Form ADV, before preparing or updating your *brochure* or *brochure supplements*.

1. Narrative Format. Part 2 of Form ADV consists of a series of items that contain disclosure requirements for your firm's *brochure* and any required supplements. The items require narrative responses. You must respond to each item in Part 2. You must include the heading for each item provided by Part 2 immediately preceding your response to that item and provide responses in the same order as the items appear in Part 2. If an item does not apply to your business, you must indicate that item is not applicable. If you have provided information in response to one item that is also responsive to another item, you may cross-reference that information in response to the other item.

2. Plain English. The items in Part 2 of Form ADV are designed to promote effective communication between you and your *clients*. Write your *brochure* and supplements in plain English, taking into consideration your *clients*' level of financial sophistication. Your *brochure* should be concise and direct. In drafting your *brochure* and *brochure supplements*, you should: (i) use short sentences; (ii) use definite, concrete, everyday words; (iii) use active voice; (iv) use tables or bullet lists for complex material, whenever possible; (v) avoid legal jargon or highly technical business terms unless you explain them or you believe that your *clients* will understand them; and (vi) avoid multiple negatives. Consider providing examples to illustrate a description of your practices or policies. The brochure should discuss only conflicts the adviser has or is reasonably likely to have, and practices in which it engages or is reasonably likely to engage. If a conflict arises or the adviser decides to engage in a practice that it has not disclosed, supplemental disclosure must be provided to clients to obtain their consent. If you have a conflict or engage in a practice with respect to some (but not all) types or classes of clients, advice, or transactions, indicate as such rather than disclosing that you "may" have the conflict or engage in the practice.

   Note: The SEC's Office of Investor Education and Advocacy has published A Plain English Handbook. You may find the handbook helpful in writing your *brochure* and supplements. For a copy of this handbook, visit the SEC's web site at<www.sec.gov/news/extra/handbook.htm> or call 1-800-732-0330.

3. Disclosure Obligations as a Fiduciary. Under federal and state law, you are a fiduciary and must make full disclosure to your *clients* of all material facts relating to the advisory relationship. As a fiduciary, you also must seek to avoid conflicts of interest with your clients, and, at a minimum, make full disclosure of all material conflicts of interest between you and your *clients* that could affect the advisory relationship. This obligation

requires that you provide the client with sufficiently specific facts so that the client is able to understand the conflicts of interest you have and the business practices in which you engage, and can give informed consent to such conflicts or practices or reject them. To satisfy this obligation, you therefore may have to disclose to *clients* information not specifically required by Part 2 of Form ADV or in more detail than the brochure items might otherwise require. You may disclose this additional information to *clients* in your *brochure* or by some other means.

4. <u>Full and Truthful Disclosure</u>. All information in your *brochure* and *brochure supplements* must be true and may not omit any material facts.

5. <u>Filing</u>. You must file your *brochure(s)* (and amendments) through the IARD system using the text-searchable Adobe Portable Document Format ("PDF"). See SEC rules 203-1 and 204-1 and similar state rules. If you are registered or are registering with the SEC, you are not required to file your *brochure supplements* through the IARD or otherwise. You must, however, preserve a copy of the supplements and make them available to SEC staff upon request. See SEC rule 204-2(a)(14). If you are registered or are registering with one or more *state securities authorities*, you must file a copy of the *brochure supplement* for each *supervised person* doing business in that state.

Instructions for Part 2A of Form ADV: Preparing Your Firm *Brochure*

1. To whom must we deliver a firm *brochure*? You must give a firm *brochure* to each *client*. You must deliver the *brochure* even if your advisory agreement with the *client* is oral. See SEC rule 204-3(b) and similar state rules.

   If you are registered with the SEC, you are not required to deliver your *brochure* to either (i) *clients* who receive only *impersonal investment advice* from you and who will pay you less than $500 per year or (ii) *clients* that are SEC-registered investment companies or business development companies (the *client* must be registered under the Investment Company Act of 1940 or be a business development company as defined in that Act, and the advisory contract must meet the requirements of section 15(c) of that Act). See SEC rule 204-3(c).

   Note: Even if you are not required to give a *brochure* to a *client*, as a fiduciary you may still be required to provide your *clients* with similar information, particularly material information about your conflicts of interest and about your disciplinary information. If you are not required to give a *client* a *brochure*, you may make any required disclosures to that *client* by delivery of your *brochure* or through some other means.

2. When must we deliver a *brochure* to *clients*?

   - You must give a firm *brochure* to each *client* before or at the time you enter into an advisory agreement with that *client*. See SEC rule 204-3(b) and similar state rules.
   - Each year you must (i) deliver, within 120 days of the end of your fiscal year, to each *client* a free updated *brochure* that either includes a summary of material changes or is accompanied by a summary of material changes, or (ii) deliver to each *client* a summary of material changes that includes an offer to provide a copy of the updated *brochure* and information on how a *client* may obtain the *brochure*. See SEC rule 204-3(b) and similar state rules.
   - You do not have to deliver an interim amendment to *clients* unless the amendment includes information in response to Item 9 of Part 2A (disciplinary information). An interim amendment can be in the form of a document describing the material facts relating to the amended disciplinary event. See SEC rule 204-3(b) and similar state rules.

   Note: As a fiduciary, you have an ongoing obligation to inform your *clients* of any material information that could affect the advisory relationship. As a result, between *annual updating amendments* you must disclose material changes to such information to *clients* even if those changes do not trigger delivery of an interim amendment. See General Instructions for Part 2 of Form ADV, Instruction 3.

3. May we deliver our *brochure* electronically? Yes. The SEC has published interpretive guidance on delivering documents electronically, which you can find at <www.sec.gov/rules/concept/33-7288.txt>.

4. When must we update our *brochure*? You must update your *brochure*: (i) each year at the time you file your *annual updating amendment*; and (ii) promptly whenever any information in the *brochure* becomes materially inaccurate. You are not required to update your *brochure* between annual amendments solely because the amount of *client* assets you manage has changed or because your fee schedule has changed. However, if you are updating your *brochure* for a separate reason in between annual amendments, and the amount of *client* assets you manage listed in response to Item 4.E or your fee schedule listed in response to Item 5.A has become materially inaccurate, you should update that item(s) as part of the interim amendment. All updates to your *brochure* must be filed through the IARD system and maintained in your files. See SEC rules 204-1 and 204-2(a)(14) and similar state rules.

5. We are filing our *annual updating amendment*. The last *brochure*(s) that we filed does not contain any materially inaccurate information. Do we have to prepare a summary of material changes? No, as long as you

have not filed any interim amendments making material changes to the *brochure* that you filed with last year's *annual updating amendment.* If you do not have to prepare a summary of material changes, you do not have to deliver a summary of material changes or a *brochure* to your existing *clients* that year. See SEC rule 204-3(b). If you are a state-registered adviser, you should contact the appropriate *state securities authorities* to determine whether you must make an annual offer of the brochure.

6. Do we need to include the summary of material changes that we prepare in response to Item 2 with *our annual updating amendment* filing on IARD? Yes, you need to include the summary in your *annual updating amendment.* Item 2 permits you to include the summary as part of the *brochure* (on the cover page or the page immediately following the cover page) or to create a separate document containing the summary. If you include the summary as part of your *brochure,* the summary will be part of the *annual updating amendment* filing that you submit on IARD. If your summary of material changes is a separate document, you must attach the summary as an exhibit to your *brochure* and upload your *brochure* and the summary together in a single, text-searchable file in Adobe Portable Document Format on IARD for your *annual updating amendment.*

   Note: If you include the summary of material changes in your *brochure,* and you revise or update your *brochure* between *annual updating amendments,* you should consider whether you should update the summary as part of that other-than annual amendment to avoid confusing or misleading *clients* reading the updated *brochure.*

7. We have determined that we have no *clients* to whom we must deliver a *brochure.* Must we prepare one? No, but see note to Instruction 1 above.

8. May we include a summary of the *brochure* at the beginning of our *brochure*? Yes. Although it is not required, you may choose to include a summary of the *brochure* at the beginning of your *brochure.* Such summary, however, may not substitute for the summary of material changes required by Item 2 of Part 2A.

9. We offer several advisory services. May we prepare multiple firm *brochures*? Yes. If you offer substantially different types of advisory services, you may opt to prepare separate *brochures* so long as each *client* receives all applicable information about services and fees. Each *brochure* may omit information that does not apply to the advisory services and fees it describes. For example, your firm *brochure* sent to your *clients* who invest only in the United States can omit information about your advisory services and fees relating to offshore investments. See SEC rule 204-3(e) and similar state rules. If you prepare separate *brochures* you must file each *brochure* (and any amendments) through the IARD system as required in SEC rules 203-1 and 204-1 and similar state rules.

10. We *sponsor* a *wrap fee program.* Is there a different *brochure* that we need to deliver to our wrap fee *clients*? Yes. If you *sponsor* a *wrap fee program,* you must deliver a *wrap fee program brochure* to your wrap fee *clients.* The disclosure requirements for preparing a *wrap fee program brochure* appear in Part 2A, Appendix 1 of Form ADV. If your entire advisory business is *sponsoring wrap fee programs,* you do not need to prepare a firm *brochure* separate from your *wrap fee program brochure(s).* See SEC rule 204-3(d) and similar state rules.

11. We provide portfolio management services to *clients* in *wrap fee programs* that we do not *sponsor.* Which *brochure* must we deliver to these *clients*? You must deliver your *brochure* prepared in accordance with Part 2A (not Appendix 1) to your wrap fee *clients.* You also must deliver to these *clients* any *brochure supplements* required by Part 2B of Form ADV.

12. May we include information not required by an item in our *brochure*? Yes. If you include information not required by an item, however, you may not include so much additional information that the required information is obscured.

13. Item 18 requires us to give our *clients* an audited balance sheet. May any public accountant perform the audit? Your auditor must be independent. Article 2 of SEC Regulation S-X sets out the general rules for auditor

independence. Please note that these requirements may be different from the rules of professional organizations.

14. We are a new firm. Do we need a *brochure*? Yes. Respond to items in Part 2A of Form ADV based on the advisory services you propose to provide and the practices, policies and procedures you propose to adopt.

15. We are a "separately identifiable department or division" (SID) of a bank. Must our *brochure* discuss our bank's general business practices? No. Information you include in your firm *brochure* (or in *brochure supplements*) should be information about you, the SID, and your business practices, rather than general information about your bank.

Part 2A of Form ADV: Firm *Brochure*

Item 1 Cover Page

A. The cover page of your *brochure* must state your name, business address, contact information, website address (if you have one), and the date of the *brochure*.

Note: If you primarily conduct advisory business under a name different from your full legal name, and you have disclosed your business name in Item 1.B of Part 1A of Form ADV, then you may use your business name throughout your *brochure*.

B. Display on the cover page of your *brochure* the following statement or other clear and concise language conveying the same information, and identifying the document as a "brochure":

This brochure provides information about the qualifications and business practices of [your name]. If you have any questions about the contents of this brochure, please contact us at [telephone number and/or email address]. The information in this brochure has not been approved or verified by the United States Securities and Exchange Commission or by any state securities authority.

Additional information about [your name] also is available on the SEC's website at www.adviserinfo.sec.gov.

C. If you refer to yourself as a "registered investment adviser" or describe yourself as being "registered," include a statement that registration does not imply a certain level of skill or training.

Item 2 Material Changes

If you are amending your *brochure* for your annual update and it contains material changes from your last annual update, identify and discuss those changes on the cover page of the *brochure* or on the page immediately following the cover page, or as a separate document accompanying the *brochure*. You must state clearly that you are discussing only material changes since the last annual update of your *brochure*, and you must provide the date of the last annual update of your *brochure*.

Note: You do not have to separately provide this information to a *client* or prospective *client* who has not received a previous version of your *brochure*.

Item 3 Table of Contents

Provide a table of contents to your *brochure*.

Note: Your table of contents must be detailed enough so that your *clients* can locate topics easily. Your *brochure* must follow the same order, and contain the same headings, as the items listed in Part 2A.

Item 4 Advisory Business

A. Describe your advisory firm, including how long you have been in business. Identify your principal owner(s).

Notes: (1) For purposes of this item, your principal owners include the *persons* you list as owning 25% or more of your firm on Schedule A of Part 1A of Form ADV (Ownership Codes C, D or E). (2) If you are a publicly held company without a 25% shareholder, simply disclose that you are publicly held. (3) If an individual or company owns 25% or more of your firm through subsidiaries, you must identify the individual or parent company and intermediate subsidiaries. If you are an SEC-registered adviser, you must identify intermediate subsidiaries that are publicly held, but not other intermediate subsidiaries. If you are a state-registered adviser, you must identify all intermediate subsidiaries.

B. Describe the types of advisory services you offer. If you hold yourself out as specializing in a particular type of advisory service, such as financial planning, quantitative analysis, or market timing, explain the nature of that service in greater detail. If you provide investment advice only with respect to limited types of investments, explain the type of investment advice you offer, and disclose that your advice is limited to those types of investments.

C. Explain whether (and, if so, how) you tailor your advisory services to the individual needs of *clients*. Explain whether *clients* may impose restrictions on investing in certain securities or types of securities.

D. If you participate in *wrap fee programs* by providing portfolio management services, (1) describe the differences, if any, between how you manage wrap fee accounts and how you manage other accounts, and (2) explain that you receive a portion of the wrap fee for your services.

E. If you manage *client* assets, disclose the amount of *client* assets you manage on a *discretionary basis* and the amount of *client* assets you manage on a non-*discretionary basis*. Disclose the date "as of" which you calculated the amounts.

Note: Your method for computing the amount of "*client* assets you manage" can be different from the method for computing "regulatory assets under management" required for Item 5.F in Part 1A. However, if you choose to use a different method to compute "*client* assets you manage," you must keep documentation describing the method you use. The amount you disclose may be rounded to the nearest $100,000. Your "as of" date must not be more than 90 days before the date you last updated your *brochure* in response to this Item 4.E.

Item 5 Fees and Compensation

A. Describe how you are compensated for your advisory services. Provide your fee schedule. Disclose whether the fees are negotiable.

Note: If you are an SEC-registered adviser, you do not need to include this information in a *brochure* that is delivered only to qualified purchasers as defined in section 2(a)(51)(A) of the Investment Company Act of 1940.

B. Describe whether you deduct fees from *clients'* assets or bill *clients* for fees incurred. If *clients* may select either method, disclose this fact. Explain how often you bill *clients* or deduct your fees.

C. Describe any other types of fees or expenses *clients* may pay in connection with your advisory services, such as custodian fees or mutual fund expenses. Disclose that *clients* will incur brokerage and other transaction costs, and direct *clients* to the section(s) of your *brochure* that discuss brokerage.

D. If your *clients* either may or must pay your fees in advance, disclose this fact. Explain how a *client* may obtain a refund of a pre-paid fee if the advisory contract is terminated before the end of the billing period. Explain how you will determine the amount of the refund.

E. If you or any of your *supervised persons* accepts compensation for the sale of securities or other investment products, including asset-based sales charges or service fees from the sale of mutual funds, disclose this fact and respond to Items 5.E.1, 5.E.2, 5.E.3 and 5.E.4.

1. Explain that this practice presents a conflict of interest and gives you or your *supervised persons* an incentive to recommend investment products based on the compensation received, rather than on a *client's* needs. Describe generally how you address conflicts that arise, including your procedures for

disclosing the conflicts to *clients*. If you primarily recommend mutual funds, disclose whether you will recommend "no-load" funds.

2. Explain that *clients* have the option to purchase investment products that you recommend through other brokers or agents that are not affiliated with you.

3. If more than 50% of your revenue from advisory *clients* results from commissions and other compensation for the sale of investment products you recommend to your *clients*, including asset-based distribution fees from the sale of mutual funds, disclose that commissions provide your primary or, if applicable, your exclusive compensation.

4. If you charge advisory fees in addition to commissions or markups, disclose whether you reduce your advisory fees to offset the commissions or markups.

Note: If you receive compensation in connection with the purchase or sale of securities, you should carefully consider the applicability of the broker-dealer registration requirements of the Securities Exchange Act of 1934 and any applicable state securities statutes.

Item 6 *Performance-Based Fees* and Side-By-Side Management

If you or any of your *supervised persons* accepts *performance-based fees* – that is, fees based on a share of capital gains on or capital appreciation of the assets of a *client* (such as a *client* that is a hedge fund or other pooled investment vehicle) – disclose this fact. If you or any of your *supervised persons* manage both accounts that are charged a *performance-based fee* and accounts that are charged another type of fee, such as an hourly or flat fee or an asset-based fee, disclose this fact. Explain the conflicts of interest that you or your *supervised persons* face by managing these accounts at the same time, including that you or your *supervised persons* have an incentive to favor accounts for which you or your *supervised persons* receive a *performance-based fee*, and describe generally how you address these conflicts.

Item 7 Types of *Clients*

Describe the types of *clients* to whom you generally provide investment advice, such as individuals, trusts, investment companies, or pension plans. If you have any requirements for opening or maintaining an account, such as a minimum account size, disclose the requirements.

Item 8 Methods of Analysis, Investment Strategies and Risk of Loss

A. Describe the methods of analysis and investment strategies you use in formulating investment advice or managing assets. Explain that investing in securities involves risk of loss that *clients* should be prepared to bear.

B. For each significant investment strategy or method of analysis you use, explain the material risks involved. If the method of analysis or strategy involves significant or unusual risks, discuss these risks in detail. If your primary strategy involves frequent trading of securities, explain how frequent trading can affect investment performance, particularly through increased brokerage and other transaction costs and taxes.

C. If you recommend primarily a particular type of security, explain the material risks involved. If the type of security involves significant or unusual risks, discuss these risks in detail.

Item 9 Disciplinary Information

If there are legal or disciplinary events that are material to a *client's* or prospective *client's* evaluation of your advisory business or the integrity of your management, disclose all material facts regarding those events.

Items 9.A, 9.B, and 9.C list specific legal and disciplinary events presumed to be material for this Item. If your advisory firm or a *management person* has been *involved* in one of these events, you must disclose it under this Item for ten years following the date of the event, unless (1) the event was resolved in your or the *management person's* favor, or was reversed, suspended or vacated, or (2) you have rebutted the presumption of materiality to determine that the event is not material (see Note below). For purposes of calculating this ten-year period, the "date" of an event is the date that the final *order*, judgment, or decree was entered, or the date that any rights of appeal from preliminary *orders*, judgments or decrees lapsed.

Items 9.A, 9.B, and 9.C do not contain an exclusive list of material disciplinary events. If your advisory firm or a *management person* has been *involved* in a legal or disciplinary event that is not listed in Items 9.A, 9.B, or 9.C, but nonetheless is material to a *client's* or prospective *client's* evaluation of your advisory business or the integrity of its management, you must disclose the event. Similarly, even if more than ten years have passed since the date of the event, you must disclose the event if it is so serious that it remains material to a *client's* or prospective *client's* evaluation.

A. A criminal or civil action in a domestic, foreign or military court of competent jurisdiction in which your firm or a *management person*

1. was convicted of, or pled guilty or nolo contendere ("no contest") to (a) any *felony*; (b) a *misdemeanor* that *involved* investments or an *investment-related* business, fraud, false statements or omissions, wrongful taking of property, bribery, perjury, forgery, counterfeiting, or extortion; or (c) a conspiracy to commit any of these offenses;

2. is the named subject of a pending criminal *proceeding* that involves an *investment-related* business, fraud, false statements or omissions, wrongful taking of property, bribery, perjury, forgery, counterfeiting, extortion, or a conspiracy to commit any of these offenses;

3. was *found* to have been *involved* in a violation of an *investment-related* statute or regulation; or

4. was the subject of any *order*, judgment, or decree permanently or temporarily enjoining, or otherwise limiting, your firm or a *management person* from engaging in any *investment-related* activity, or from violating any *investment-related* statute, rule, or *order*.

B. An administrative *proceeding* before the SEC, any other federal regulatory agency, any state regulatory agency, or any *foreign financial regulatory authority* in which your firm or a *management person*

1. was *found* to have caused an *investment-related* business to lose its authorization to do business; or

2. was *found* to have been *involved* in a violation of an *investment-related* statute or regulation and was the subject of an *order* by the agency or authority

(a) denying, suspending, or revoking the authorization of your firm or a *management person* to act in an *investment-related* business;

(b) barring or suspending your firm's or a *management person's* association with an *investment-related* business;

(c) otherwise significantly limiting your firm's or a *management person's investment-related* activities; or

(d) imposing a civil money penalty of more than $2,500 on your firm or a *management person.*

C. A *self-regulatory organization (SRO) proceeding* in which your firm or a *management person*

1. was *found* to have caused an *investment-related* business to lose its authorization to do business; or

2. was *found* to have been *involved* in a violation of the *SRO's* rules and was: (i) barred or suspended from membership or from association with other members, or was expelled from membership; (ii) otherwise significantly limited from *investment-related* activities; or (iii) fined more than $2,500.

Note: You may, under certain circumstances, rebut the presumption that a disciplinary event is material. If an event is immaterial, you are not required to disclose it. When you review a legal or disciplinary event involving your firm or a *management person* to determine whether it is appropriate to rebut the presumption of materiality, you should consider all of the following factors: (1) the proximity of the *person involved* in the disciplinary event to the advisory function; (2) the nature of the infraction that led to the disciplinary event; (3) the severity of the disciplinary sanction; and (4) the time elapsed since the date of the disciplinary event. If you conclude that the materiality presumption has been overcome, you must prepare and maintain a file memorandum of your determination in your records. See SEC rule 204-2(a)(14)(iii).

Item 10 Other Financial Industry Activities and Affiliations

A. If you or any of your *management persons* are registered, or have an application pending to register, as a broker-dealer or a registered representative of a broker-dealer, disclose this fact.

B. If you or any of your *management persons* are registered, or have an application pending to register, as a futures commission merchant, commodity pool operator, a commodity trading advisor, or an associated person of the foregoing entities, disclose this fact.

C. Describe any relationship or arrangement that is material to your advisory business or to your *clients* that you or any of your *management persons* have with any *related person* listed below. Identify the *related person* and if the relationship or arrangement creates a material conflict of interest with *clients*, describe the nature of the conflict and how you address it.

1. broker-dealer, municipal securities dealer, or government securities dealer or broker
2. investment company or other pooled investment vehicle (including a mutual fund, closed-end investment company, unit investment trust, private investment company or "hedge fund," and offshore fund)
3. other investment adviser or financial planner
4. futures commission merchant, commodity pool operator, or commodity trading advisor
5. banking or thrift institution
6. accountant or accounting firm
7. lawyer or law firm
8. insurance company or agency
9. pension consultant
10. real estate broker or dealer
11. sponsor or syndicator of limited partnerships.

D. If you recommend or select other investment advisers for your *clients* and you receive compensation directly or indirectly from those advisers that creates a material conflict of interest, or if you have other business relationships with those advisers that create a material conflict of interest, describe these practices and discuss the material conflicts of interest these practices create and how you address them.

Item 11 Code of Ethics, Participation or Interest in *Client* Transactions and Personal Trading

A. If you are an SEC-registered adviser, briefly describe your code of ethics adopted pursuant to SEC rule 204A-1 or similar state rules. Explain that you will provide a copy of your code of ethics to any *client* or prospective *client* upon request.

B. If you or a *related person* recommends to *clients*, or buys or sells for *client* accounts, securities in which you or a *related person* has a material financial interest, describe your practice and discuss the conflicts of interest it presents. Describe generally how you address conflicts that arise.

Examples: (1) You or a *related person*, as principal, buys securities from (or sells securities to) your *clients*; (2) you or a *related person* acts as general partner in a partnership in which you solicit *client* investments; or (3) you or a *related person* acts as an investment adviser to an investment company that you recommend to *clients*.

C. If you or a *related person* invests in the same securities (or related securities, *e.g.*, warrants, options or futures) that you or a *related person* recommends to *clients*, describe your practice and discuss the conflicts of interest this presents and generally how you address the conflicts that arise in connection with personal trading.

D. If you or a *related person* recommends securities to *clients*, or buys or sells securities for *client* accounts, at or about the same time that you or a *related person* buys or sells the same securities for your own (or the *related person's* own) account, describe your practice and discuss the conflicts of interest it presents. Describe generally how you address conflicts that arise.

Note: The description required by Item 11.A may include information responsive to Item 11.B, C or D. If so, it is not necessary to make repeated disclosures of the same information. You do not have to provide disclosure in response to Item 11.B, 11.C, or 11.D with respect to securities that are not "reportable securities" under SEC rule 204A-1(e)(10) and similar state rules.

Item 12 Brokerage Practices

A. Describe the factors that you consider in selecting or recommending broker-dealers for *client* transactions and determining the reasonableness of their compensation (*e.g.*, commissions).

1. Research and Other Soft Dollar Benefits. If you receive research or other products or services other than execution from a broker-dealer or a third party in connection with *client* securities transactions ("soft dollar benefits"), disclose your practices and discuss the conflicts of interest they create.

   Note: Your disclosure and discussion must include all soft dollar benefits you receive, including, in the case of research, both proprietary research (created or developed by the broker-dealer) and research created or developed by a third party.

   a. Explain that when you use *client* brokerage commissions (or markups or markdowns) to obtain research or other products or services, you receive a benefit because you do not have to produce or pay for the research, products or services.

   b. Disclose that you may have an incentive to select or recommend a broker-dealer based on your interest in receiving the research or other products or services, rather than on your *clients*' interest in receiving most favorable execution.

c. If you may cause *clients* to pay commissions (or markups or markdowns) higher than those charged by other broker-dealers in return for soft dollar benefits (known as paying-up), disclose this fact.

d. Disclose whether you use soft dollar benefits to service all of your *clients*' accounts or only those that paid for the benefits. Disclose whether you seek to allocate soft dollar benefits to *client* accounts proportionately to the soft dollar credits the accounts generate.

e. Describe the types of products and services you or any of your *related persons* acquired with *client* brokerage commissions (or markups or markdowns) within your last fiscal year.

Note: This description must be specific enough for your *clients* to understand the types of products or services that you are acquiring and to permit them to evaluate possible conflicts of interest. Your description must be more detailed for products or services that do not qualify for the safe harbor in section 28(e) of the Securities Exchange Act of 1934, such as those services that do not aid in investment decision-making or trade execution. Merely disclosing that you obtain various research reports and products is not specific enough.

f. Explain the procedures you used during your last fiscal year to direct *client* transactions to a particular broker-dealer in return for soft dollar benefits you received.

2. Brokerage for *Client* Referrals. If you consider, in selecting or recommending broker-dealers, whether you or a *related person* receives *client* referrals from a broker-dealer or third party, disclose this practice and discuss the conflicts of interest it creates.

a. Disclose that you may have an incentive to select or recommend a broker-dealer based on your interest in receiving *client* referrals, rather than on your *clients*' interest in receiving most favorable execution.

b. Explain the procedures you used during your last fiscal year to direct *client* transactions to a particular broker-dealer in return for *client* referrals.

3. Directed Brokerage.

a. If you routinely recommend, request or require that a *client* direct you to execute transactions through a specified broker-dealer, describe your practice or policy. Explain that not all advisers require their *clients* to direct brokerage. If you and the broker-dealer are affiliates or have another economic relationship that creates a material conflict of interest, describe the relationship and discuss the conflicts of interest it presents. Explain that by directing brokerage you may be unable to achieve most favorable execution of *client* transactions, and that this practice may cost *clients* more money.

b. If you permit a *client* to direct brokerage, describe your practice. If applicable, explain that you may be unable to achieve most favorable execution of *client* transactions. Explain that directing brokerage may cost *clients* more money. For example, in a directed brokerage account, the *client* may pay higher brokerage commissions because you may not be able to aggregate orders to reduce transaction costs, or the *client* may receive less favorable prices.

Note: If your *clients* only have directed brokerage arrangements subject to most favorable execution of *client* transactions, you do not need to respond to the last sentence of Item 12.A.3.a. or to the second or third sentences of Item 12.A.3.b.

B. Discuss whether and under what conditions you aggregate the purchase or sale of securities for various *client* accounts. If you do not aggregate orders when you have the opportunity to do so, explain your practice and describe the costs to *clients* of not aggregating.

Item 13 Review of Accounts

A. Indicate whether you periodically review *client* accounts or financial plans. If you do, describe the frequency and nature of the review, and the titles of the *supervised persons* who conduct the review.

B. If you review *client* accounts on other than a periodic basis, describe the factors that trigger a review.

C. Describe the content and indicate the frequency of regular reports you provide to *clients* regarding their accounts. State whether these reports are written.

Item 14 *Client* Referrals and Other Compensation

A. If someone who is not a *client* provides an economic benefit to you for providing investment advice or other advisory services to your *clients*, generally describe the arrangement, explain the conflicts of interest, and describe how you address the conflicts of interest. For purposes of this Item, economic benefits include any sales awards or other prizes.

B. If you or a *related person* directly or indirectly compensates any *person* who is not your *supervised person* for *client* referrals, describe the arrangement and the compensation.

Note: If you compensate any *person* for *client* referrals, you should consider whether SEC rule 206(4)-3 or similar state rules regarding solicitation arrangements and/or state rules requiring registration of *investment adviser representatives* apply.

Item 15 *Custody*

If you have *custody* of *client* funds or securities and a qualified custodian sends quarterly, or more frequent, account statements directly to your *clients*, explain that *clients* will receive account statements from the broker-dealer, bank or other qualified custodian and that *clients* should carefully review those statements. If your *clients* also receive account statements from you, your explanation must include a statement urging *clients* to compare the account statements they receive from the qualified custodian with those they receive from you.

Item 16 Investment Discretion

If you accept *discretionary authority* to manage securities accounts on behalf of *clients*, disclose this fact and describe any limitations *clients* may (or customarily do) place on this authority. Describe the procedures you follow before you assume this authority (*e.g.,* execution of a power of attorney).

Item 17 Voting *Client* Securities

A. If you have, or will accept, authority to vote *client* securities, briefly describe your voting policies and procedures, including those adopted pursuant to SEC rule 206(4)-6. Describe whether (and, if so, how) your *clients* can direct your vote in a particular solicitation. Describe how you address conflicts of interest between you and your *clients* with respect to voting their securities. Describe how *clients* may obtain information from you about how you voted their securities. Explain to *clients* that they may obtain a copy of your proxy voting policies and procedures upon request.

B. If you do not have authority to vote *client* securities, disclose this fact. Explain whether *clients* will receive their proxies or other solicitations directly from their custodian or a transfer agent or from you, and discuss whether (and, if so, how) *clients* can contact you with questions about a particular solicitation.

Item 18 Financial Information

A. If you require or solicit prepayment of more than $1,200 in fees per *client*, six months or more in advance, include a balance sheet for your most recent fiscal year.

1. The balance sheet must be prepared in accordance with generally accepted accounting principles, audited by an independent public accountant, and accompanied by a note stating the principles used to prepare it, the basis of securities included, and any other explanations required for clarity.

2. Show parenthetically the market or fair value of securities included at cost.

3. Qualifications of the independent public accountant and any accompanying independent public accountant's report must conform to Article 2 of SEC Regulation S-X.

Note: If you are a sole proprietor, show investment advisory business assets and liabilities separate from other business and personal assets and liabilities. You may aggregate other business and personal assets unless advisory business liabilities exceed advisory business assets.

Note: If you have not completed your first fiscal year, include a balance sheet dated not more than 90 days prior to the date of your *brochure.*

Exception: You are not required to respond to Item 18.A of Part 2A if you also are: (i) a qualified custodian as defined in SEC rule 206(4)-2 or similar state rules; or (ii) an insurance company.

B. If you have *discretionary authority* or *custody* of *client* funds or securities, or you require or solicit prepayment of more than $1,200 in fees per *client*, six months or more in advance, disclose any financial condition that is reasonably likely to impair your ability to meet contractual commitments to *clients.*

Note: With respect to Items 18.A and 18.B, if you are registered or are registering with one or more of the *state securities authorities*, the dollar amount reporting threshold for including the required balance sheet and for making the required financial condition disclosures is more than $500 in fees per *client*, six months or more in advance.

C. If you have been the subject of a bankruptcy petition at any time during the past ten years, disclose this fact, the date the petition was first brought, and the current status.

If you are registering or are registered with one or more *state securities authorities*, you must respond to the following additional Item.

Item 19 Requirements for State-Registered Advisers

A. Identify each of your principal executive officers and *management persons*, and describe their formal education and business background. If you have supplied this information elsewhere in your Form ADV, you do not need to repeat it in response to this Item.

B. Describe any business in which you are actively engaged (other than giving investment advice) and the approximate amount of time spent on that business. If you have supplied this information elsewhere in your Form ADV, you do not need to repeat it in response to this Item.

C. In addition to the description of your fees in response to Item 5 of Part 2A, if you or a *supervised person* are compensated for advisory services with *performance-based fees*, explain how these fees will be calculated. Disclose specifically that performance-based compensation may create an incentive for the adviser to recommend an investment that may carry a higher degree of risk to the *client*.

D. If you or a *management person* has been *involved* in one of the events listed below, disclose all material facts regarding the event.

1. An award or otherwise being *found* liable in an arbitration claim alleging damages in excess of $2,500, *involving* any of the following:

(a) an investment or an *investment-related* business or activity;
(b) fraud, false statement(s), or omissions;
(c) theft, embezzlement, or other wrongful taking of property;
(d) bribery, forgery, counterfeiting, or extortion; or
(e) dishonest, unfair, or unethical practices.

2. An award or otherwise being *found* liable in a civil, *self-regulatory organization*, or administrative *proceeding involving* any of the following:

(a) an investment or an *investment-related* business or activity;
(b) fraud, false statement(s), or omissions;
(c) theft, embezzlement, or other wrongful taking of property;
(d) bribery, forgery, counterfeiting, or extortion; or
(e) dishonest, unfair, or unethical practices.

E. In addition to any relationship or arrangement described in response to Item 10.C. of Part 2A, describe any relationship or arrangement that you or any of your *management persons* have with any issuer of securities that is not listed in Item 10.C. of Part 2A.

Instructions for Part 2A Appendix 1 of Form ADV:
Preparing Your *Wrap Fee Program Brochure*

Read all the instructions, including General Instructions for Form ADV, General Instructions for Part 2 of Form ADV, Instructions for Part 2A of Form ADV, and the instructions below, before preparing or updating your *wrap fee program brochure.*

1. Who must deliver a *wrap fee program brochure*? If you *sponsor* a *wrap fee program*, you must give a *wrap fee program brochure* to each *client* of the *wrap fee program.*

   However, if a *wrap fee program* that you *sponsor* has multiple *sponsors* and another *sponsor* creates and delivers to your *wrap fee program clients* a *wrap fee program brochure* that includes all the information required in your *wrap brochure,* you do not have to create or deliver a separate *wrap fee program brochure.*

   A *wrap fee program brochure* takes the place of your advisory firm *brochure* required by Part 2A of Form ADV, but only for *clients* of *wrap fee programs* that you *sponsor.* See SEC rule 204-3(d) and similar state rules.

2. When must a *wrap fee program brochure* be delivered?

   - You must give a *wrap fee program brochure* to each *client* of the *wrap fee program* before or at the time the *client* enters into a *wrap fee program* contract. See SEC rule 204-3(b) and similar state rules.
   - Each year you must (i) deliver, within 120 days of the end of your fiscal year, to each *client* a free updated *wrap fee program brochure* that either includes a summary of material changes or is accompanied by a summary of material changes, or (ii) deliver to each *client* a summary of material changes that includes an offer to provide a copy of the updated *wrap fee program brochure* and information on how a *client* may obtain the *wrap fee program brochure.* See SEC rule 204-3(b) and similar state rules.
   - You do not have to deliver an interim amendment to *clients* unless the amendment includes information in response to Item 9 of Part 2A (disciplinary information). An interim amendment can be in the form of a document describing the material facts relating to the amended disciplinary event. See SEC rule 204-3(b) and similar state rules.

   Note: As a fiduciary, you have an ongoing obligation to inform your *clients* of any material information that could affect the advisory relationship. As a result, between *annual updating amendments* you must disclose material changes to such information to *clients* even if those changes do not trigger delivery of an interim amendment. See General Instructions for Part 2 of Form ADV, Instruction 3.

3. When must we update our *wrap fee program brochure*? You must update your *wrap fee program brochure*: (i) each year at the time you file your *annual updating amendment*, and (ii) promptly whenever any information in the *wrap fee program brochure* becomes materially inaccurate. You are not required to update your *wrap fee program brochure* between annual amendments solely because your fee schedule has changed. However, if you are updating your *wrap fee program brochure* for a separate reason in between annual amendments, and your fee schedule listed in response to Item 4.A has become materially inaccurate, you should update that item as part of the interim amendment. All updates to your *wrap fee program brochure* must be filed through the IARD system and maintained in your files. See SEC rules 204-1 and 204-2(a)(14) and similar state rules.

4. May we deliver our *wrap fee program brochure* electronically? Yes. The SEC has published interpretive guidance on delivering documents electronically, which you can find at <www.sec.gov/rules/concept/33-7288.txt>.

5. What if we *sponsor* more than one *wrap fee program*? You may prepare a single *wrap fee program brochure* describing all the *wrap fee programs* you *sponsor*, or you may prepare separate *wrap fee program brochures* that describe one or more of your *wrap fee programs.* If you prepare separate *brochures*, each *brochure* must state that you *sponsor* other *wrap fee programs* and must explain how the *client* can obtain *brochures* for the other programs.

6. We provide portfolio management services under a *wrap fee program* that we *sponsor*. Must we deliver both our *wrap fee program brochure* and our firm *brochure* to our *wrap fee program clients*? No, just the *wrap fee program brochure*. If you or your *supervised persons* provide portfolio management services under a *wrap fee program* that you also *sponsor*, your *wrap fee program brochure* must describe the investments and investment strategies you (or your *supervised persons*) will use as portfolio managers. This requirement appears in Item 6.C of this Appendix.

7. We provide other advisory services outside of our *wrap fee programs*. May we combine our *wrap fee program brochure* into our firm *brochure* for *clients* receiving these other services? No. Your *wrap fee program brochure* must address only the *wrap fee programs* you *sponsor*. See SEC rule 204-3(d)(1) and similar state rules.

8. Must we also deliver *brochure supplements* to *wrap fee program clients*? Yes. A *wrap fee program brochure* does not take the place of any supplements required by Part 2B of Form ADV.

Part 2A Appendix 1 of Form ADV: *Wrap Fee Program Brochure*

Item 1 Cover Page

A. The cover page of your *wrap fee program brochure* must state your name, business address, contact information, web site address (if you have one), and the date of the *wrap fee program brochure*.

Note: If you primarily conduct advisory business under a name different from your full legal name, and you have disclosed your business name in Item 1.B of Part 1A of Form ADV, then you may use your business name throughout your *wrap fee program brochure*.

B. Display on the cover page of your *wrap fee program brochure* the following (or other clear and concise language conveying the same information) and identifying the document as a "wrap fee program brochure":

This wrap fee program brochure provides information about the qualifications and business practices of [your name]. If you have any questions about the contents of this brochure, please contact us at [telephone number and/or email address]. The information in this brochure has not been approved or verified by the United States Securities and Exchange Commission or by any state securities authority.

Additional information about [your name] also is available on the SEC's website at www.adviserinfo.sec.gov.

D. If you refer to yourself as a "registered investment adviser" or describe yourself as being "registered," include a statement that registration does not imply a certain level of skill or training.

Item 2 Material Changes

If you are amending your *wrap fee program brochure* for your annual update and it contains material changes from your last annual update, identify and discuss those changes on the page immediately following the cover page of the *wrap fee program brochure* or as a separate document accompanying the *brochure*. You must clearly state that you are discussing only material changes since the last annual update of the *wrap fee program brochure*, and must provide the date of the last annual update to the *wrap fee program brochure*.

Notes: You do not have to provide this information to a *client* or prospective *client* who has not received a previous version of your *wrap fee program brochure*.

Item 3 Table of Contents

Provide a table of contents to your *wrap fee program brochure*.

Note: Your table of contents must be detailed enough so that your *clients* can locate topics easily. Your *wrap fee program brochure* must follow the same order, and contain the same headings, as the items listed in this Appendix 1.

Item 4 Services, Fees and Compensation

A. Describe the services, including the types of portfolio management services, provided under each program. Indicate the wrap fee charged for each program or, if fees vary according to a schedule, provide your fee schedule. Indicate whether fees are negotiable and identify the portion of the total fee, or the range of fees, paid to portfolio managers.

B. Explain that the program may cost the *client* more or less than purchasing such services separately and describe the factors that bear upon the relative cost of the program, such as the cost of the services if provided separately and the trading activity in the *client's* account.

C. Describe any fees that the *client* may pay in addition to the wrap fee, and describe the circumstances under which *clients* may pay these fees, including, if applicable, mutual fund expenses and mark-ups, mark-downs, or spreads paid to market makers.

D. If the *person* recommending the *wrap fee program* to the *client* receives compensation as a result of the *client's* participation in the program, disclose this fact. Explain, if applicable, that the amount of this compensation may be more than what the *person* would receive if the *client* participated in your other programs or paid separately for investment advice, brokerage, and other services. Explain that the *person*, therefore, may have a financial incentive to recommend the *wrap fee program* over other programs or services.

Item 5 Account Requirements and Types of *Clients*

If a *wrap fee program* imposes any requirements to open or maintain an account, such as a minimum account size, disclose these requirements. If there is a minimum amount for assets placed with each portfolio manager as well as a minimum account size for participation in the *wrap fee program*, disclose and explain these requirements. To the extent applicable to your *wrap fee program clients*, describe the types of *clients* to whom you generally provide investment advice, such as individuals, trusts, investment companies, or pension plans.

Item 6 Portfolio Manager Selection and Evaluation

A. Describe how you select and review portfolio managers, your basis for recommending or selecting portfolio managers for particular *clients*, and your criteria for replacing or recommending the replacement of portfolio managers for the program and for particular *clients*.

   1. Describe any standards you use to calculate portfolio manager performance, such as industry standards or standards used solely by you.

   2. Indicate whether you review, or whether any third-party reviews, performance information to determine or verify its accuracy or its compliance with presentation standards. If so, briefly describe the nature of the review and the name of any third party conducting the review.

   3. If applicable, explain that neither you nor a third-party reviews portfolio manager performance information, and/or that performance information may not be calculated on a uniform and consistent basis.

B. Disclose whether any of your *related persons* act as a portfolio manager for a *wrap fee program* described in the *wrap fee program brochure*. Explain the conflicts of interest that you face because of this arrangement and describe how you address these conflicts of interest. Disclose whether *related person* portfolio managers are subject to the same selection and review as the other portfolio managers that participate in the *wrap fee program*. If they are not, describe how you select and review *related person* portfolio managers.

C. If you, or any of your *supervised persons* covered under your investment adviser registration, act as a portfolio manager for a *wrap fee program* described in the *wrap fee program brochure*, respond to Items 4.B, 4.C, 4.D (Advisory Business), 6 (*Performance-Based Fees* and Side-By-Side Management), 8.A (Methods of Analysis, Investment Strategies and Risk of Loss) and 17 (Voting *Client* Securities) of Part 2A of Form ADV.

Item 7 *Client* Information Provided to Portfolio Managers

Describe the information about *clients* that you communicate to the *clients*' portfolio managers, and how often or under what circumstances you provide updated information.

Item 8 *Client* Contact with Portfolio Managers

Explain any restrictions placed on *clients*' ability to contact and consult with their portfolio managers.

Item 9 Additional Information

A. Respond to Item 9 (Disciplinary Information) and Item 10 (Other Financial Industry Activities and Affiliations) of Part 2A of Form ADV.

B. Respond to Items 11 (Code of Ethics, Participation or Interest in *Client* Transactions and Personal Trading), 13 (Review of Accounts), 14 (*Client* Referrals and Other Compensation), and 18 (Financial Information) of Part 2A of Form ADV, as applicable to your wrap fee *clients*.

If you are registered or are registering with one or more *state securities authorities*, you must respond to the following additional Item.

Item 10 Requirements for State-Registered Advisers

Respond to Item 19.E of Part 2A of Form ADV.

Instructions for Part 2B of Form ADV: Preparing a *Brochure Supplement*

1. For which *supervised persons* must we prepare a *brochure supplement*? As an initial matter, if you have no *clients* to whom you must deliver a *brochure supplement* (see Instruction 2 below), then you need not prepare any *brochure supplements*. Otherwise, you must prepare a *brochure supplement* for the following *supervised persons*:

   (i) Any *supervised person* who formulates investment advice for a *client* and has direct *client* contact; and

   (ii) Any *supervised person* who has *discretionary authority* over a *client's* assets, even if the *supervised person* has no direct *client* contact. See SEC rule 204-3(b)(2) and similar state rules.

   Note: No supplement is required for a *supervised person* who has no direct *client* contact and has *discretionary authority* over a *client*'s assets only as part of a team. In addition, if discretionary advice is provided by a team comprised of more than five *supervised persons*, *brochure supplements* need only be provided for the five *supervised persons* with the most significant responsibility for the day-to-day discretionary advice provided to the *client*. See SEC rule 204-3(b) and similar state rules.

2. To whom must we deliver *brochure supplements*? Are there any exceptions?

   You must deliver to a *client* the *brochure supplements* for each *supervised person* who provides advisory services to that *client*. However, there are three categories of *clients* to whom you are not required to deliver *supplements*. See SEC rule 204-3(c) and similar state rules.

   First, you are not required to deliver supplements to *clients* to whom you are not required to deliver a firm *brochure* (or a *wrap fee program brochure*).

   Second, you are not required to deliver supplements to *clients* who receive only *impersonal investment advice*, even if they receive a firm *brochure*.

   Third, you are not required to deliver supplements to *clients* who are individuals who would be "qualified clients" of your firm under SEC rule 205-3(d)(1)(iii). Those *persons* are:

   (i) Any executive officers, directors, trustees, general partners, or *persons* serving in a similar capacity, of your firm; or

   (ii) Any employees of your firm (other than employees performing solely clerical, secretarial or administrative functions) who, in connection with their regular functions or duties, participate in the investment activities of your firm and have been performing such functions or duties for at least 12 months.

3. When must we deliver a supplement to a *client*?

- You must deliver the supplement for a *supervised person* before or at the time that *supervised person* begins to provide advisory services to a *client*.
- You also must deliver to *clients* any update to the supplement that amends information in response to Item 3 of Part 2B (disciplinary information). Such an amendment can be in the form of a "sticker" that identifies the information that has become inaccurate and provides the new information and the date of the sticker.

  Note: As a fiduciary, you have a continuing obligation to inform your *clients* of any material information that could affect the advisory relationship. As a result, between *annual updating amendments* you must disclose material changes to *clients* even if those changes do not trigger delivery of an updated supplement.

You may have a *supervised person* deliver supplements (including his own) on your behalf. Furthermore, if you are an SEC-registered adviser, you not required to file *brochure supplements* or updates, but you must maintain copies of them. See Instruction 5 of SEC General Instructions for Part 2 of Form ADV.

4. When must we update *brochure supplements*? You must update *brochure supplements* promptly whenever any information in them becomes materially inaccurate.

5. May we deliver *brochure supplements* electronically? Yes. You may deliver supplements using electronic media. The SEC has published interpretive guidance on delivering documents electronically, which you can find at <www.sec.gov/rules/concept/33-7288.txt>. If you deliver a supplement electronically, you may disclose in that supplement that the *supervised person* has a disciplinary event and provide a hyperlink to either the BrokerCheck or the IAPD systems.

6. Must *brochure supplements* be separate documents? No. If your firm *brochure* includes all the information required in a *brochure supplement*, you do not need a separate supplement. Smaller firms with just a few *supervised persons* may find it easier to include all supplement information in their firm *brochure*, while larger firms may prefer to use a firm *brochure* and separate supplements. If supplement information is included in the firm *brochure*, however, the supplements must be included at the end of the brochure. In addition, each supplement must follow the same order as the supplement items listed in Part 2B, and contain the same headings.

   You may prepare supplements for groups of *supervised persons*. A group supplement, or a firm *brochure* presenting supplement information about *supervised persons*, must present information in a separate section for each *supervised person*.

7. Must an adviser who is a sole proprietor provide his own *brochure supplement* to *clients*? No, if that information is included in the firm *brochure*.

8. May we include information not required by an item in a *brochure supplement*? Yes. If you include information not required by an item, however, you may not include so much additional information that the required information is obscured.

9. Are we required to file the *brochure supplements*? If you are registered or are registering with the SEC, you are not required to file your *brochure supplements*, but you are required to maintain copies of all supplements and amendments to supplements in your files. See SEC rule 204-2(a)(14)(i). If you are registered or are registering with one or more *state securities authorities*, you must file through IARD a copy of the *brochure supplement* for each *supervised person* doing business in that state.

Part 2B of Form ADV: *Brochure Supplement*

Item 1 Cover Page

A. Include the following on the cover page of the supplement:

1. The *supervised person's* name, business address and telephone number (if different from yours).
2. Your firm's name, business address and telephone number. If your firm *brochure* uses a business name for your firm, use the same business name for the firm in the supplement.
3. The date of the supplement.

B. Display on the cover page statements containing the following or other clear and concise language conveying the same information, and identifying the document as a "brochure supplement:"

This brochure supplement provides information about [name of *supervised person*] that supplements the [name of advisory firm] brochure. You should have received a copy of that brochure. Please contact [service center or name and/or title of your contact *person*] if you did not receive [name of advisory firm]'s brochure or if you have any questions about the contents of this supplement.

Additional information about [name of *supervised person*] is available on the SEC's website at www.adviserinfo.sec.gov.

Note: You do not have to include this statement directing *clients* to the public website unless the *supervised person* is an *investment adviser representative* required to register with *state securities authorities*. The above information must be on the cover page of the supplement but need not be the only information on the cover page of the supplement. If other information is included on the cover page of the supplement, the above information must be on the top of the first page of the supplement.

Item 2 Educational Background and Business Experience

Disclose the *supervised person's* name, age (or year of birth), formal education after high school, and business background (including an identification of the specific positions held) for the preceding five years. If the *supervised person* has no high school education, no formal education after high school, or no business background, disclose this fact. You may list any professional designations held by the *supervised person*, but if you do so, you must provide a sufficient explanation of the minimum qualifications required for each designation to allow *clients* to understand the value of the designation.

Item 3 Disciplinary Information

If there are legal or disciplinary events material to a *client's* or prospective *client's* evaluation of the *supervised person*, disclose all material facts regarding those events.

Items 3.A, 3.B, 3.C, and 3.D below list specific legal and disciplinary events presumed to be material for this Item. If the *supervised person* has been *involved* in one of these events, you must disclose it under this Item for ten years following the date of the event, unless (1) the event was resolved in the *supervised person's* favor, or was reversed, suspended or vacated, or (2) you have rebutted the presumption of materiality to determine that the event is not material (see Note below). For purposes of calculating this ten-year period, the "date" of an event is the date the final *order*, judgment, or decree was entered, or the date any rights of appeal from preliminary *orders*, judgments or decrees lapsed.

Items 3.A, 3.B, 3.C, and 3.D do not contain an exclusive list of material disciplinary events. If the *supervised person* has been *involved* in a legal or disciplinary event that is not listed in Items 3.A, 3.B, 3.C, or 3.D but is material to a *client's* or prospective *client's* evaluation of the *supervised person's* integrity, you must disclose the

event. Similarly, even if more than ten years have passed since the date of the event, you must disclose the event if it is so serious that it remains currently material to a *client's* or prospective *client's* evaluation.
If you deliver a supplement electronically and if a particular disclosure required below for the *supervised person* is provided through either the Financial Industry Regulatory Authority's (FINRA) BrokerCheck system or the IAPD, you may satisfy that particular disclosure obligation by including in that supplement (i) a statement that the *supervised person* has a disciplinary history, the details of which can be found on FINRA's BrokerCheck system or the IAPD, and (ii) a hyperlink to the relevant system with a brief explanation of how the *client* can access the disciplinary history. The BrokerCheck link is www.finra.org/brokercheck; the IAPD link is www.adviserinfo.sec.gov.

A. A criminal or civil action in a domestic, foreign or military court of competent jurisdiction in which the *supervised person*

 1. was convicted of, or pled guilty or nolo contendere ("no contest") to (a) any *felony*; (b) a *misdemeanor* that *involved* investments or an *investment-related* business, fraud, false statements or omissions, wrongful taking of property, bribery, perjury, forgery, counterfeiting, or extortion; or (c) a conspiracy to commit any of these offenses;

 2. is the named subject of a pending criminal *proceeding* that involves an *investment-related* business, fraud, false statements or omissions, wrongful taking of property, bribery, perjury, forgery, counterfeiting, extortion, or a conspiracy to commit any of these offenses;

 3. was *found* to have been *involved* in a violation of an *investment-related* statute or regulation; or

 4. was the subject of any *order*, judgment, or decree permanently or temporarily enjoining, or otherwise limiting, the *supervised person* from engaging in any *investment-related* activity, or from violating any *investment-related* statute, rule, or *order*.

B. An administrative *proceeding* before the SEC, any other federal regulatory agency, any state regulatory agency, or any *foreign financial regulatory authority* in which the *supervised person*

 1. was *found* to have caused an *investment-related* business to lose its authorization to do business; or

 2. was *found* to have been *involved* in a violation of an *investment-related* statute or regulation and was the subject of an *order* by the agency or authority

 (a) denying, suspending, or revoking the authorization of the *supervised person* to act in an *investment-related* business;

 (b) barring or suspending the *supervised person's* association with an *investment-related* business;

 (c) otherwise significantly limiting the *supervised person's investment-related* activities; or

 (d) imposing a civil money penalty of more than $2,500 on the *supervised person*.

C. A *self-regulatory organization (SRO) proceeding* in which the *supervised person*

 1. was *found* to have caused an *investment-related* business to lose its authorization to do business; or

 2. was *found* to have been *involved* in a violation of the *SRO's* rules and was: (i) barred or suspended from membership or from association with other members, or was expelled from membership; (ii) otherwise significantly limited from *investment-related* activities; or (iii) fined more than $2,500.

D. Any other hearing or formal adjudication in which a professional attainment, designation, or license of the *supervised person* was revoked or suspended because of a violation of rules relating to professional conduct. If the *supervised person* resigned (or otherwise relinquished the attainment, designation, or license) in anticipation of such a hearing or formal adjudication (and the adviser knows, or should have known, of such resignation or relinquishment), disclose the event.

Note: You may, under certain circumstances, rebut the presumption that a disciplinary event is material. If an event is immaterial, you are not required to disclose it. When you review a legal or disciplinary event involving the *supervised person* to determine whether it is appropriate to rebut the presumption of materiality, you should consider all of the following factors: (1) the proximity of the *supervised person* to the advisory function; (2) the nature of the infraction that led to the disciplinary event; (3) the severity of the disciplinary sanction; and (4) the time elapsed since the date of the disciplinary event. If you conclude that the materiality presumption has been overcome, you must prepare and maintain a file memorandum of your determination in your records. See SEC rule 204-2(a)(14)(iii) and similar state rules.

Item 4 Other Business Activities

A. If the *supervised person* is actively engaged in any *investment-related* business or occupation, including if the *supervised person* is registered, or has an application pending to register, as a broker-dealer, registered representative of a broker-dealer, futures commission merchant ("FCM"), commodity pool operator ("CPO"), commodity trading advisor ("CTA"), or an associated *person* of an FCM, CPO, or CTA, disclose this fact and describe the business relationship, if any, between the advisory business and the other business.

1. If a relationship between the advisory business and the *supervised person's* other financial industry activities creates a material conflict of interest with *clients*, describe the nature of the conflict and generally how you address it.

2. If the *supervised person* receives commissions, bonuses or other compensation based on the sale of securities or other investment products, including as a broker-dealer or registered representative, and including distribution or service ("trail") fees from the sale of mutual funds, disclose this fact. If this compensation is not cash, explain what type of compensation the *supervised person* receives. Explain that this practice gives the *supervised person* an incentive to recommend investment products based on the compensation received, rather than on the *client's* needs.

B. If the *supervised person* is actively engaged in any business or occupation for compensation not discussed in response to Item 4.A, above, and the other business activity or activities provide a substantial source of the *supervised person's* income or involve a substantial amount of the *supervised person's* time, disclose this fact and describe the nature of that business. If the other business activities represent less than 10 percent of the *supervised person's* time and income, you may presume that they are not substantial.

Item 5 Additional Compensation

If someone who is not a *client* provides an economic benefit to the *supervised person* for providing advisory services, generally describe the arrangement. For purposes of this Item, economic benefits include sales awards and other prizes, but do not include the *supervised person's* regular salary. Any bonus that is based, at least in part, on the number or amount of sales, *client* referrals, or new accounts should be considered an economic benefit, but other regular bonuses should not.

Item 6 Supervision

Explain how you *supervise* the *supervised person*, including how you monitor the advice the *supervised person* provides to *clients*. Provide the name, title and telephone number of the *person* responsible for supervising the *supervised person's* advisory activities on behalf of your firm.

If you are registered or are registering with one or more *state securities authorities*, you must respond to the following additional Item.

Item 7 Requirements for State-Registered Advisers

A. In addition to the events listed in Item 3 of Part 2B, if the *supervised person* has been *involved* in one of the events listed below, disclose all material facts regarding the event.

1. An award or otherwise being *found* liable in an arbitration claim alleging damages in excess of $2,500, *involving* any of the following:

   (a) an investment or an *investment-related* business or activity;
   (b) fraud, false statement(s), or omissions;
   (c) theft, embezzlement, or other wrongful taking of property;
   (d) bribery, forgery, counterfeiting, or extortion; or
   (e) dishonest, unfair, or unethical practices.

2. An award or otherwise being *found* liable in a civil, *self-regulatory organization*, or administrative *proceeding involving* any of the following:

   (a) an investment or an *investment-related* business or activity;
   (b) fraud, false statement(s), or omissions;
   (c) theft, embezzlement, or other wrongful taking of property;
   (d) bribery, forgery, counterfeiting, or extortion; or
   (e) dishonest, unfair, or unethical practices.

B. If the *supervised person* has been the subject of a bankruptcy petition, disclose that fact, the date the petition was first brought, and the current status.

FORM ADV (Paper Version)

- **UNIFORM APPLICATION FOR INVESTMENT ADVISER REGISTRATION**
  AND
- **REPORT BY EXEMPT REPORTING ADVISERS**

DOMESTIC INVESTMENT ADVISER EXECUTION PAGE

You must complete the following Execution Page to Form ADV. This execution page must be signed and attached to your initial submission of Form ADV to the SEC and all amendments.

Appointment of Agent for Service of Process

By signing this Form ADV Execution Page, you, the undersigned adviser, irrevocably appoint the Secretary of State or other legally designated officer, of the state in which you maintain your *principal office and place of business* and any other state in which you are submitting a *notice filing*, as your agents to receive service, and agree that such *persons* may accept service on your behalf, of any notice, subpoena, summons, *order* instituting *proceedings*, demand for arbitration, or other process or papers, and you further agree that such service may be made by registered or certified mail, in any federal or state action, administrative *proceeding* or arbitration brought against you in any place subject to the jurisdiction of the United States, if the action, *proceeding* or arbitration (a) arises out of any activity in connection with your investment advisory business that is subject to the jurisdiction of the United States, and (b) is *founded*, directly or indirectly, upon the provisions of: (i) the Securities Act of 1933, the Securities Exchange Act of 1934, the Trust Indenture Act of 1939, the Investment Company Act of 1940, or the Investment Advisers Act of 1940, or any rule or regulation under any of these acts, or (ii) the laws of the state in which you maintain your *principal office and place of business* or of any state in which you are submitting a *notice filing*.

Signature

I, the undersigned, sign this Form ADV on behalf of, and with the authority of, the investment adviser. The investment adviser and I both certify, under penalty of perjury under the laws of the United States of America, that the information and statements made in this ADV, including exhibits and any other information submitted, are true and correct, and that I am signing this Form ADV Execution Page as a free and voluntary act.

I certify that the adviser's books and records will be preserved and available for inspection as required by law. Finally, I authorize any *person* having *custody* or possession of these books and records to make them available to federal and state regulatory representatives.

Signature: ______________________________ Date: ________________________

Printed Name: ___________________________ Title: ________________________

Adviser *CRD* Number: ____________________

SEC 1707 (09-11)
File 4 of 4

FORM ADV (Paper Version)

- **UNIFORM APPLICATION FOR INVESTMENT ADVISER REGISTRATION AND**
- **REPORT BY EXEMPT REPORTING ADVISERS**

STATE-REGISTERED INVESTMENT ADVISER EXECUTION PAGE

You must complete the following Execution Page to Form ADV. This execution page must be signed and attached to your initial application for state registration and all amendments to registration.

1. Appointment of Agent for Service of Process

By signing this Form ADV Execution Page, you, the undersigned adviser, irrevocably appoint the legally designated officers and their successors, of the state in which you maintain your *principal office and place of business* and any other state in which you are applying for registration or amending your registration, as your agents to receive service, and agree that such *persons* may accept service on your behalf, of any notice, subpoena, summons, *order* instituting *proceedings*, demand for arbitration, or other process or papers, and you further agree that such service may be made by registered or certified mail, in any federal or state action, administrative *proceeding* or arbitration brought against you in any place subject to the jurisdiction of the United States, if the action, *proceeding* or arbitration (a) arises out of any activity in connection with your investment advisory business that is subject to the jurisdiction of the United States, and (b) is *founded*, directly or indirectly, upon the provisions of: (i) the Securities Act of 1933, the Securities Exchange Act of 1934, the Trust Indenture Act of 1939, the Investment Company Act of 1940, or the Investment Advisers Act of 1940, or any rule or regulation under any of these acts, or (ii) the laws of the state in which you maintain your *principal office and place of business* or of any state in which you are applying for registration, or amending your registration.

2. State-Registered Investment Adviser Affidavit

If you are subject to state regulation, by signing this Form ADV, you represent that, you are in compliance with the registration requirements of the state in which you maintain your *principal place of business* and are in compliance with the bonding, capital, and recordkeeping requirements of that state.

Signature

I, the undersigned, sign this Form ADV on behalf of, and with the authority of, the investment adviser. The investment adviser and I both certify, under penalty of perjury under the laws of the United States of America, that the information and statements made in this ADV, including exhibits and any other information submitted, are true and correct, and that I am signing this Form ADV Execution Page as a free and voluntary act.

I certify that the adviser's books and records will be preserved and available for inspection as required by law. Finally, I authorize any *person* having custody or possession of these books and records to make them available to federal and state regulatory representatives.

Signature: ______________________________ Date: ________________________

Printed Name: ______________________________ Title: ________________________

Adviser *CRD* Number: ______________________

FORM ADV (Paper Version)

- **UNIFORM APPLICATION FOR INVESTMENT ADVISER REGISTRATION**
  AND
- **REPORT BY EXEMPT REPORTING ADVISERS**

***NON-RESIDENT* INVESTMENT ADVISER EXECUTION**	**PAGE 1**

You must complete the following Execution Page to Form ADV. This execution page must be signed and attached to your initial submission of Form ADV to the SEC and all amendments.

1. Appointment of Agent for Service of Process

By signing this Form ADV Execution Page, you, the undersigned adviser, irrevocably appoint each of the Secretary of the SEC, and the Secretary of State or other legally designated officer, of any other state in which you are submitting a *notice filing*, as your agents to receive service, and agree that such *persons* may accept service on your behalf, of any notice, subpoena, summons, *order* instituting *proceedings*, demand for arbitration, or other process or papers, and you further agree that such service may be made by registered or certified mail, in any federal or state action, administrative *proceeding* or arbitration brought against you in any place subject to the jurisdiction of the United States, if the action, *proceeding* or arbitration (a) arises out of any activity in connection with your investment advisory business that is subject to the jurisdiction of the United States, and (b) is *founded*, directly or indirectly, upon the provisions of: (i) the Securities Act of 1933, the Securities Exchange Act of 1934, the Trust Indenture Act of 1939, the Investment Company Act of 1940, or the Investment Advisers Act of 1940, or any rule or regulation under any of these acts, or (ii) the laws of any state in which you are submitting a *notice filing*.

2. Appointment and Consent: Effect on Partnerships

If you are organized as a partnership, this irrevocable power of attorney and consent to service of process will continue in effect if any partner withdraws from or is admitted to the partnership, provided that the admission or withdrawal does not create a new partnership. If the partnership dissolves, this irrevocable power of attorney and consent shall be in effect for any action brought against you or any of your former partners.

3. *Non-Resident* Investment Adviser Undertaking Regarding Books and Records

By signing this Form ADV, you also agree to provide, at your own expense, to the U.S. Securities and Exchange Commission at its principal office in Washington D.C., at any Regional or District Office of the Commission, or at any one of its offices in the United States, as specified by the Commission, correct, current, and complete copies of any or all records that you are required to maintain under Rule 204-2 under the Investment Advisers Act of 1940. This undertaking shall be binding upon you, your heirs, successors and assigns, and any *person* subject to your written irrevocable consents or powers of attorney or any of your general partners and *managing agents*.

Signature

I, the undersigned, sign this Form ADV on behalf of, and with the authority of, the *non-resident* investment adviser. The investment adviser and I both certify, under penalty of perjury under the laws of the United States of America, that the information and statements made in this ADV, including exhibits and any other information submitted, are true and correct, and that I am signing this Form ADV Execution Page as a free and voluntary act.

I certify that the adviser's books and records will be preserved and available for inspection as required by law. Finally, I authorize any *person* having custody or possession of these books and records to make them available to federal and state regulatory representatives.

Signature: ______________________________ Date: ________________________

Printed Name: ______________________________ Title: ________________________

Adviser *CRD* Number: ______________________

Resources

There are a multitude of resources available online that will assist you with your Advisers Act compliance activities. The most important ones are listed here:

www.iard.com/GetStarted.asp
How to get started

www.sec.gov/pdf/handbook.pdf
Plain English handbook

www.sec.gov/divisions/investment/advoverview.htm
Regarding your role as fiduciary.

www.adviserinfo.sec.gov
Form ADV/Investment Adviser Search

www.sec.gov/about/forms/formadv-instructions.pdf
Instructions to Form ADV Part 1

www.sec.gov/about/forms/formadv-part2.pdf
Instructions to Form ADV Part 2

www.sec.gov/divisions/marketreg/tmcompliance/modelprivacyform-secg.htm
Model Privacy Notice

www.sec.gov/investment/
SEC guidance and alerts on a number of Advisers Act topics

www.investmentadviser.org/eweb/
Investment Adviser Association website

www.nasaa.org/
North American Securities Administrators website

www.nasaa.org/about-us/contact-us/contact-your-regulator/
Contact information for state securities regulators

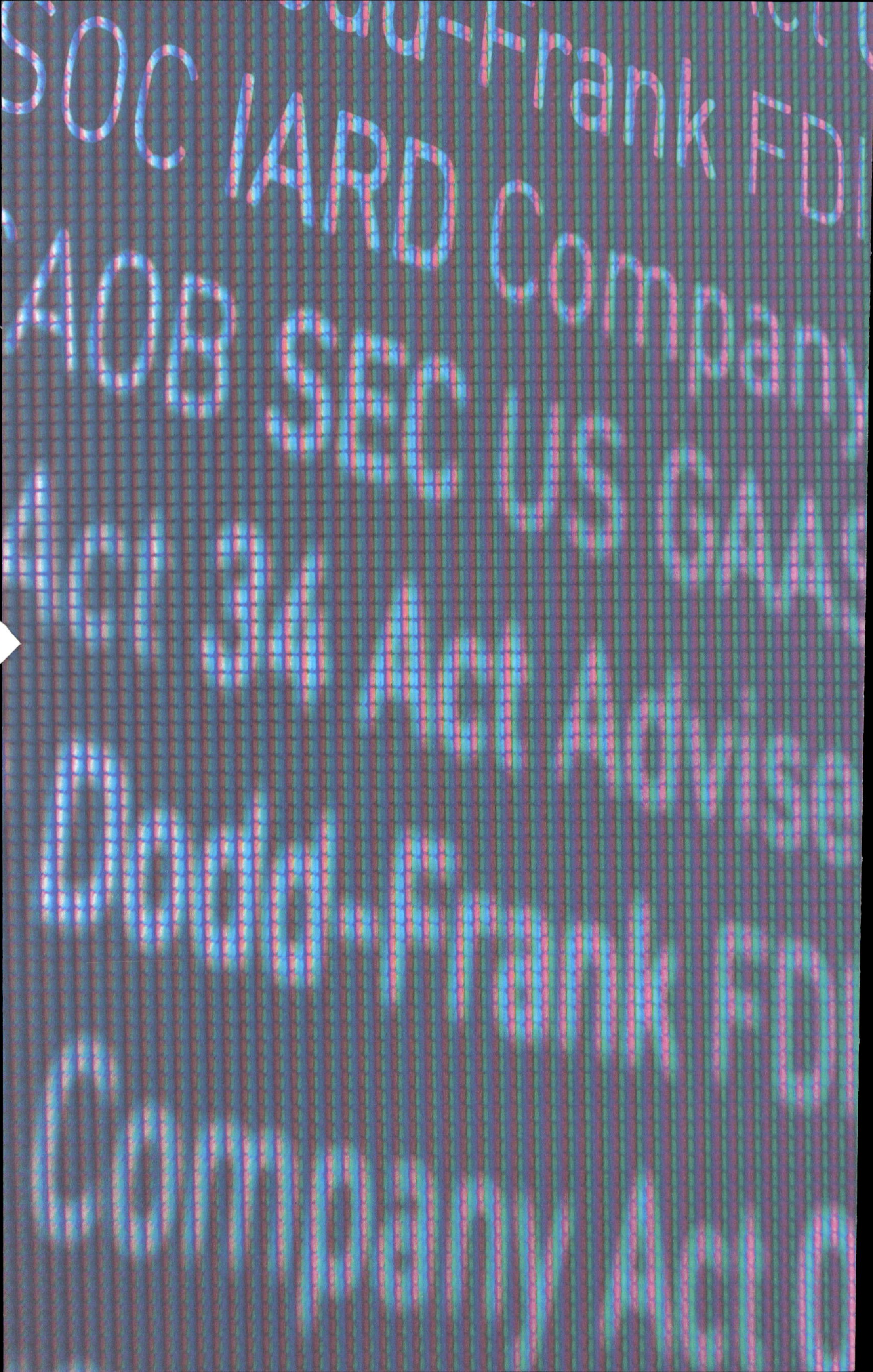
SOC IARD
SEC US
Dodd-Frank
Company

Glossary

This glossary contains the key players and definitions for the main terms necessary to understand the Advisers Act and this book. Furthermore, any references to sections are to the relevant sections of the Advisers Act and references to rules are to the respective rules and regulations promulgated under it, unless otherwise specified.

33 Act: The Securities Act of 1933, and the rules and regulations promulgated thereunder.

34 Act: The Securities Exchange Act of 1934, and the rules and regulations promulgated thereunder.

Advisers Act: The Investment Advisers Act of 1940, and the rules and regulations promulgated under it.

CFTC: Commodity Futures Trading Commission

CRD: Central Registration Depository

Dodd-Frank: The Dodd-Frank Wall Street Reform and Consumer Protection Act

FDIC: Federal Deposit Insurance Corporation

FINRA: Financial Industry Regulatory Authority, Inc.

FSOC: Financial Stability Oversight Council

IARD: Investment Adviser Registration Depository, a one-stop electronic filing system for investment advisers.

Investment Company Act: The Investment Company Act of 1940, and the rules and regulations promulgated under it.

OFR: Office of Financial Research

PCAOB: Public Company Accounting Oversight Board

SEC: Securities and Exchange Commission

US GAAS: Generally Accepted Auditing Standards in the United States

US GAAP: Generally Accepted Accounting Principles in the United States

Index

NOTE: Page references in *italics* refer to figures.

G

H

I

L

S